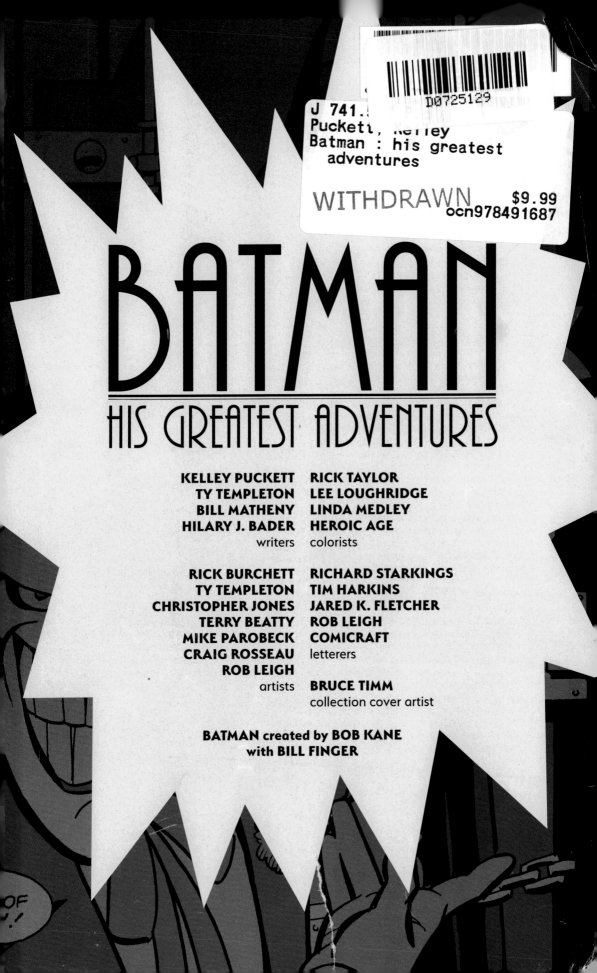

BATMAN
HIS GREATEST ADVENTURES

KELLEY PUCKETT	**RICK TAYLOR**
TY TEMPLETON	**LEE LOUGHRIDGE**
BILL MATHENY	**LINDA MEDLEY**
HILARY J. BADER	**HEROIC AGE**
writers	colorists
RICK BURCHETT	**RICHARD STARKINGS**
TY TEMPLETON	**TIM HARKINS**
CHRISTOPHER JONES	**JARED K. FLETCHER**
TERRY BEATTY	**ROB LEIGH**
MIKE PAROBECK	**COMICRAFT**
CRAIG ROSSEAU	letterers
ROB LEIGH	
artists	**BRUCE TIMM**
	collection cover artist

BATMAN created by **BOB KANE**
with **BILL FINGER**

SCOTT PETERSON, NACHIE CASTRO, DARREN VINCENZO, JOAN HILTY Editors – Original Series
JOSEPH ILLIDGE Associate Editor – Original Series
HARVEY RICHARDS Assistant Editor – Original Series
JEB WOODARD Group Editor – Collected Editions
ERIKA ROTHBERG Editor – Collected Edition
STEVE COOK Design Director – Books
LOUIS PRANDI Publication Design

BOB HARRAS Senior VP – Editor-in-Chief, DC Comics

DIANE NELSON President
DAN DiDIO Publisher
JIM LEE Publisher
GEOFF JOHNS President & Chief Creative Officer
AMIT DESAI Executive VP – Business & Marketing Strategy, Direct to Consumer & Global Franchise Management
SAM ADES Senior VP – Direct to Consumer
BOBBIE CHASE VP – Talent Development
MARK CHIARELLO Senior VP – Art, Design & Collected Editions
JOHN CUNNINGHAM Senior VP – Sales & Trade Marketing
ANNE DePIES Senior VP – Business Strategy, Finance & Administration
DON FALLETTI VP – Manufacturing Operations
LAWRENCE GANEM VP – Editorial Administration & Talent Relations
ALISON GILL Senior VP – Manufacturing & Operations
HANK KANALZ Senior VP – Editorial Strategy & Administration
JAY KOGAN VP – Legal Affairs
THOMAS LOFTUS VP – Business Affairs
JACK MAHAN VP – Business Affairs
NICK J. NAPOLITANO VP – Manufacturing Administration
EDDIE SCANNELL VP – Consumer Marketing
COURTNEY SIMMONS Senior VP – Publicity & Communications
JIM (SKI) SOKOLOWSKI VP – Comic Book Specialty Sales & Trade Marketing
NANCY SPEARS VP – Mass, Book, Digital Sales & Trade Marketing

BATMAN: HIS GREATEST ADVENTURES

Published by DC Comics. Compilation and all new material Copyright © 2017 DC Comics. All Rights Reserved. Originally published in single magazine form in BATMAN ADVENTURES 3, BATMAN ADVENTURES 11,
BATMAN ADVENTURES 19, BATMAN AND ROBIN ADVENTURES 4, BATMAN BEYOND 1, THE BATMAN STRIKES
6. Copyright © 1992, 1994, 1996, 1999, 2004, 2005 DC Comics. All Rights Reserved. All characters, their distinctive
likenesses and related elements featured in this publication are trademarks of DC Comics. The stories, characters
and incidents featured in this publication are entirely fictional. DC Comics does not read or accept unsolicited
submissions of ideas, stories or artwork.
DC Comics, 2900 West Alameda Ave., Burbank, CA 91505
Printed by Vanguard Graphics, LLC, Ithaca, NY, USA. 8/11/17. First Printing.
ISBN: 978-1-4012-7693-5
Library of Congress Cataloging-in-Publication Data is available.

MIX
Paper from
responsible sources
FSC® C016956
www.fsc.org

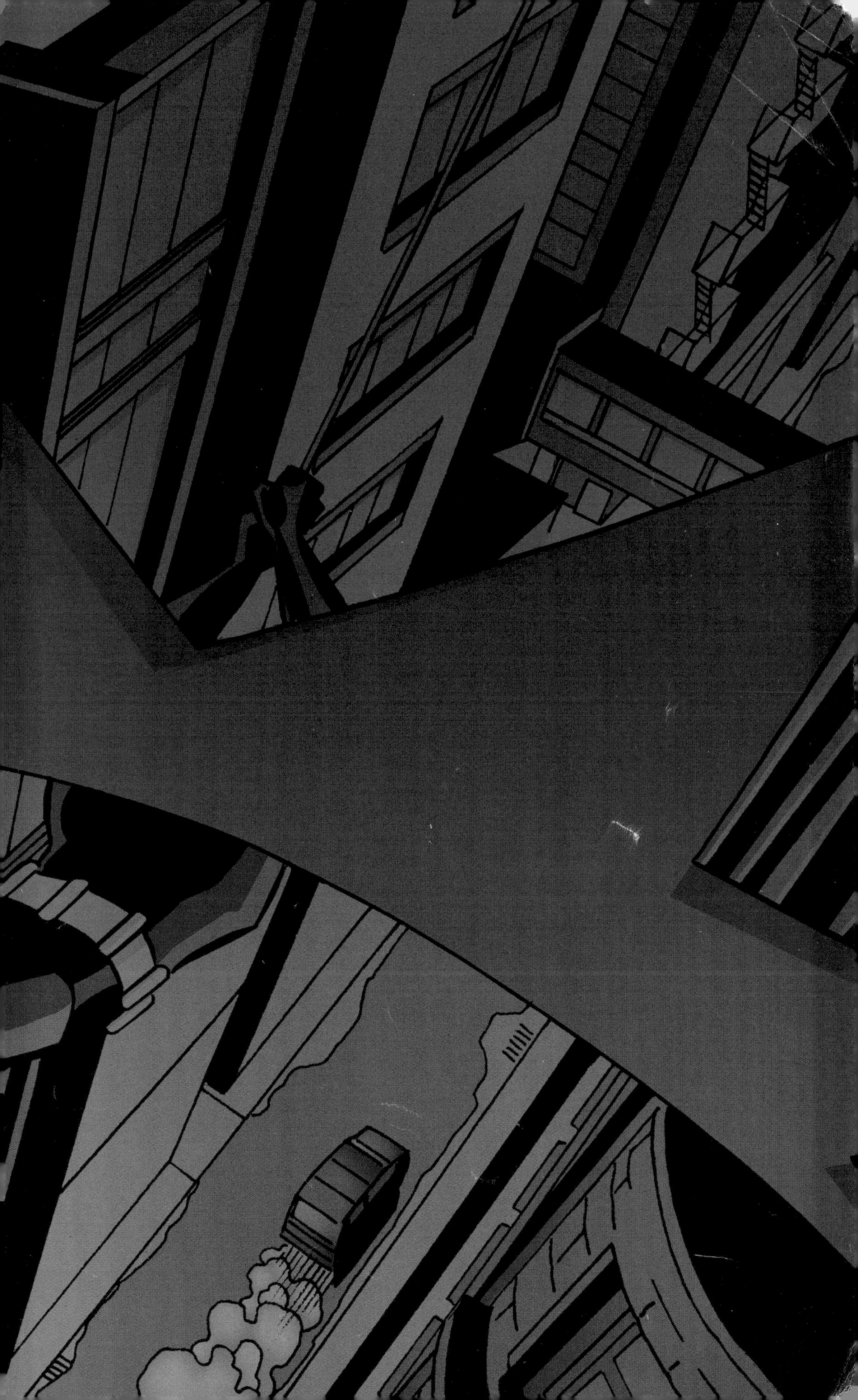

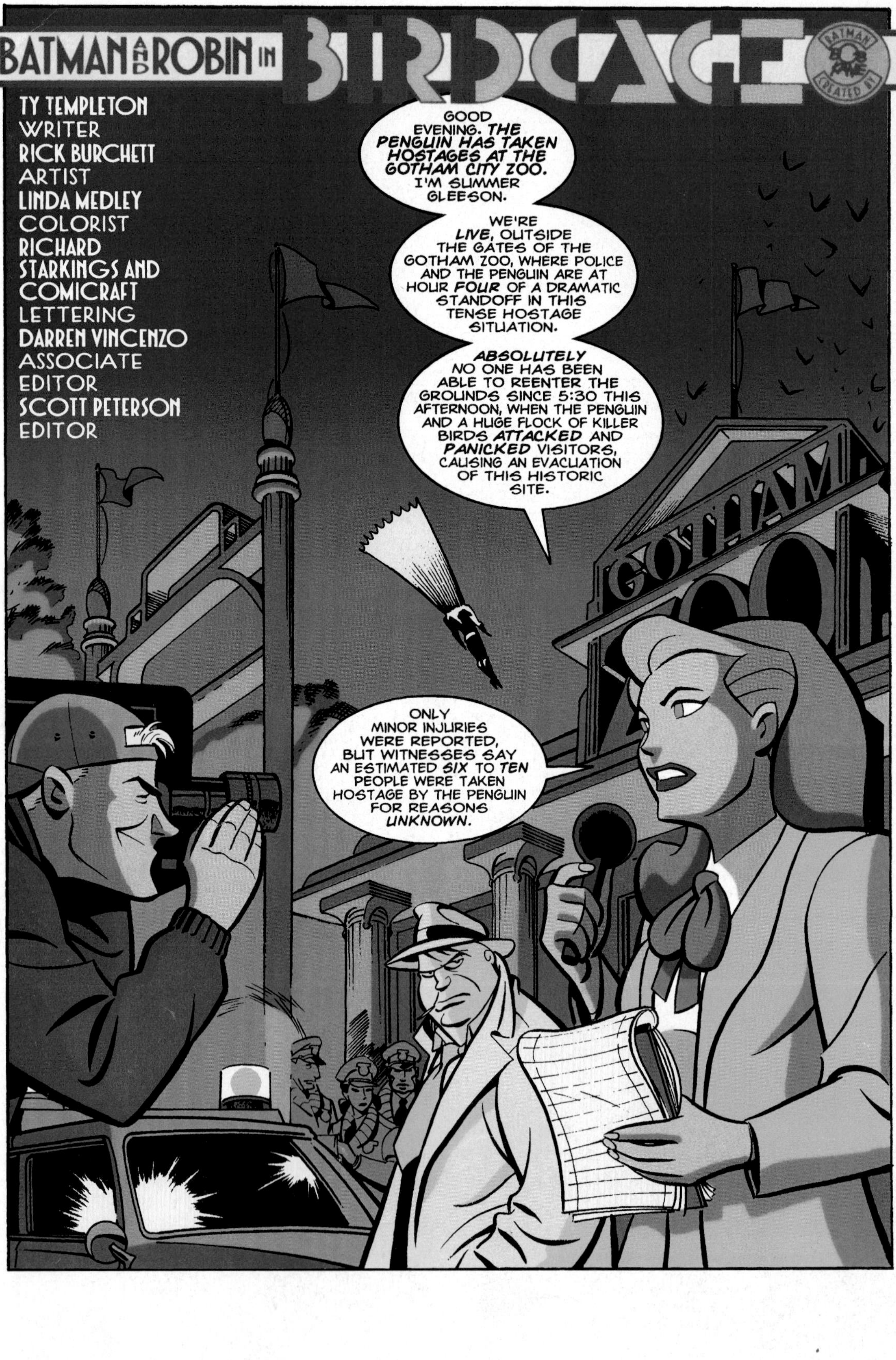
BATMAN AND ROBIN IN BIRDCAGE
BATMAN CREATED BY BOB KANE
TY TEMPLETON WRITER
RICK BURCHETT ARTIST
LINDA MEDLEY COLORIST
RICHARD STARKINGS AND COMICRAFT LETTERING
DARREN VINCENZO ASSOCIATE EDITOR
SCOTT PETERSON EDITOR
GOOD EVENING. THE PENGUIN HAS TAKEN HOSTAGES AT THE GOTHAM CITY ZOO. I'M SUMMER GLEESON.
WE'RE LIVE, OUTSIDE THE GATES OF THE GOTHAM ZOO, WHERE POLICE AND THE PENGUIN ARE AT HOUR FOUR OF A DRAMATIC STANDOFF IN THIS TENSE HOSTAGE SITUATION.
ABSOLUTELY NO ONE HAS BEEN ABLE TO REENTER THE GROUNDS SINCE 5:30 THIS AFTERNOON, WHEN THE PENGUIN AND A HUGE FLOCK OF KILLER BIRDS ATTACKED AND PANICKED VISITORS, CAUSING AN EVACUATION OF THIS HISTORIC SITE.
GOTHAM ZOO
ONLY MINOR INJURIES WERE REPORTED, BUT WITNESSES SAY AN ESTIMATED SIX TO TEN PEOPLE WERE TAKEN HOSTAGE BY THE PENGUIN FOR REASONS UNKNOWN.

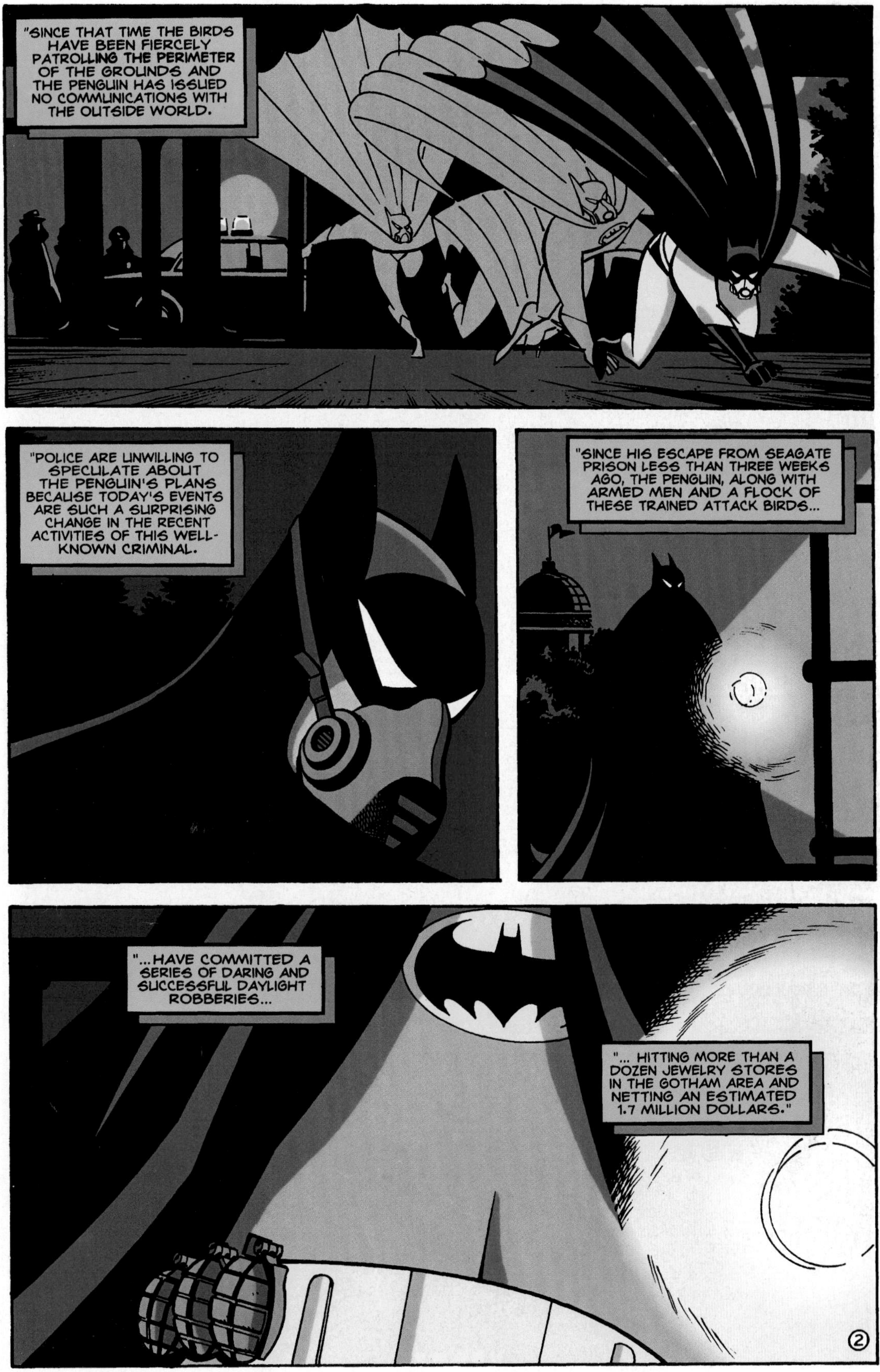
"SINCE THAT TIME THE BIRDS HAVE BEEN FIERCELY PATROLLING THE PERIMETER OF THE GROUNDS AND THE PENGUIN HAS ISSUED NO COMMUNICATIONS WITH THE OUTSIDE WORLD.
"POLICE ARE UNWILLING TO SPECULATE ABOUT THE PENGUIN'S PLANS BECAUSE TODAY'S EVENTS ARE SUCH A SURPRISING CHANGE IN THE RECENT ACTIVITIES OF THIS WELL-KNOWN CRIMINAL.
"SINCE HIS ESCAPE FROM SEAGATE PRISON LESS THAN THREE WEEKS AGO, THE PENGUIN, ALONG WITH ARMED MEN AND A FLOCK OF THESE TRAINED ATTACK BIRDS...
"...HAVE COMMITTED A SERIES OF DARING AND SUCCESSFUL DAYLIGHT ROBBERIES...
"... HITTING MORE THAN A DOZEN JEWELRY STORES IN THE GOTHAM AREA AND NETTING AN ESTIMATED 1.7 MILLION DOLLARS."
2

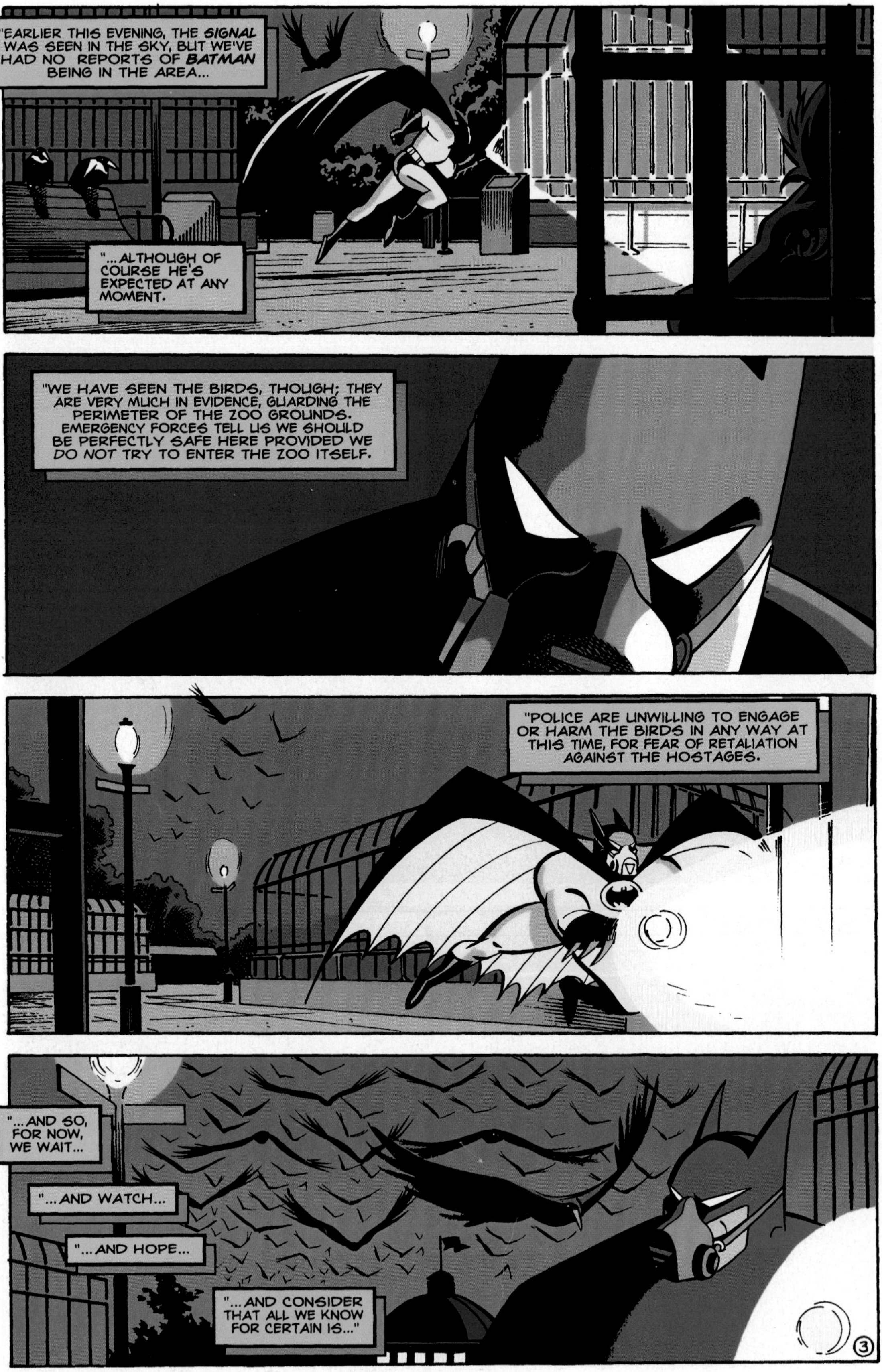
"EARLIER THIS EVENING, THE SIGNAL WAS SEEN IN THE SKY, BUT WE'VE HAD NO REPORTS OF BATMAN BEING IN THE AREA...
"...ALTHOUGH OF COURSE HE'S EXPECTED AT ANY MOMENT.
"WE HAVE SEEN THE BIRDS, THOUGH; THEY ARE VERY MUCH IN EVIDENCE, GUARDING THE PERIMETER OF THE ZOO GROUNDS. EMERGENCY FORCES TELL US WE SHOULD BE PERFECTLY SAFE HERE PROVIDED WE DO NOT TRY TO ENTER THE ZOO ITSELF.
"POLICE ARE UNWILLING TO ENGAGE OR HARM THE BIRDS IN ANY WAY AT THIS TIME, FOR FEAR OF RETALIATION AGAINST THE HOSTAGES.
"...AND SO, FOR NOW, WE WAIT...
"...AND WATCH...
"...AND HOPE...
"...AND CONSIDER THAT ALL WE KNOW FOR CERTAIN IS..."

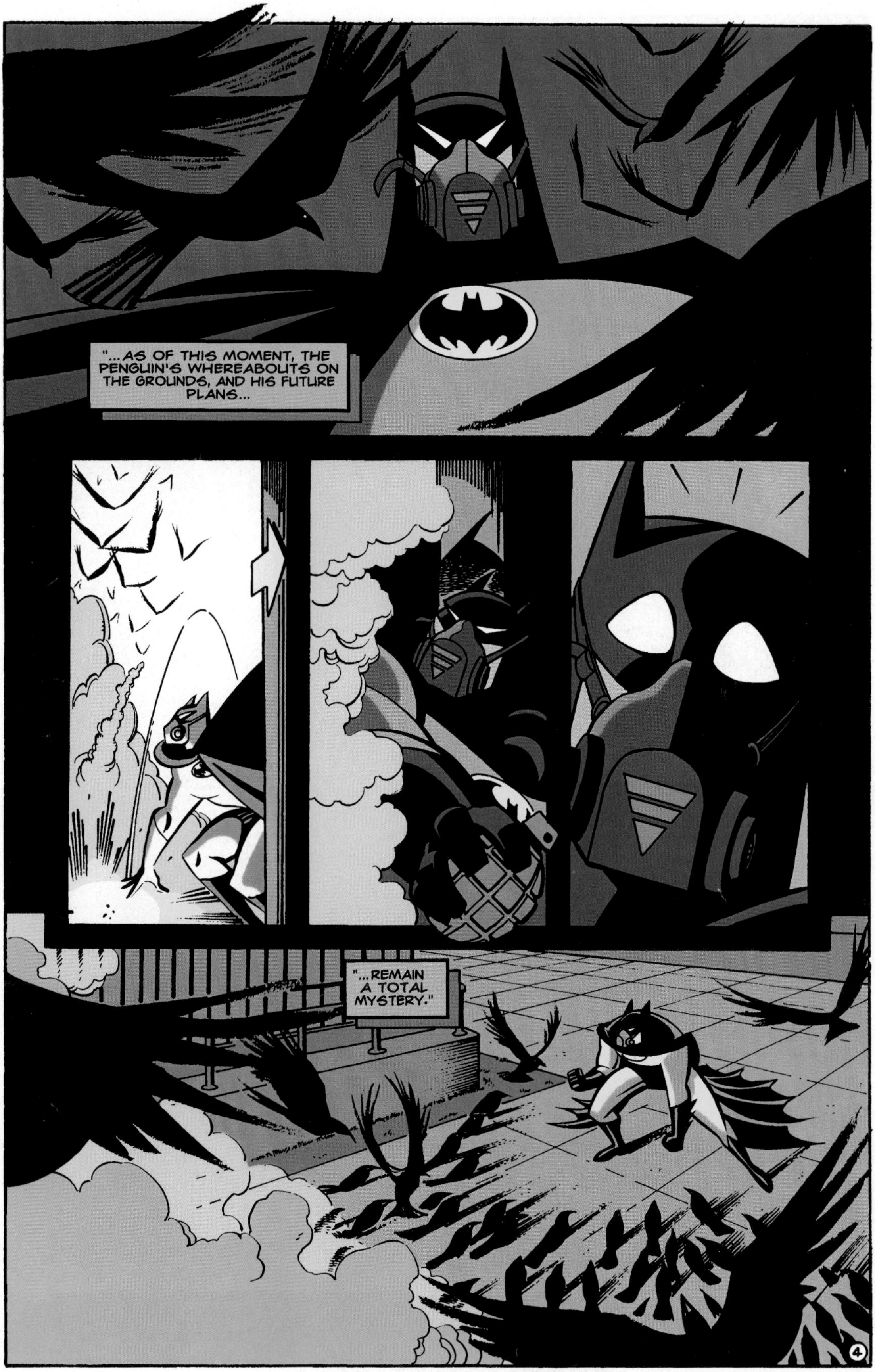
"...AS OF THIS MOMENT, THE PENGUIN'S WHEREABOUTS ON THE GROUNDS, AND HIS FUTURE PLANS...
"...REMAIN A TOTAL MYSTERY."

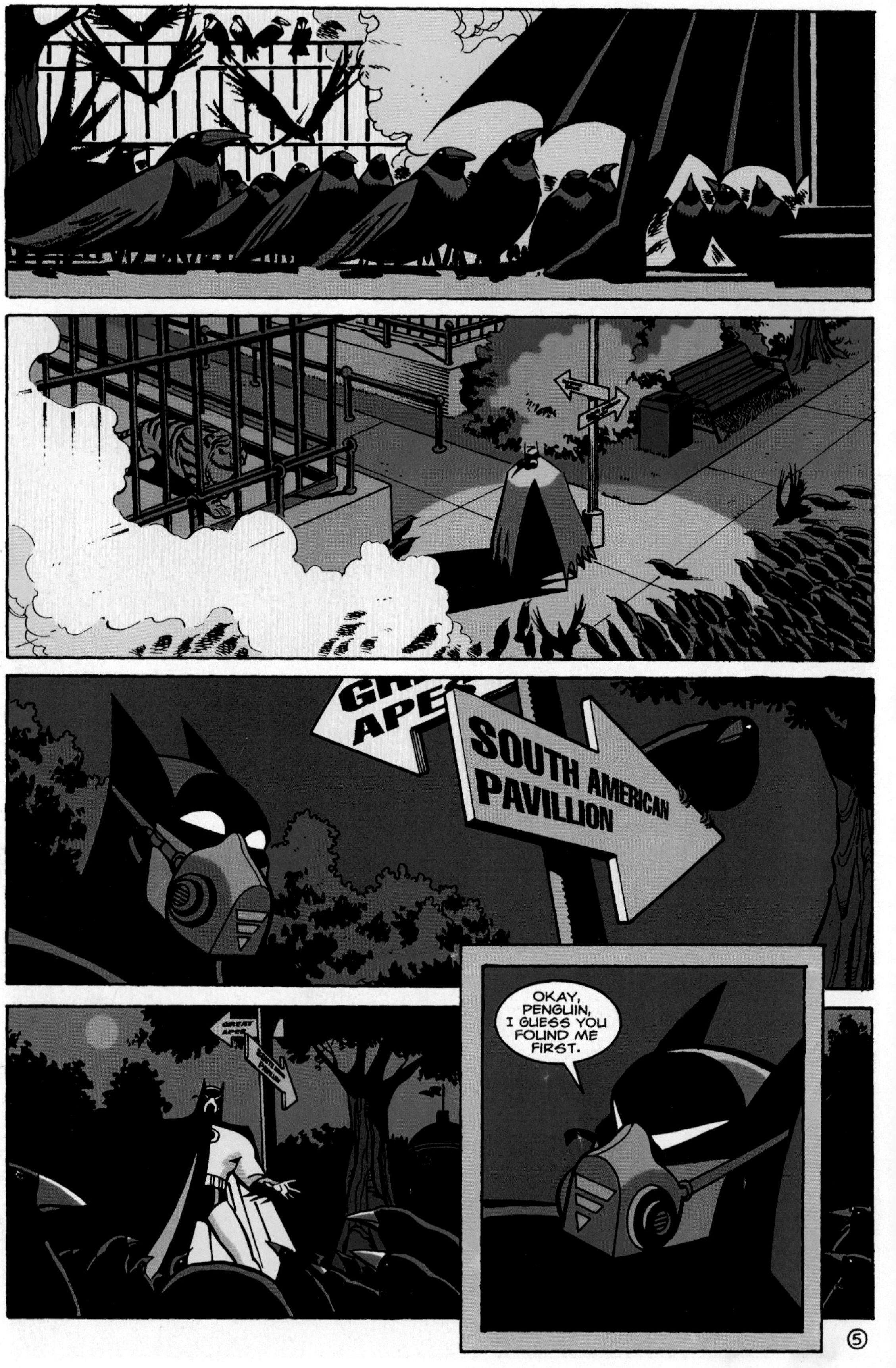
SOUTH AMERICAN PAVILLION
GREAT APES
OKAY, PENGUIN, I GUESS YOU FOUND ME FIRST.

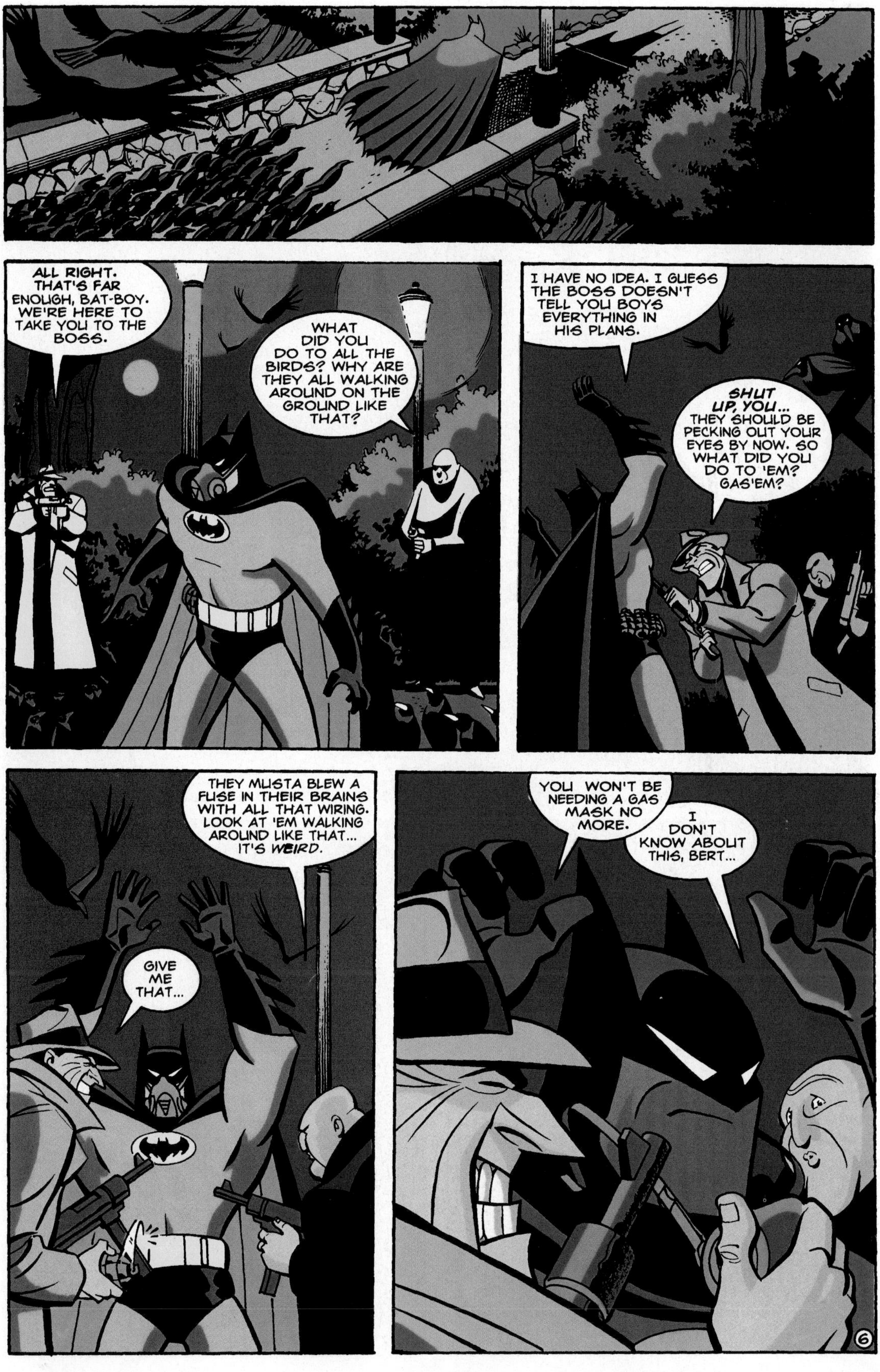
ALL RIGHT. THAT'S FAR ENOUGH, BAT-BOY. WE'RE HERE TO TAKE YOU TO THE BOSS.
WHAT DID YOU DO TO ALL THE BIRDS? WHY ARE THEY ALL WALKING AROUND ON THE GROUND LIKE THAT?
I HAVE NO IDEA. I GUESS THE BOSS DOESN'T TELL YOU BOYS EVERYTHING IN HIS PLANS.
SHUT UP, YOU... THEY SHOULD BE PECKING OUT YOUR EYES BY NOW. SO WHAT DID YOU DO TO 'EM? GAS'EM?
THEY MUSTA BLEW A FUSE IN THEIR BRAINS WITH ALL THAT WIRING. LOOK AT 'EM WALKING AROUND LIKE THAT... IT'S WEIRD.
GIVE ME THAT...
YOU WON'T BE NEEDING A GAS MASK NO MORE.
I DON'T KNOW ABOUT THIS, BERT...
6

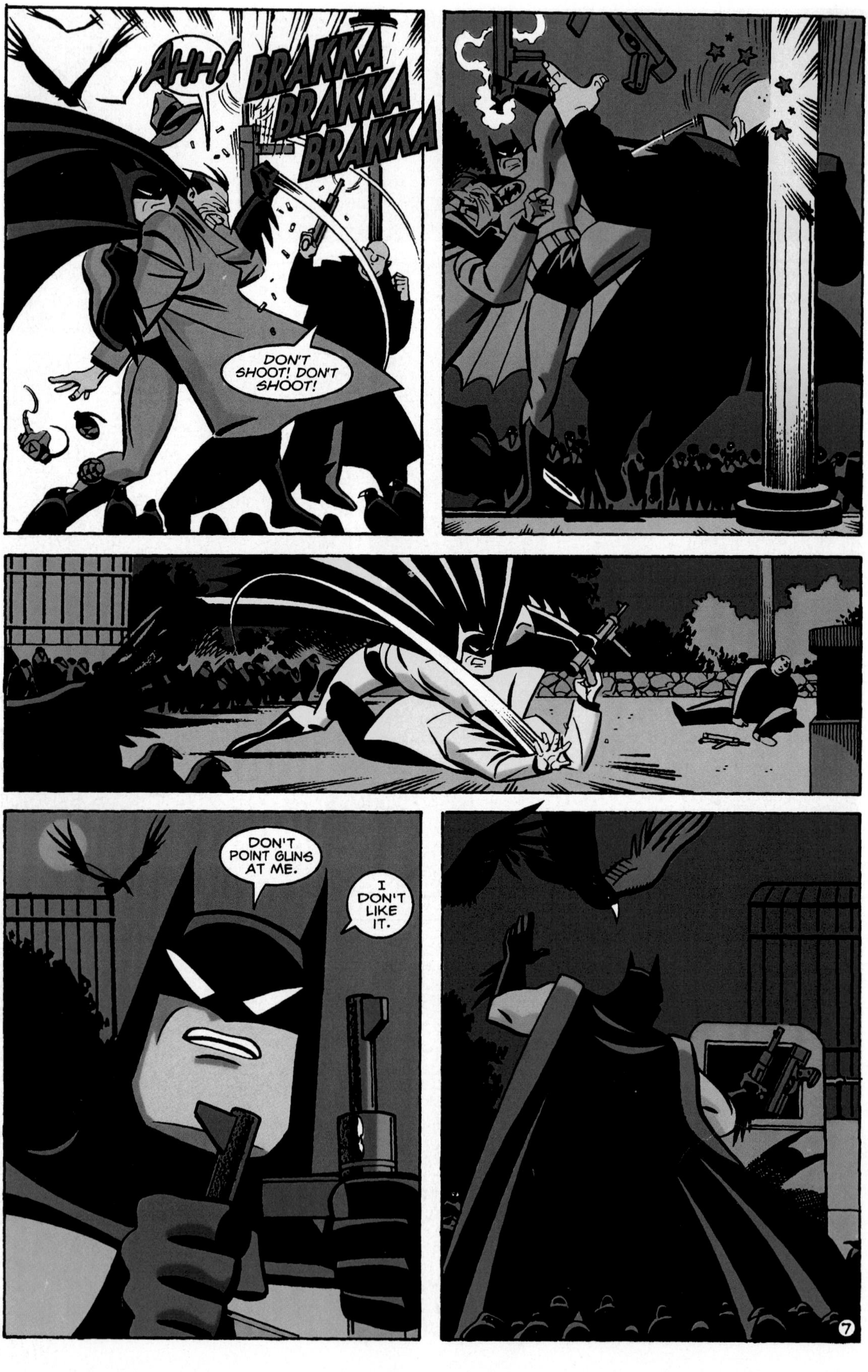
AHH!
BRAKKA BRAKKA BRAKKA
DON'T SHOOT! DON'T SHOOT!
DON'T POINT GUNS AT ME.
I DON'T LIKE IT.

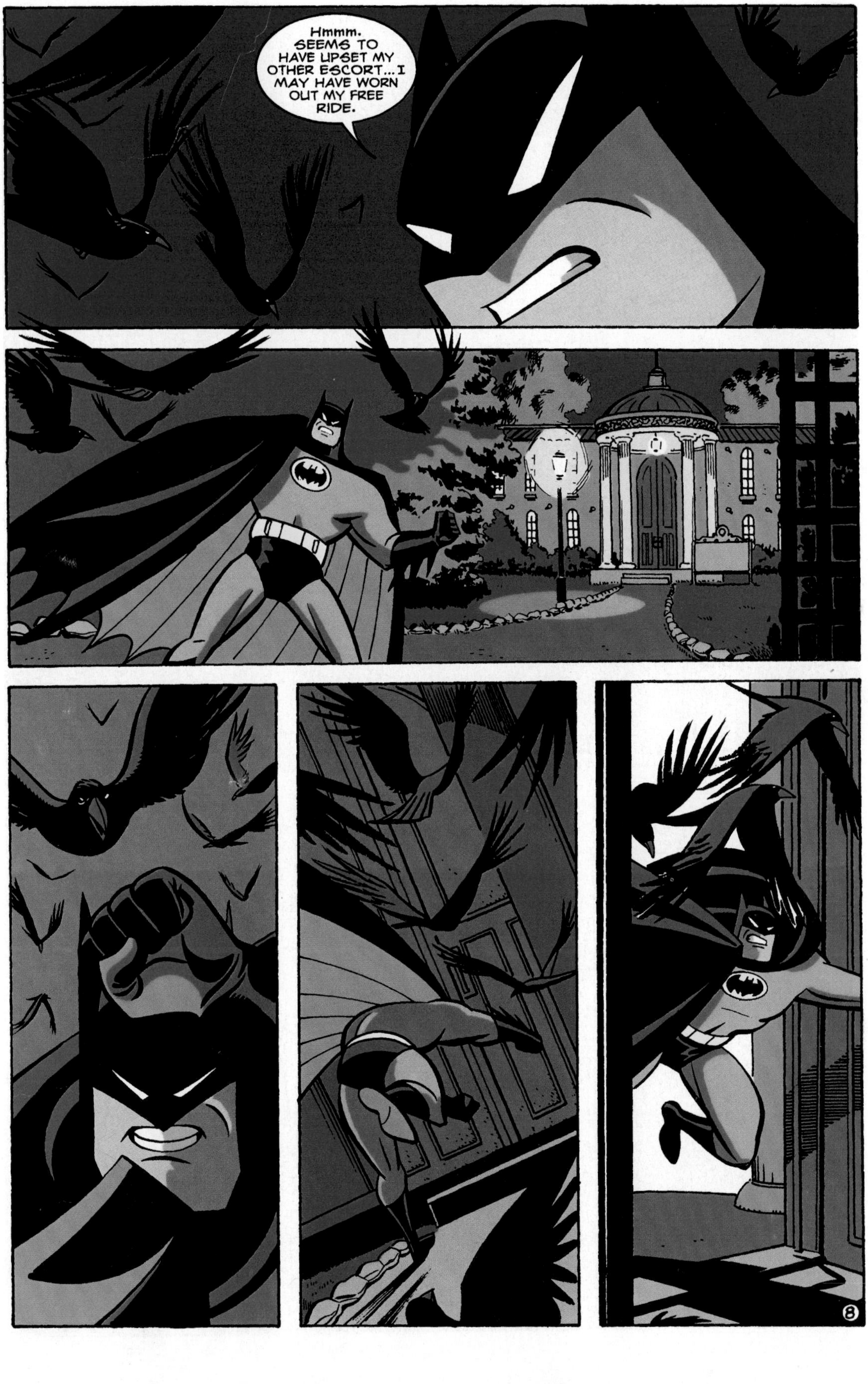
Hmmm. SEEMS TO HAVE UPSET MY OTHER ESCORT... I MAY HAVE WORN OUT MY FREE RIDE.

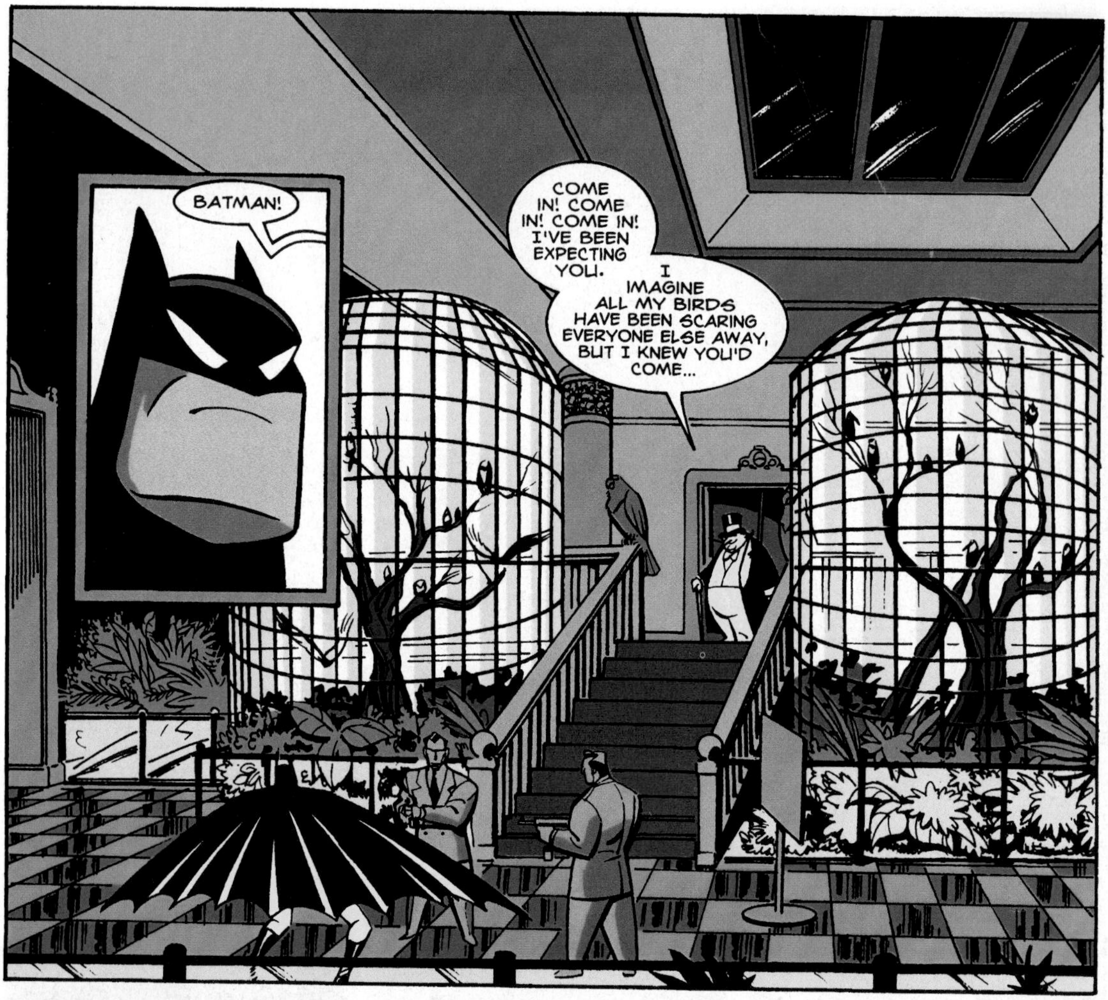
BATMAN!
COME IN! COME IN! COME IN! I'VE BEEN EXPECTING YOU.
I IMAGINE ALL MY BIRDS HAVE BEEN SCARING EVERYONE ELSE AWAY, BUT I KNEW YOU'D COME...

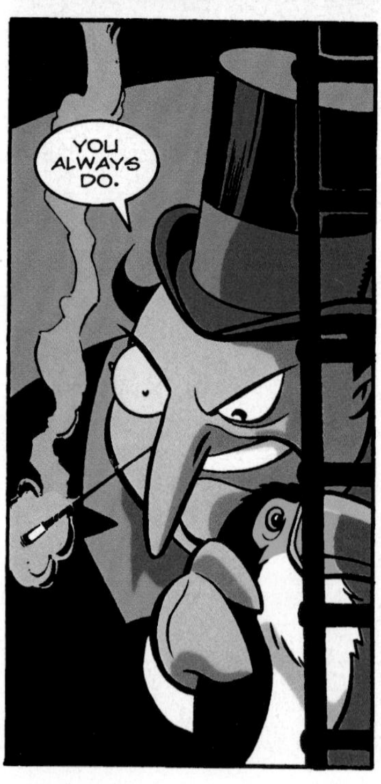
YOU ALWAYS DO.

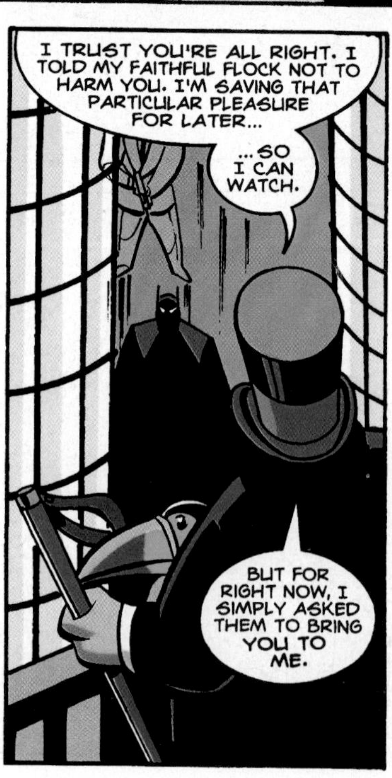
I TRUST YOU'RE ALL RIGHT. I TOLD MY FAITHFUL FLOCK NOT TO HARM YOU. I'M SAVING THAT PARTICULAR PLEASURE FOR LATER...
...SO I CAN WATCH.
BUT FOR RIGHT NOW, I SIMPLY ASKED THEM TO BRING YOU TO ME.

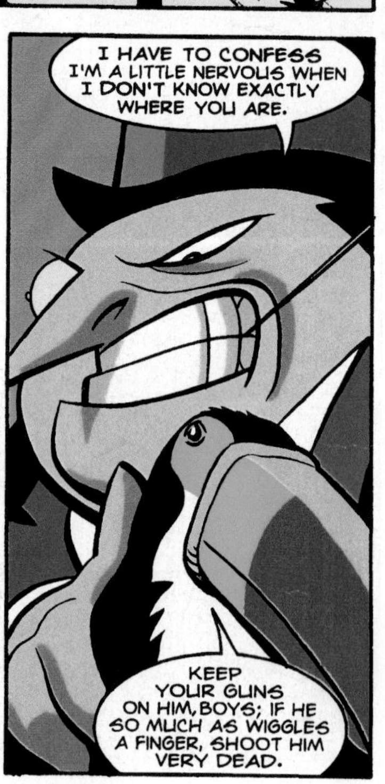
I HAVE TO CONFESS I'M A LITTLE NERVOUS WHEN I DON'T KNOW EXACTLY WHERE YOU ARE.
KEEP YOUR GUNS ON HIM, BOYS; IF HE SO MUCH AS WIGGLES A FINGER, SHOOT HIM VERY DEAD.

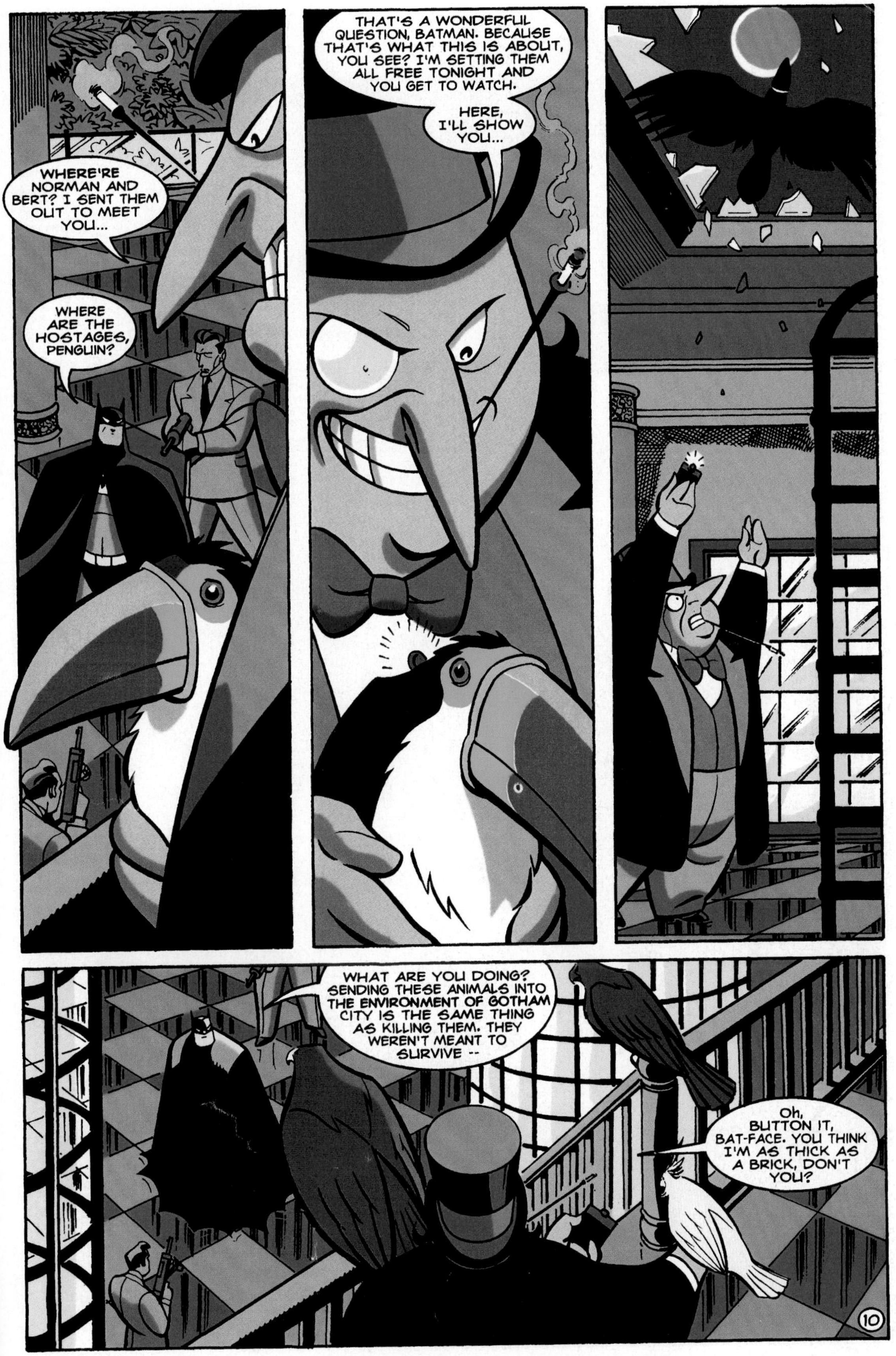
WHERE'RE NORMAN AND BERT? I SENT THEM OUT TO MEET YOU...
WHERE ARE THE HOSTAGES, PENGUIN?
THAT'S A WONDERFUL QUESTION, BATMAN. BECAUSE THAT'S WHAT THIS IS ABOUT, YOU SEE? I'M SETTING THEM ALL FREE TONIGHT AND YOU GET TO WATCH.
HERE, I'LL SHOW YOU...
WHAT ARE YOU DOING? SENDING THESE ANIMALS INTO THE ENVIRONMENT OF GOTHAM CITY IS THE SAME THING AS KILLING THEM. THEY WEREN'T MEANT TO SURVIVE --
Oh, BUTTON IT, BAT-FACE. YOU THINK I'M AS THICK AS A BRICK, DON'T YOU?
10

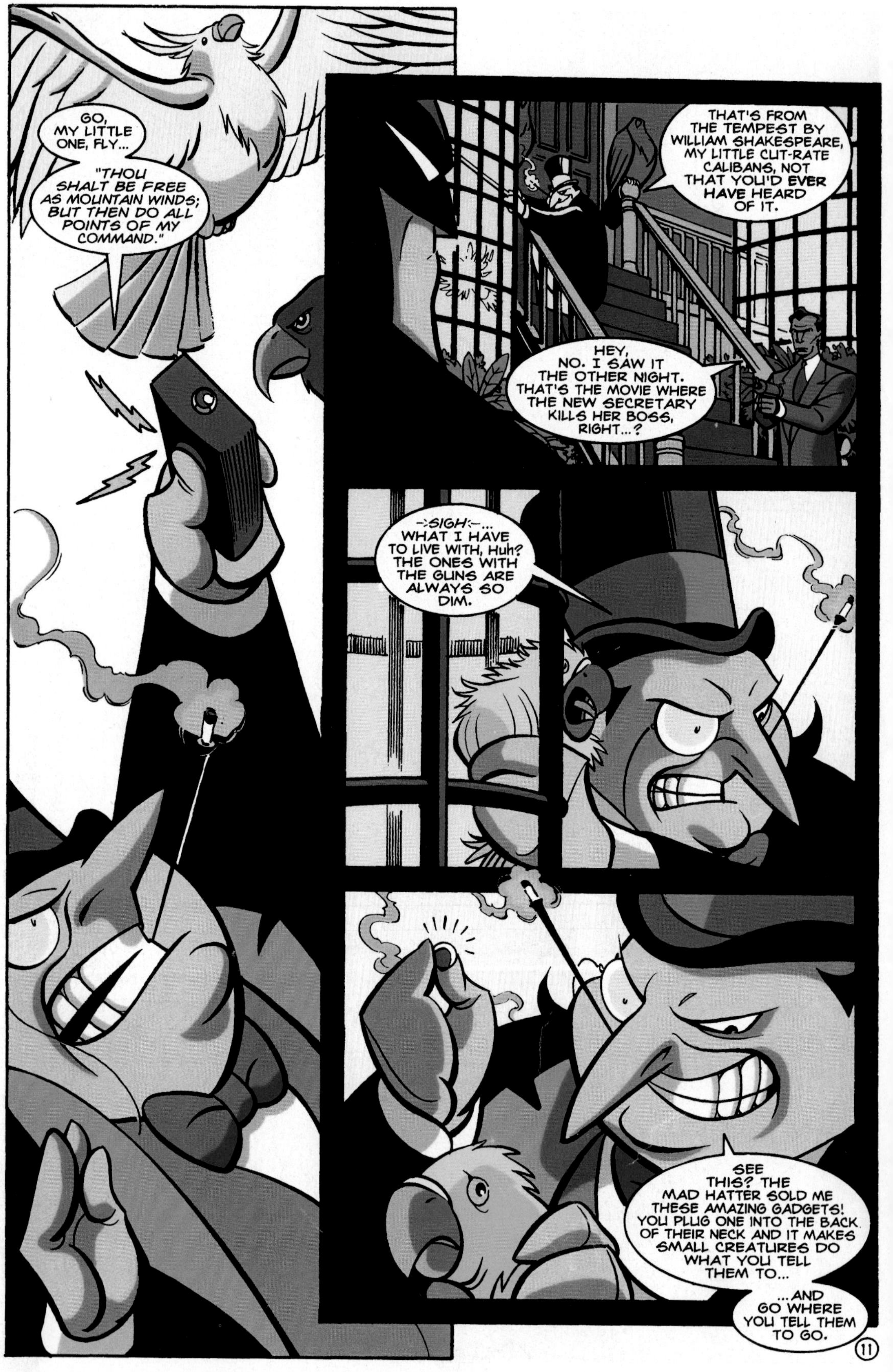
GO, MY LITTLE ONE, FLY...
"THOU SHALT BE FREE AS MOUNTAIN WINDS; BUT THEN DO ALL POINTS OF MY COMMAND."
THAT'S FROM THE TEMPEST BY WILLIAM SHAKESPEARE, MY LITTLE CUT-RATE CALIBANS, NOT THAT YOU'D **EVER HAVE** HEARD OF IT.
HEY, NO. I SAW IT THE OTHER NIGHT. THAT'S THE MOVIE WHERE THE NEW SECRETARY KILLS HER BOSS, RIGHT...?
>SIGH<... WHAT I HAVE TO LIVE WITH, Huh? THE ONES WITH THE GUNS ARE ALWAYS SO DIM.
SEE THIS? THE MAD HATTER SOLD ME THESE AMAZING GADGETS! YOU PLUG ONE INTO THE BACK OF THEIR NECK AND IT MAKES SMALL CREATURES DO WHAT YOU TELL THEM TO...
...AND GO WHERE YOU TELL THEM TO GO.

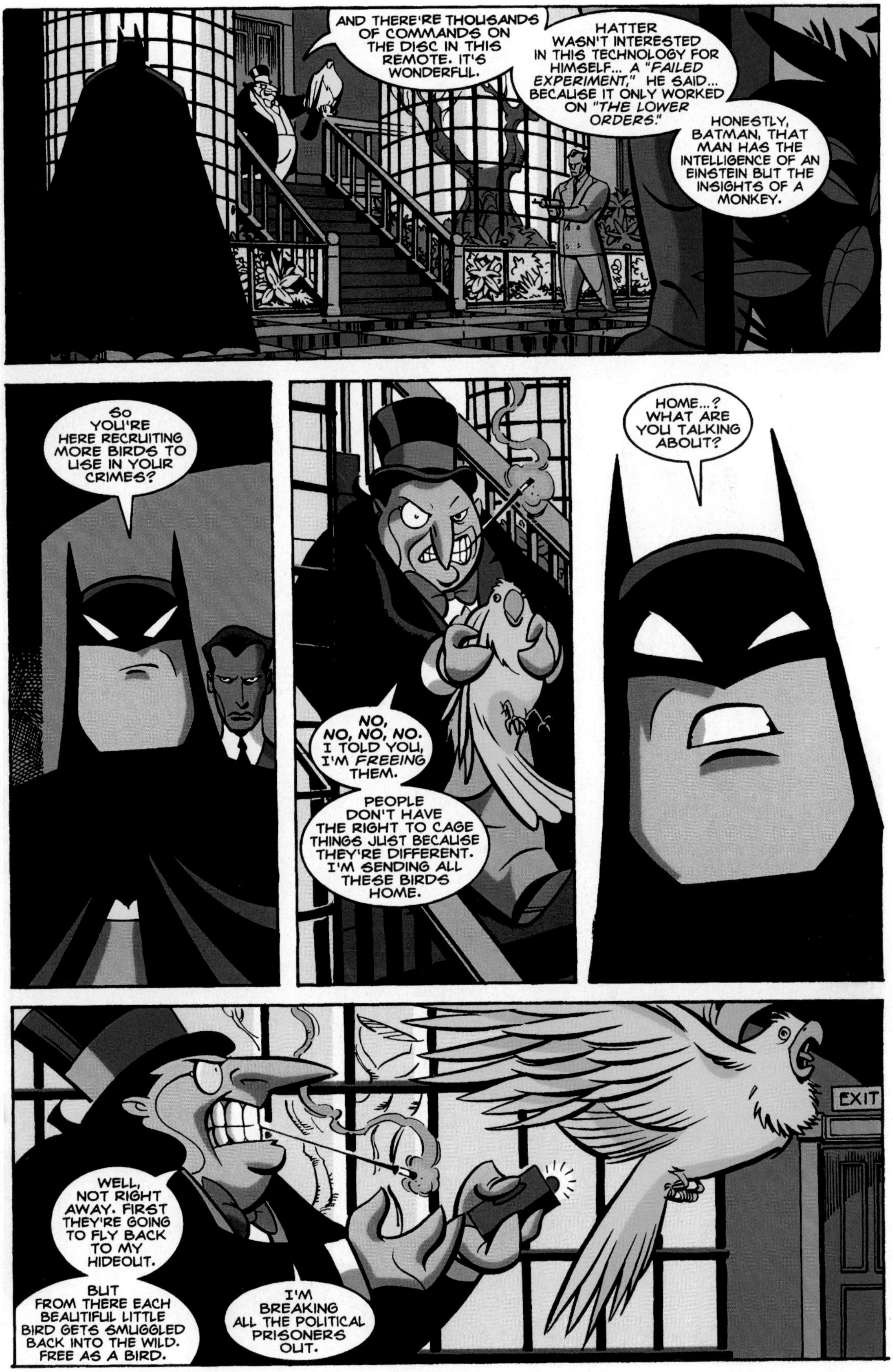
AND THERE'RE THOUSANDS OF COMMANDS ON THE DISC IN THIS REMOTE. IT'S WONDERFUL.
HATTER WASN'T INTERESTED IN THIS TECHNOLOGY FOR HIMSELF... A "FAILED EXPERIMENT," HE SAID... BECAUSE IT ONLY WORKED ON "THE LOWER ORDERS."
HONESTLY, BATMAN, THAT MAN HAS THE INTELLIGENCE OF AN EINSTEIN BUT THE INSIGHTS OF A MONKEY.
SO YOU'RE HERE RECRUITING MORE BIRDS TO USE IN YOUR CRIMES?
NO, NO, NO, NO. I TOLD YOU, I'M FREEING THEM.
PEOPLE DON'T HAVE THE RIGHT TO CAGE THINGS JUST BECAUSE THEY'RE DIFFERENT. I'M SENDING ALL THESE BIRDS HOME.
HOME...? WHAT ARE YOU TALKING ABOUT?
EXIT
WELL, NOT RIGHT AWAY. FIRST THEY'RE GOING TO FLY BACK TO MY HIDEOUT.
BUT FROM THERE EACH BEAUTIFUL LITTLE BIRD GETS SMUGGLED BACK INTO THE WILD. FREE AS A BIRD.
I'M BREAKING ALL THE POLITICAL PRISONERS OUT.

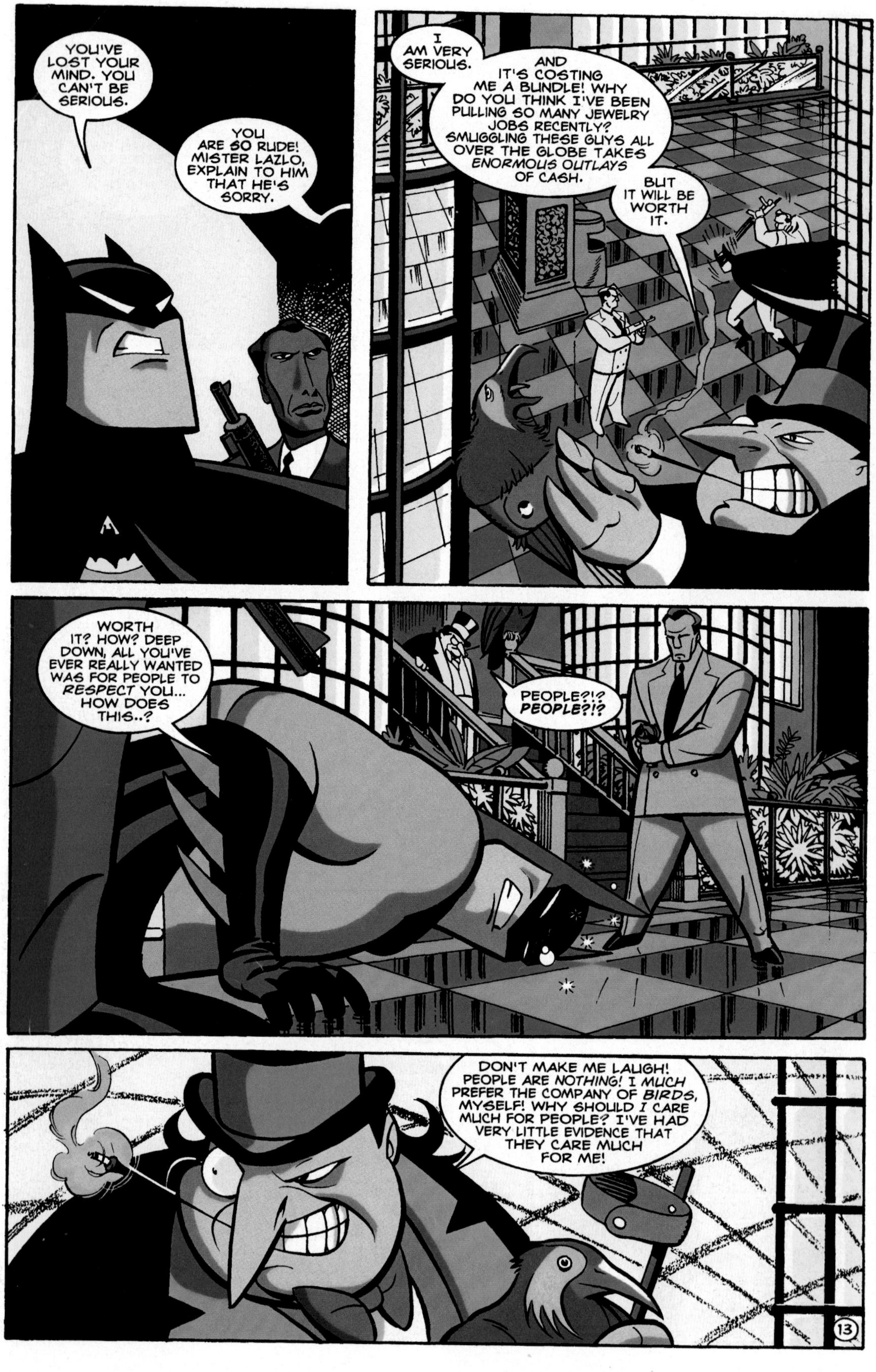
YOU'VE LOST YOUR MIND. YOU CAN'T BE SERIOUS.
YOU ARE SO RUDE! MISTER LAZLO, EXPLAIN TO HIM THAT HE'S SORRY.
I AM VERY SERIOUS.
AND IT'S COSTING ME A BUNDLE! WHY DO YOU THINK I'VE BEEN PULLING SO MANY JEWELRY JOBS RECENTLY? SMUGGLING THESE GUYS ALL OVER THE GLOBE TAKES ENORMOUS OUTLAYS OF CASH.
BUT IT WILL BE WORTH IT.
WORTH IT? HOW? DEEP DOWN, ALL YOU'VE EVER REALLY WANTED WAS FOR PEOPLE TO RESPECT YOU... HOW DOES THIS..?
PEOPLE?!? PEOPLE?!?
DON'T MAKE ME LAUGH! PEOPLE ARE NOTHING! I MUCH PREFER THE COMPANY OF BIRDS, MYSELF! WHY SHOULD I CARE MUCH FOR PEOPLE? I'VE HAD VERY LITTLE EVIDENCE THAT THEY CARE MUCH FOR ME!

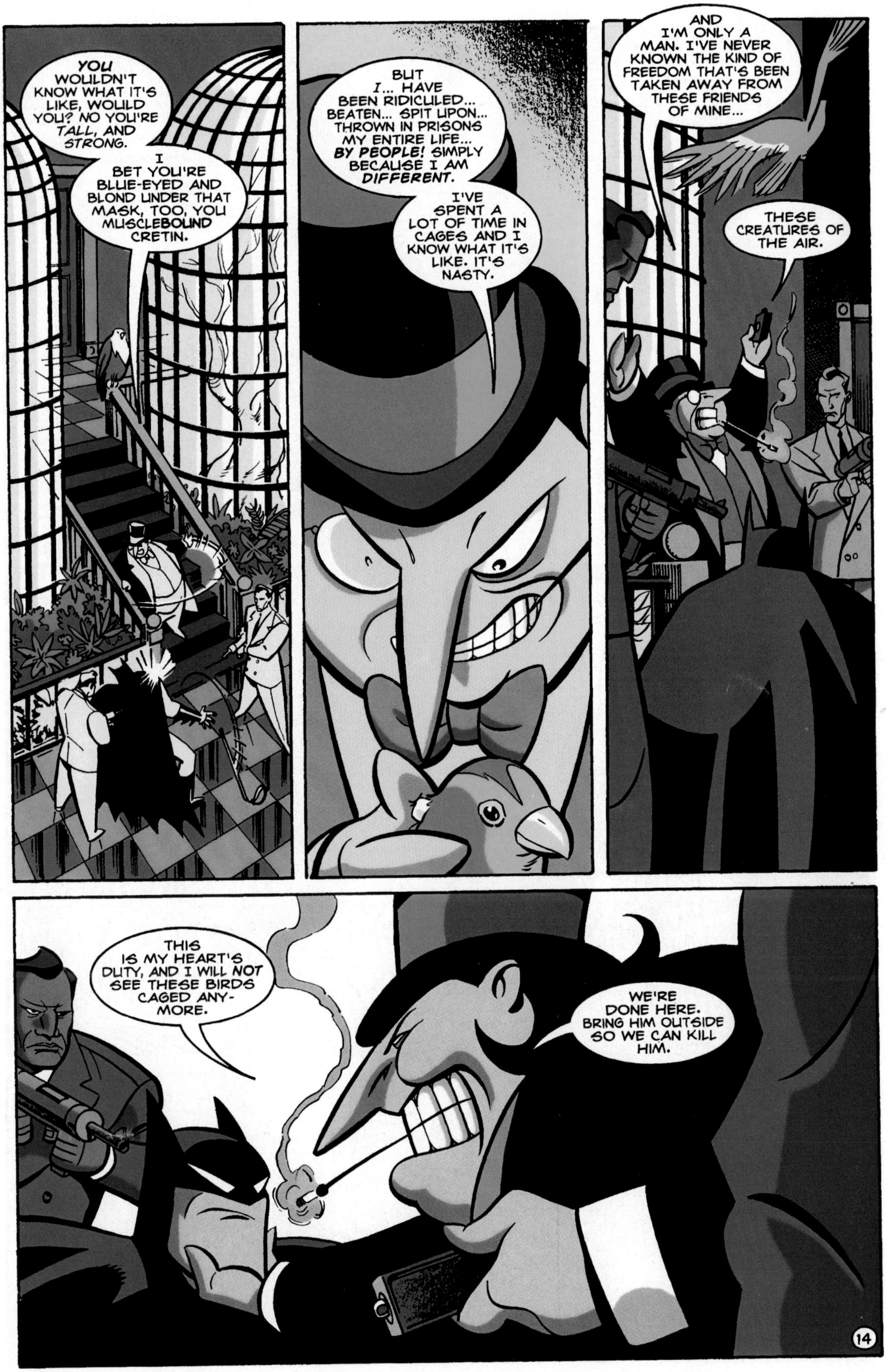
YOU WOULDN'T KNOW WHAT IT'S LIKE, WOULD YOU? NO YOU'RE TALL, AND STRONG.
I BET YOU'RE BLUE-EYED AND BLOND UNDER THAT MASK, TOO, YOU MUSCLEBOUND CRETIN.
BUT I... HAVE BEEN RIDICULED... BEATEN... SPIT UPON... THROWN IN PRISONS MY ENTIRE LIFE... BY PEOPLE! SIMPLY BECAUSE I AM DIFFERENT.
I'VE SPENT A LOT OF TIME IN CAGES AND I KNOW WHAT IT'S LIKE. IT'S NASTY.
AND I'M ONLY A MAN. I'VE NEVER KNOWN THE KIND OF FREEDOM THAT'S BEEN TAKEN AWAY FROM THESE FRIENDS OF MINE...
THESE CREATURES OF THE AIR.
THIS IS MY HEART'S DUTY, AND I WILL NOT SEE THESE BIRDS CAGED ANY-MORE.
WE'RE DONE HERE. BRING HIM OUTSIDE SO WE CAN KILL HIM.

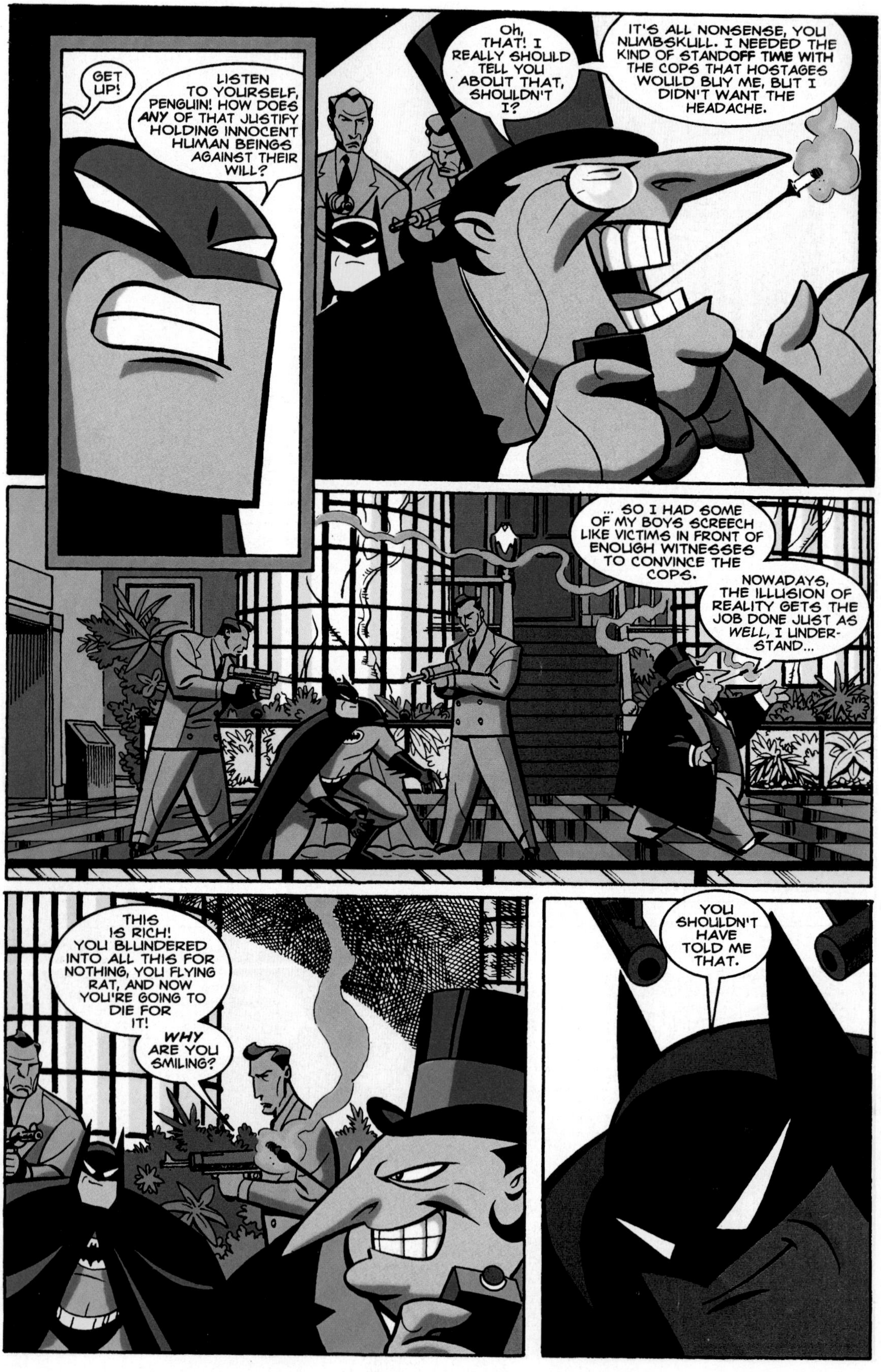
GET UP!
LISTEN TO YOURSELF, PENGUIN! HOW DOES ANY OF THAT JUSTIFY HOLDING INNOCENT HUMAN BEINGS AGAINST THEIR WILL?
Oh, THAT! I REALLY SHOULD TELL YOU ABOUT THAT, SHOULDN'T I?
IT'S ALL NONSENSE, YOU NUMBSKULL. I NEEDED THE KIND OF STANDOFF TIME WITH THE COPS THAT HOSTAGES WOULD BUY ME, BUT I DIDN'T WANT THE HEADACHE.
... SO I HAD SOME OF MY BOYS SCREECH LIKE VICTIMS IN FRONT OF ENOUGH WITNESSES TO CONVINCE THE COPS.
NOWADAYS, THE ILLUSION OF REALITY GETS THE JOB DONE JUST AS WELL, I UNDER-STAND...
THIS IS RICH! YOU BLUNDERED INTO ALL THIS FOR NOTHING, YOU FLYING RAT, AND NOW YOU'RE GOING TO DIE FOR IT!
WHY ARE YOU SMILING?
YOU SHOULDN'T HAVE TOLD ME THAT.

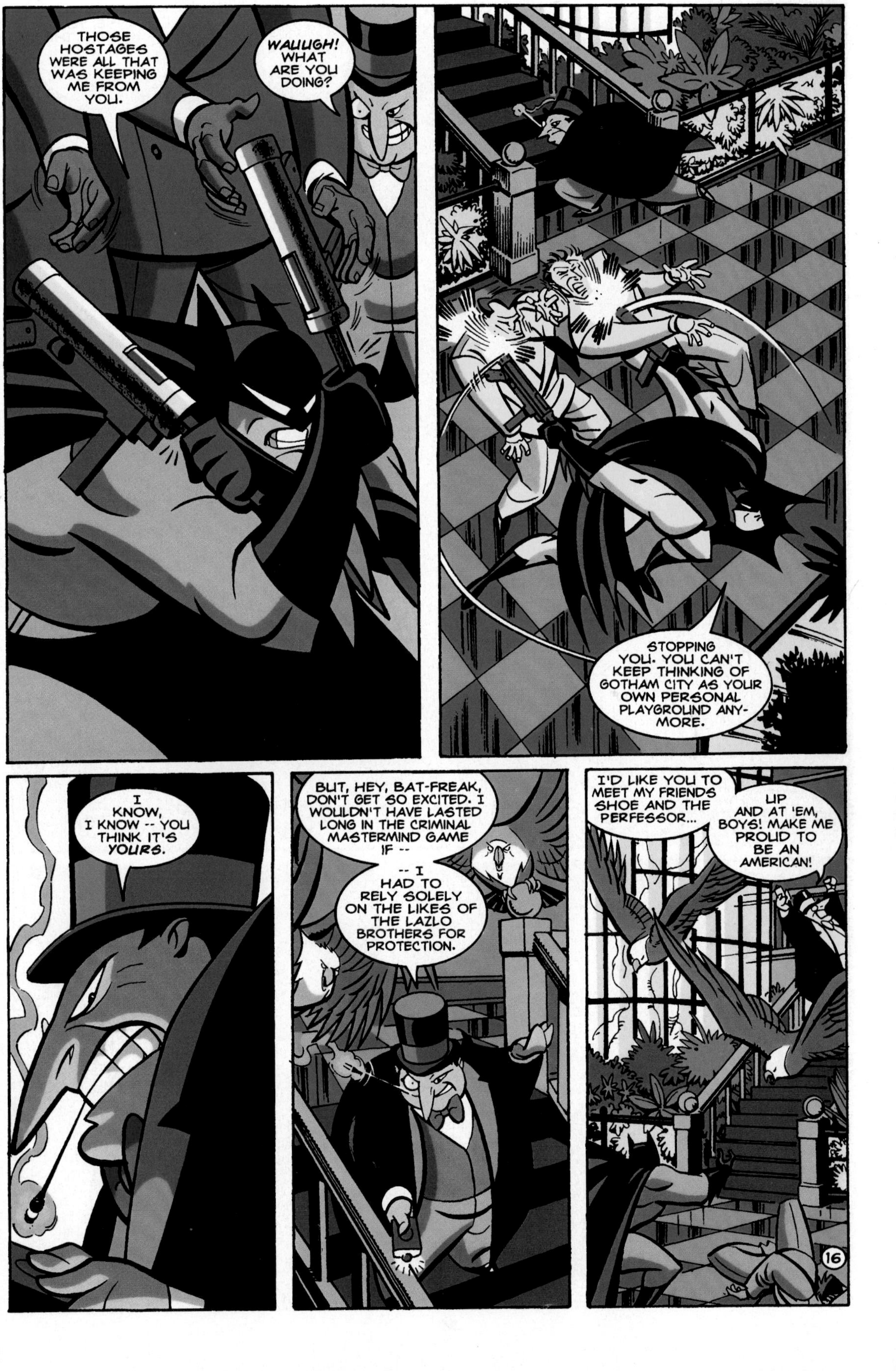
THOSE HOSTAGES WERE ALL THAT WAS KEEPING ME FROM YOU.
WAUUGH! WHAT ARE YOU DOING?
STOPPING YOU. YOU CAN'T KEEP THINKING OF GOTHAM CITY AS YOUR OWN PERSONAL PLAYGROUND ANY-MORE.
I KNOW, I KNOW -- YOU THINK IT'S YOURS.
BUT, HEY, BAT-FREAK, DON'T GET SO EXCITED. I WOULDN'T HAVE LASTED LONG IN THE CRIMINAL MASTERMIND GAME IF --
-- I HAD TO RELY SOLELY ON THE LIKES OF THE LAZLO BROTHERS FOR PROTECTION.
I'D LIKE YOU TO MEET MY FRIENDS SHOE AND THE PERFESSOR...
UP AND AT 'EM, BOYS! MAKE ME PROUD TO BE AN AMERICAN!
16

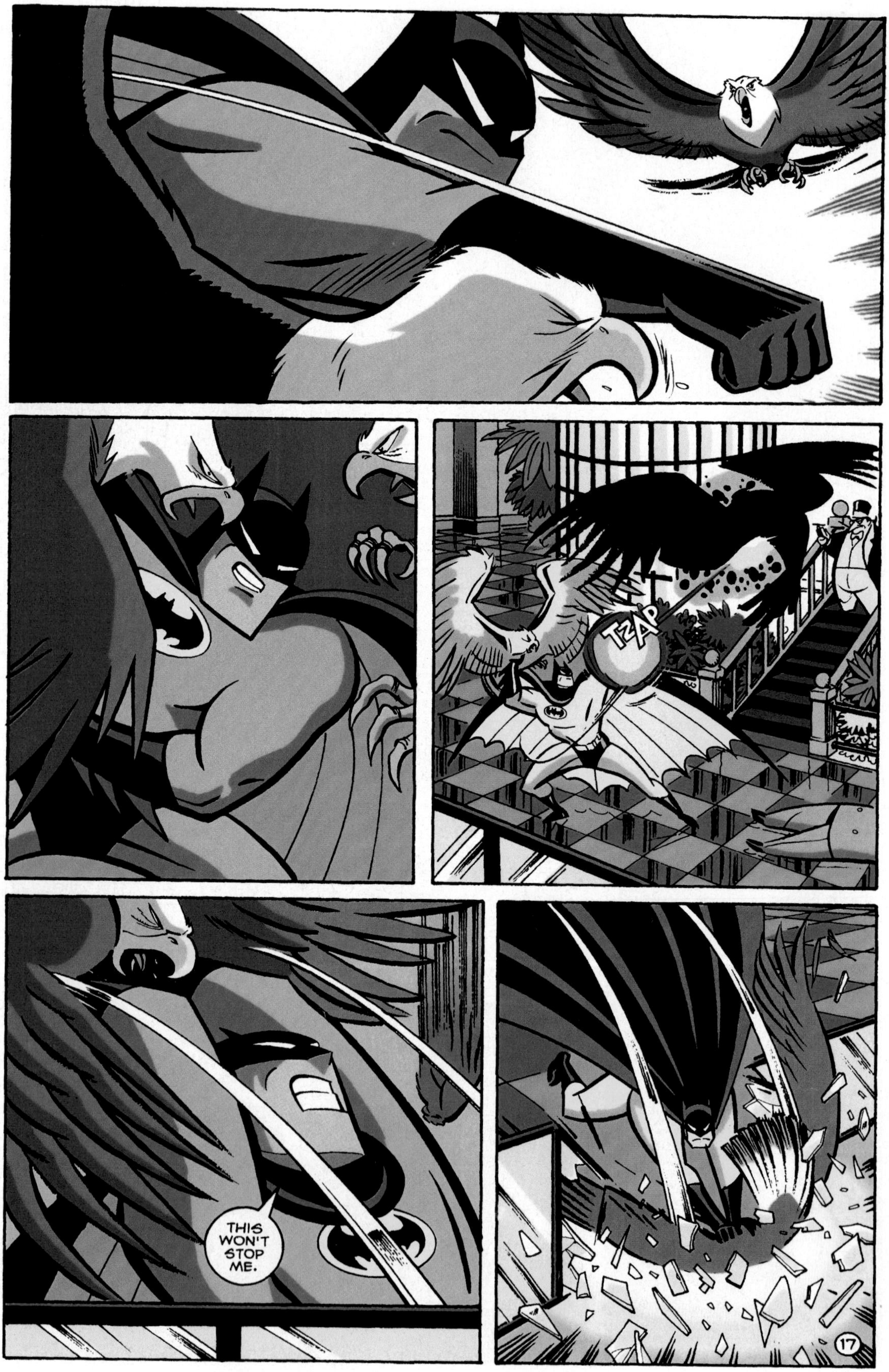
TZAP
THIS WON'T STOP ME.

YOU CLAIM TO LOVE THESE ANIMALS, PENGUIN.

SO DON'T MAKE ME HURT ANY MORE OF THEM.

A GENERAL LOSES SOLDIERS, BATMAN; IT DOESN'T MEAN HE DOESN'T LOVE THEM.

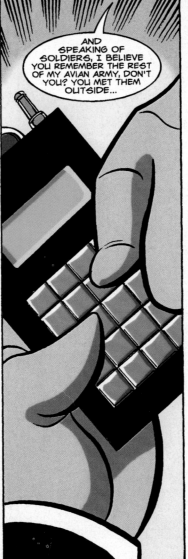

AND SPEAKING OF SOLDIERS, I BELIEVE YOU REMEMBER THE REST OF MY AVIAN ARMY, DON'T YOU? YOU MET THEM OUTSIDE...

LET'S INVITE THEM IN, SHALL WE?

18

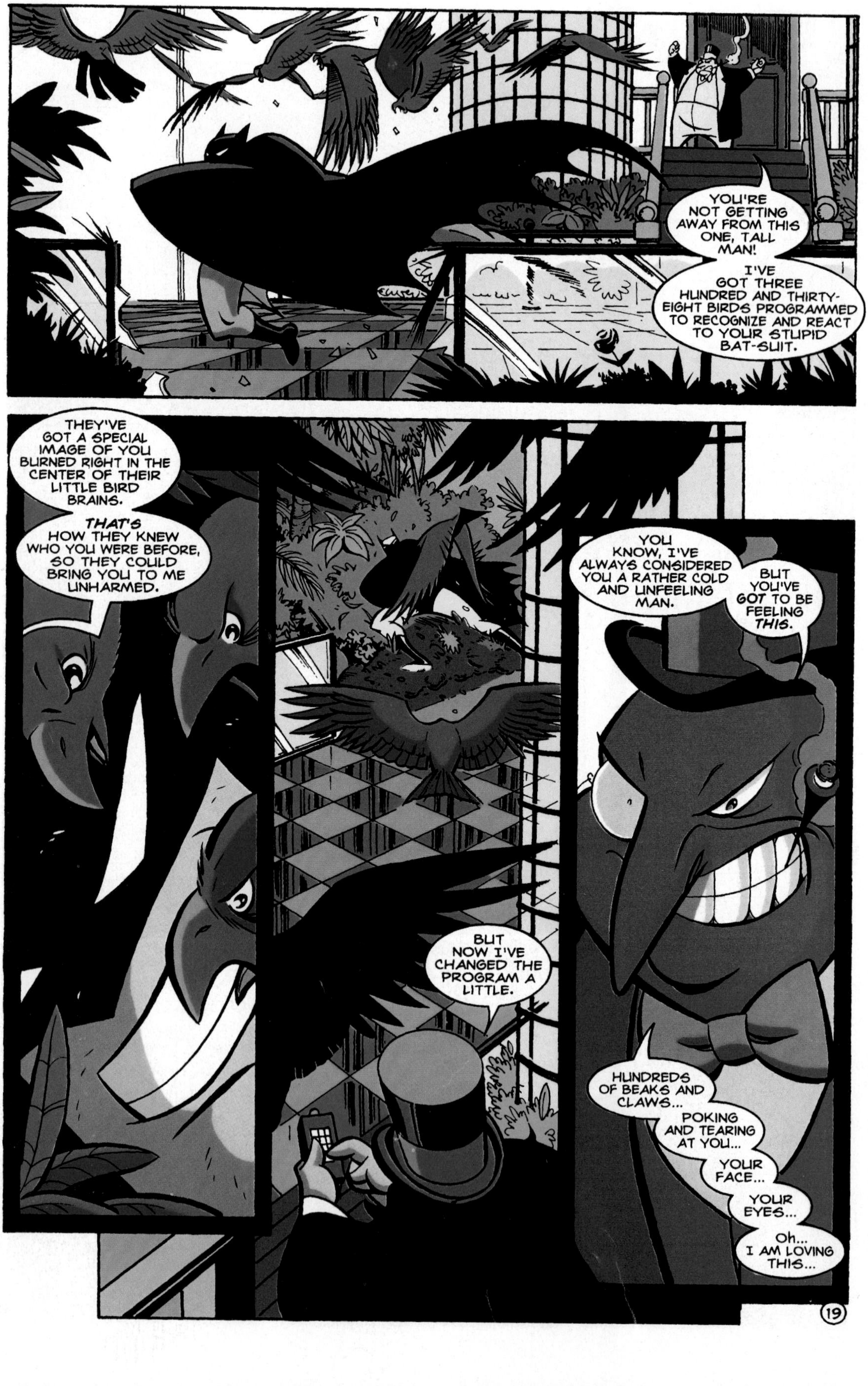
YOU'RE NOT GETTING AWAY FROM THIS ONE, TALL MAN!
I'VE GOT THREE HUNDRED AND THIRTY-EIGHT BIRDS PROGRAMMED TO RECOGNIZE AND REACT TO YOUR STUPID BAT-SUIT.
THEY'VE GOT A SPECIAL IMAGE OF YOU BURNED RIGHT IN THE CENTER OF THEIR LITTLE BIRD BRAINS.
THAT'S HOW THEY KNEW WHO YOU WERE BEFORE, SO THEY COULD BRING YOU TO ME UNHARMED.
BUT NOW I'VE CHANGED THE PROGRAM A LITTLE.
YOU KNOW, I'VE ALWAYS CONSIDERED YOU A RATHER COLD AND UNFEELING MAN.
BUT YOU'VE *GOT* TO BE FEELING *THIS*.
HUNDREDS OF BEAKS AND CLAWS...
POKING AND TEARING AT YOU...
YOUR FACE...
YOUR EYES...
Oh... I AM LOVING THIS...

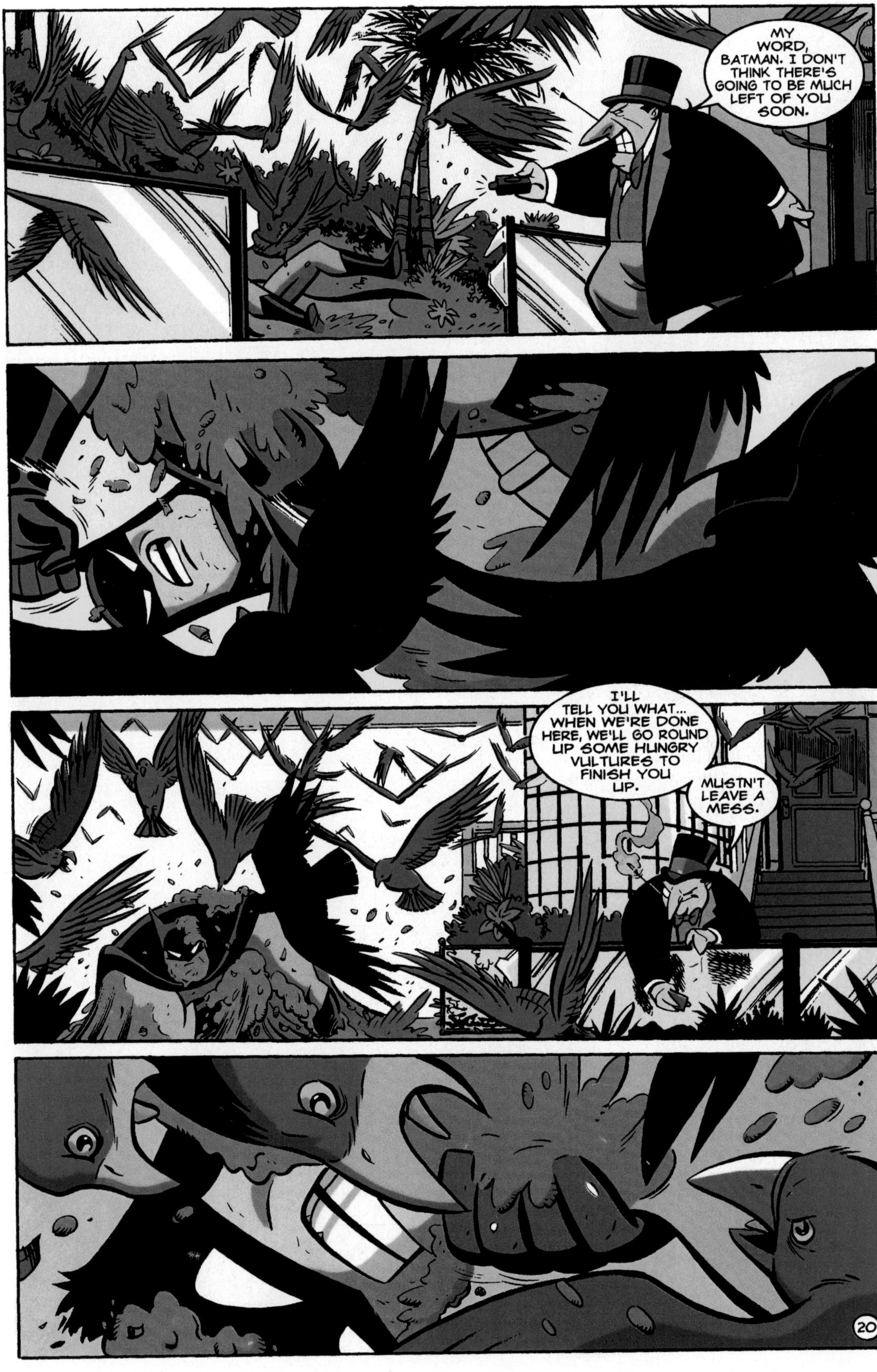
MY WORD, BATMAN. I DON'T THINK THERE'S GOING TO BE MUCH LEFT OF YOU SOON.
I'LL TELL YOU WHAT... WHEN WE'RE DONE HERE, WE'LL GO ROUND UP SOME HUNGRY VULTURES TO FINISH YOU UP.
MUSTN'T LEAVE A MESS.

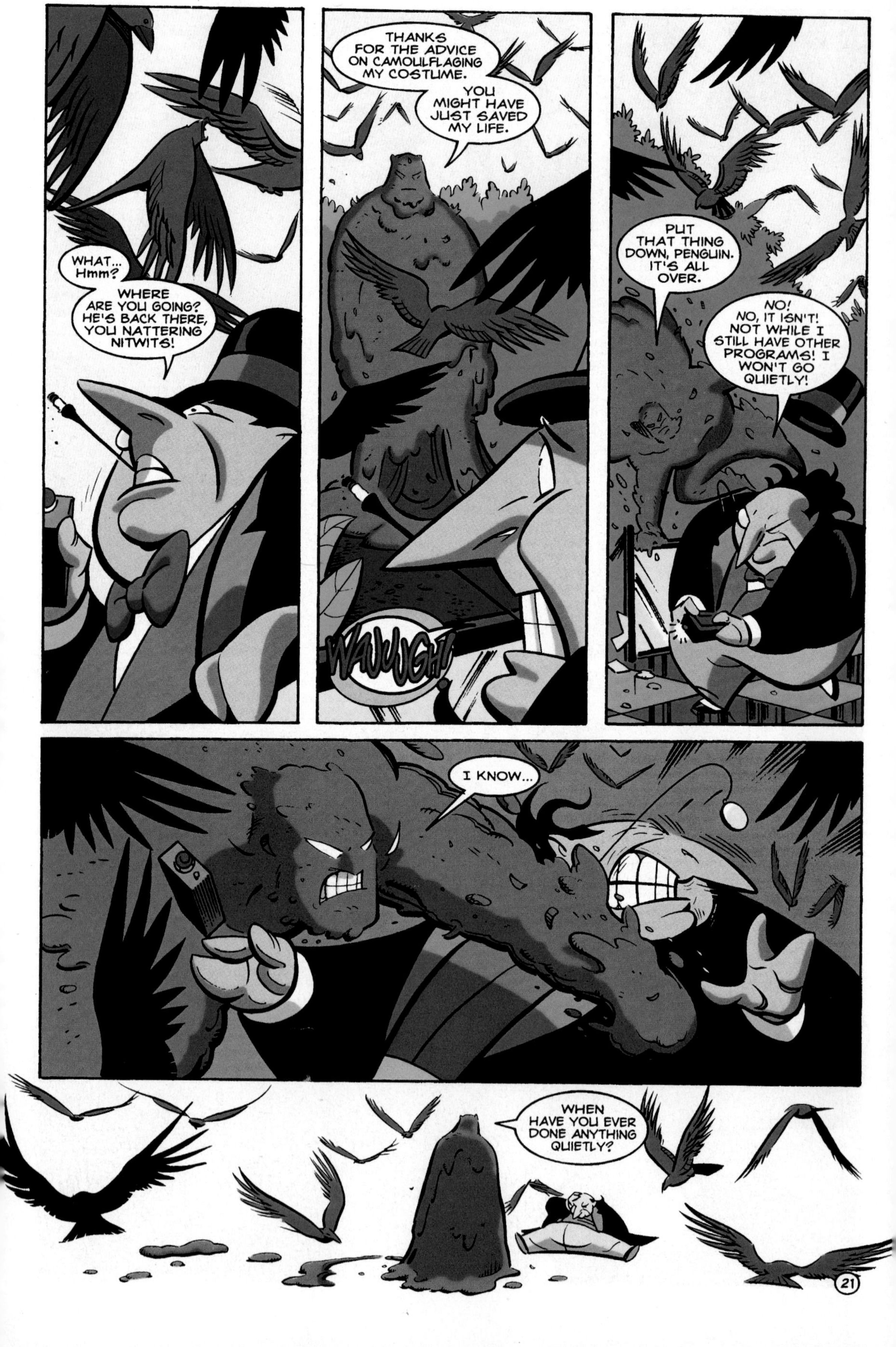

WHAT... Hmm?
WHERE ARE YOU GOING? HE'S BACK THERE, YOU NATTERING NITWITS!
THANKS FOR THE ADVICE ON CAMOUFLAGING MY COSTUME.
YOU MIGHT HAVE JUST SAVED MY LIFE.
WAUUGH!
PUT THAT THING DOWN, PENGUIN. IT'S ALL OVER.
NO! NO, IT ISN'T! NOT WHILE I STILL HAVE OTHER PROGRAMS! I WON'T GO QUIETLY!
I KNOW...
WHEN HAVE YOU EVER DONE ANYTHING QUIETLY?

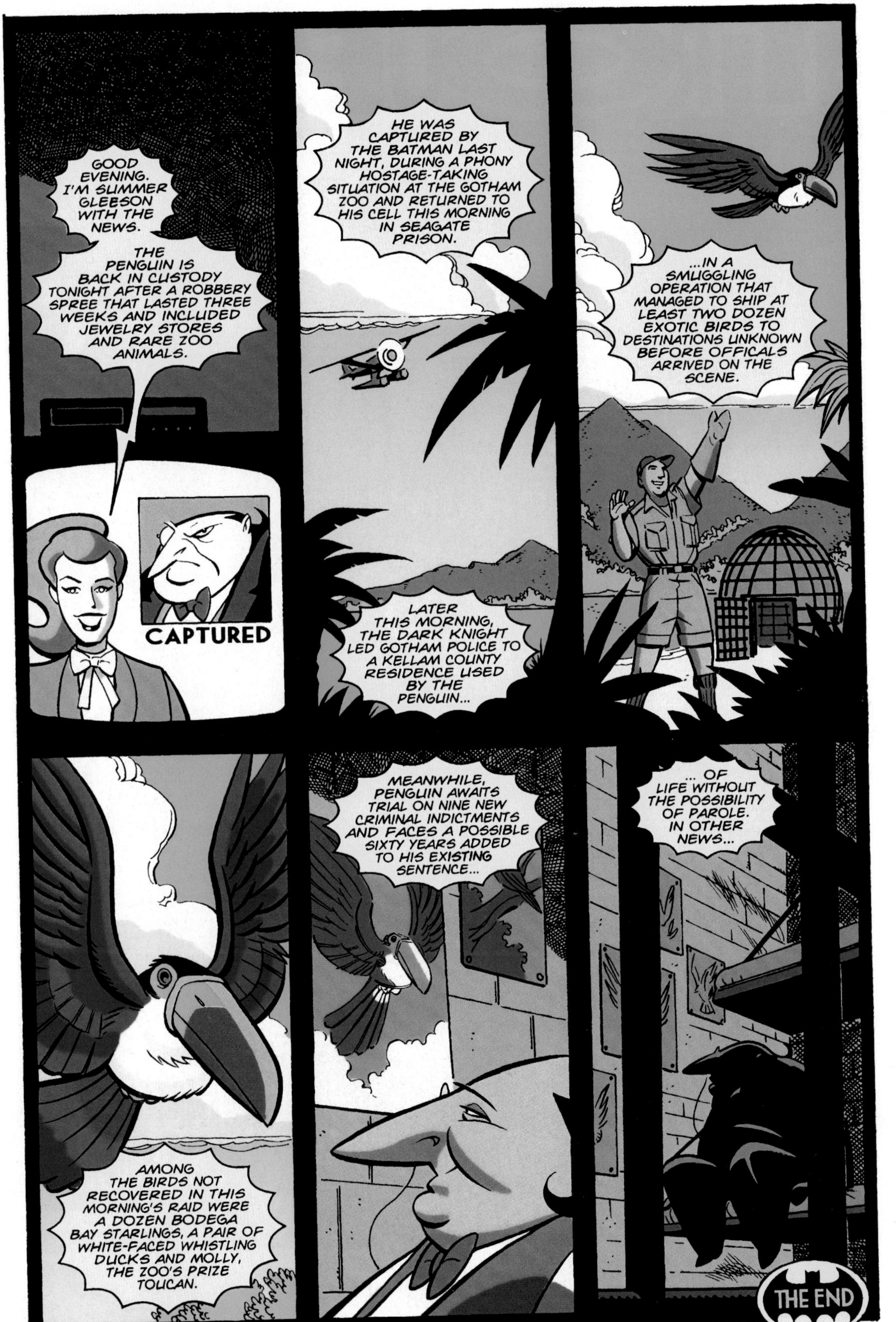
GOOD EVENING. I'M SUMMER GLEESON WITH THE NEWS.
THE PENGUIN IS BACK IN CUSTODY TONIGHT AFTER A ROBBERY SPREE THAT LASTED THREE WEEKS AND INCLUDED JEWELRY STORES AND RARE ZOO ANIMALS.
CAPTURED
HE WAS CAPTURED BY THE BATMAN LAST NIGHT, DURING A PHONY HOSTAGE-TAKING SITUATION AT THE GOTHAM ZOO AND RETURNED TO HIS CELL THIS MORNING IN SEAGATE PRISON.
LATER THIS MORNING, THE DARK KNIGHT LED GOTHAM POLICE TO A KELLAM COUNTY RESIDENCE USED BY THE PENGUIN...
...IN A SMUGGLING OPERATION THAT MANAGED TO SHIP AT LEAST TWO DOZEN EXOTIC BIRDS TO DESTINATIONS UNKNOWN BEFORE OFFICALS ARRIVED ON THE SCENE.
AMONG THE BIRDS NOT RECOVERED IN THIS MORNING'S RAID WERE A DOZEN BODEGA BAY STARLINGS, A PAIR OF WHITE-FACED WHISTLING DUCKS AND MOLLY, THE ZOO'S PRIZE TOUCAN.
MEANWHILE, PENGUIN AWAITS TRIAL ON NINE NEW CRIMINAL INDICTMENTS AND FACES A POSSIBLE SIXTY YEARS ADDED TO HIS EXISTING SENTENCE...
... OF LIFE WITHOUT THE POSSIBILITY OF PAROLE. IN OTHER NEWS...
THE END

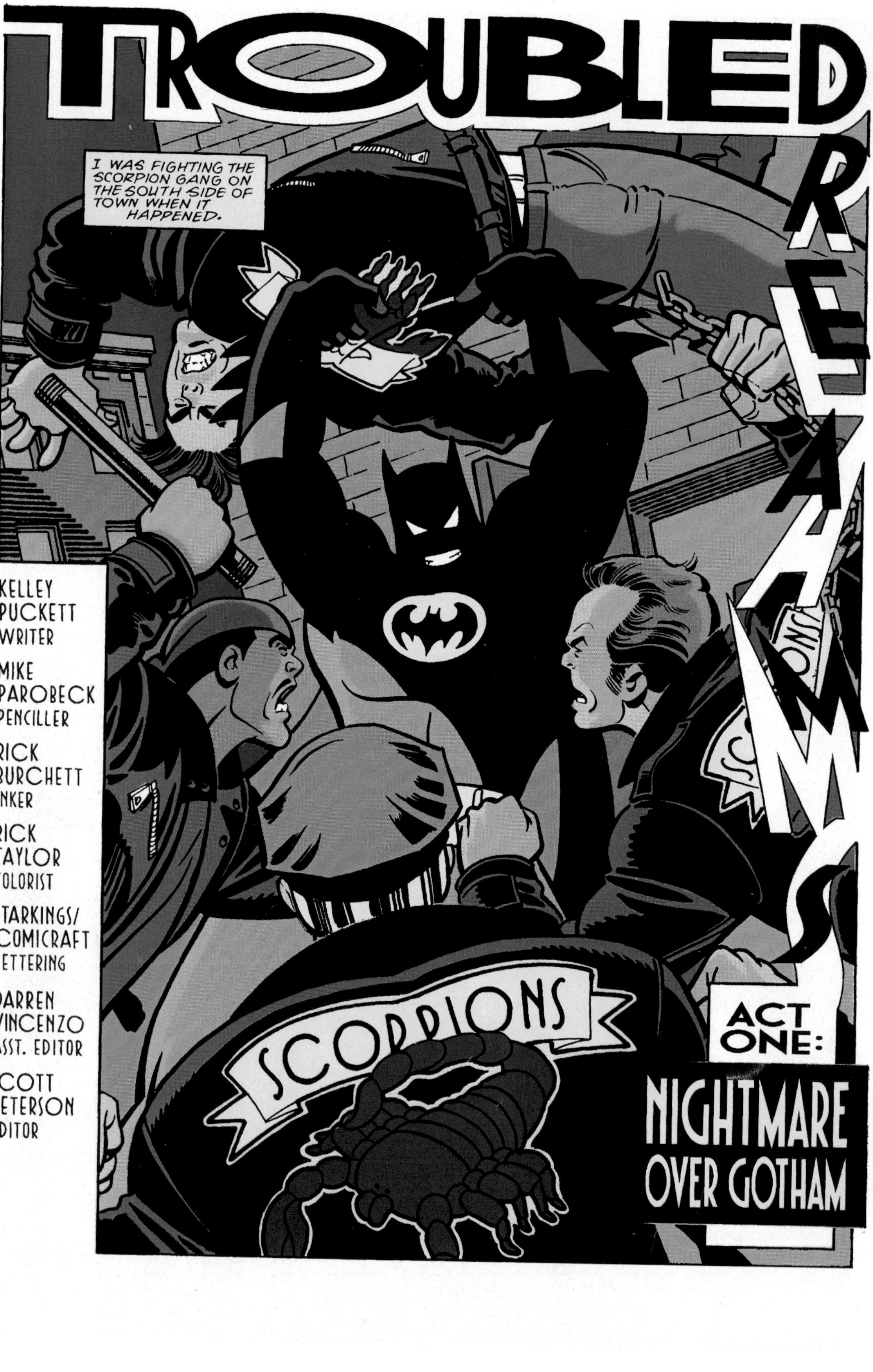
TROUBLED DREAMS
I WAS FIGHTING THE SCORPION GANG ON THE SOUTH SIDE OF TOWN WHEN IT HAPPENED.
SCORPIONS
ACT ONE:
NIGHTMARE OVER GOTHAM

KELLEY PUCKETT
WRITER

MIKE PAROBECK
PENCILLER

RICK BURCHETT
INKER

RICK TAYLOR
COLORIST

STARKINGS/ COMICRAFT
LETTERING

DARREN VINCENZO
ASST. EDITOR

SCOTT PETERSON
EDITOR

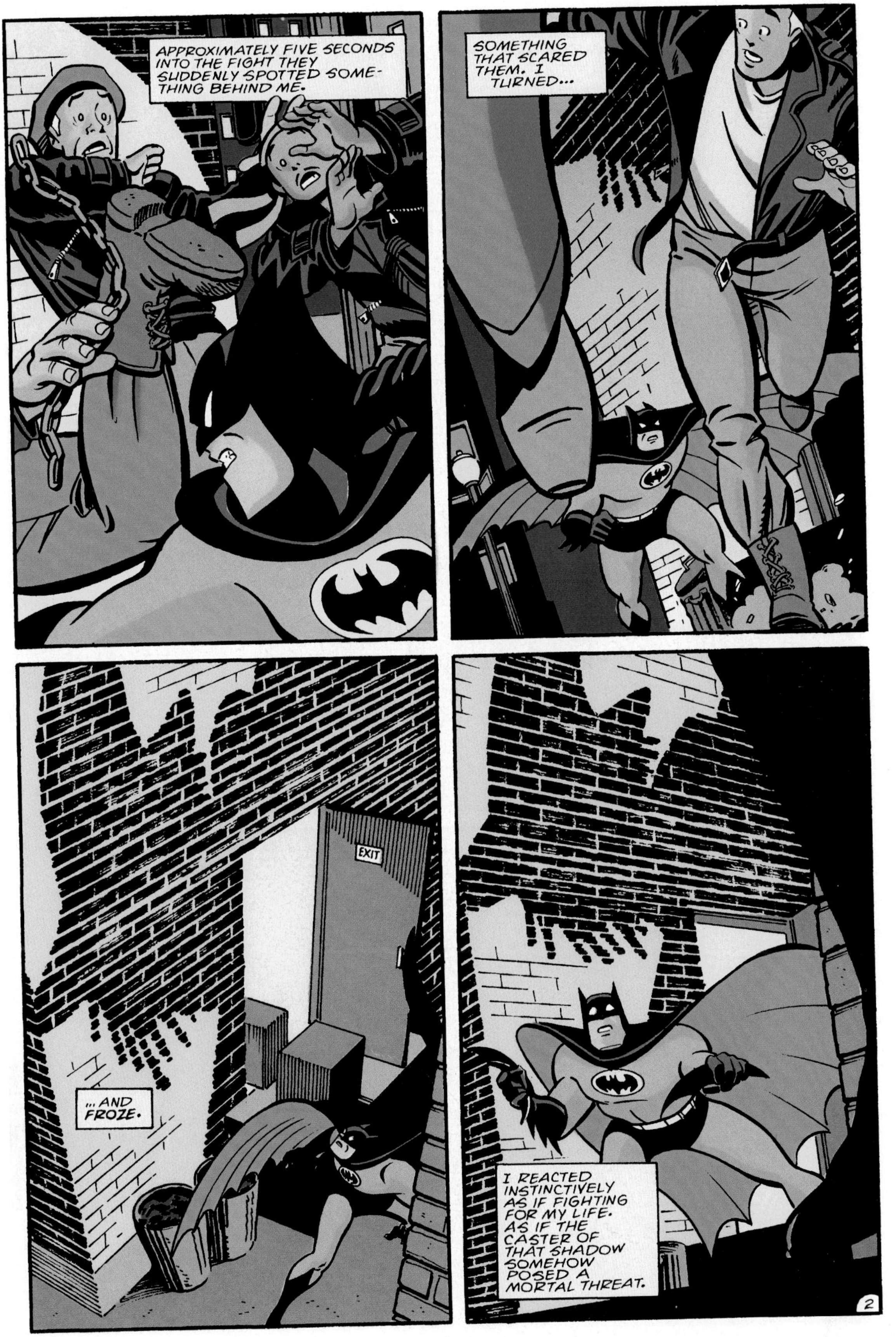
APPROXIMATELY FIVE SECONDS INTO THE FIGHT THEY SUDDENLY SPOTTED SOME-THING BEHIND ME.
SOMETHING THAT SCARED THEM. I TURNED...
...AND FROZE.
I REACTED INSTINCTIVELY AS IF FIGHTING FOR MY LIFE. AS IF THE CASTER OF THAT SHADOW SOMEHOW POSED A MORTAL THREAT.

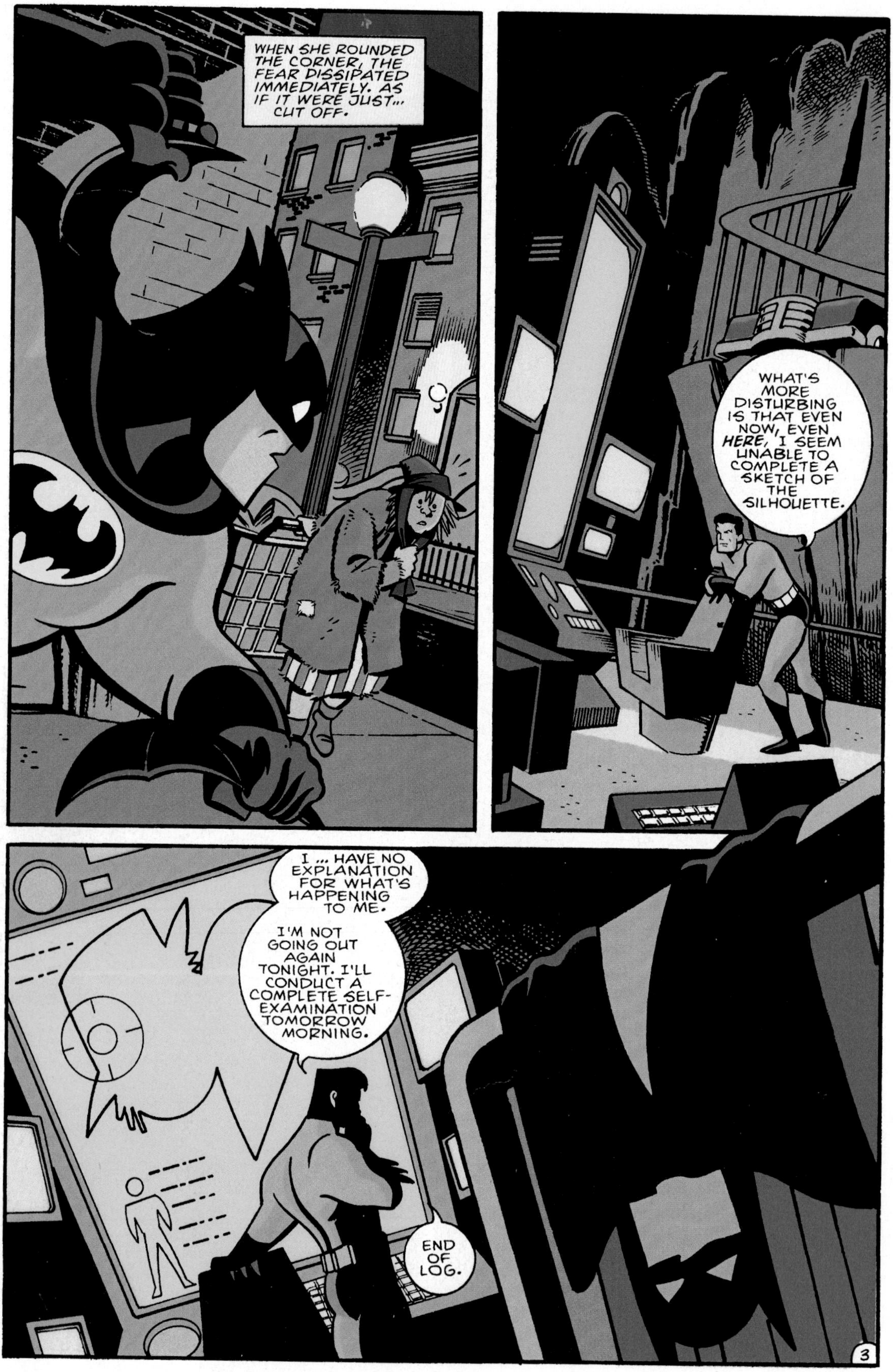
WHEN SHE ROUNDED THE CORNER, THE FEAR DISSIPATED IMMEDIATELY. AS IF IT WERE JUST... CUT OFF.
WHAT'S MORE DISTURBING IS THAT EVEN NOW, EVEN HERE, I SEEM UNABLE TO COMPLETE A SKETCH OF THE SILHOUETTE.
I ... HAVE NO EXPLANATION FOR WHAT'S HAPPENING TO ME.
I'M NOT GOING OUT AGAIN TONIGHT. I'LL CONDUCT A COMPLETE SELF-EXAMINATION TOMORROW MORNING.
END OF LOG.
3

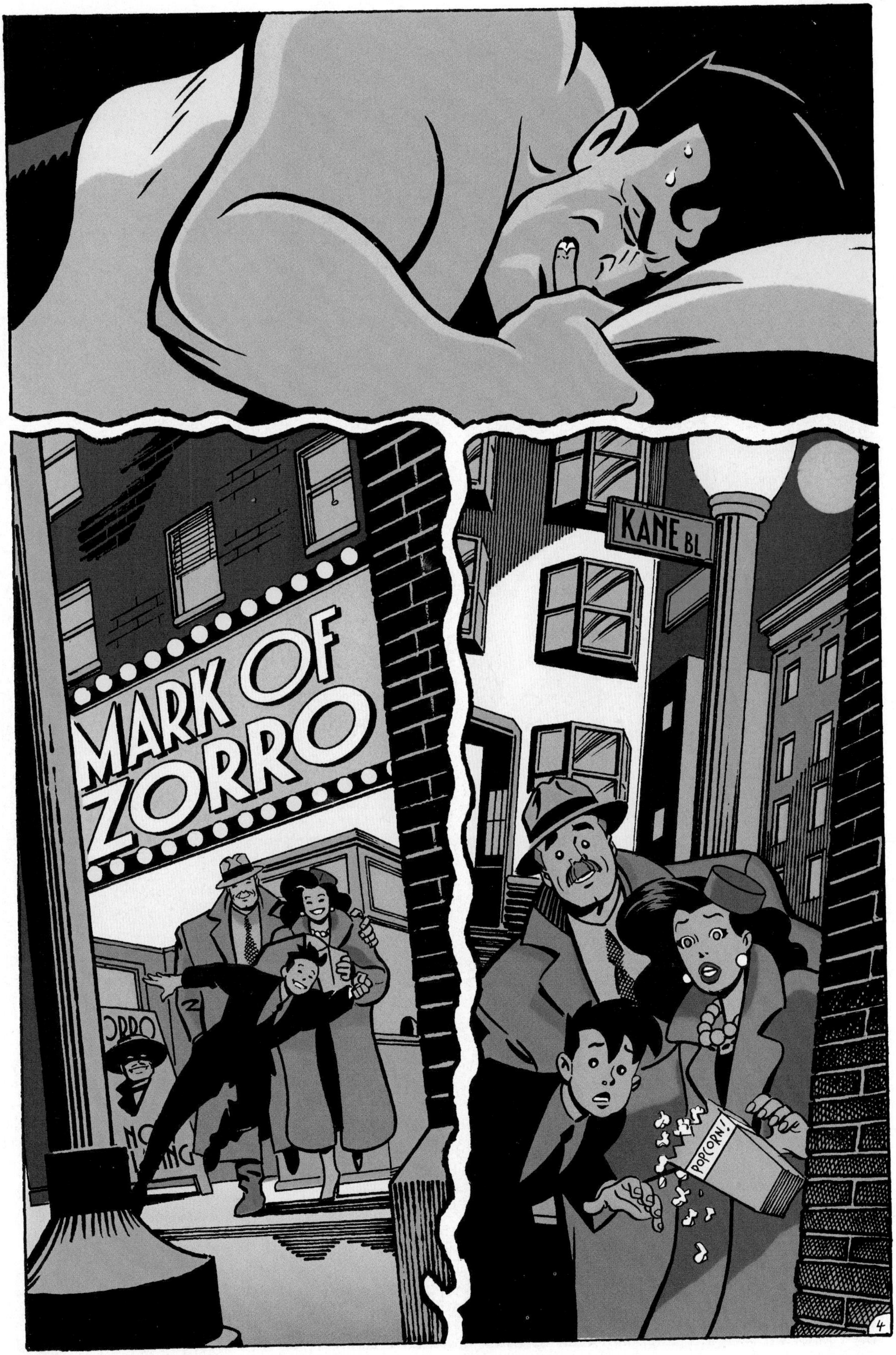
KANE BL
MARK OF ZORRO
ZORRO
POPCORN!

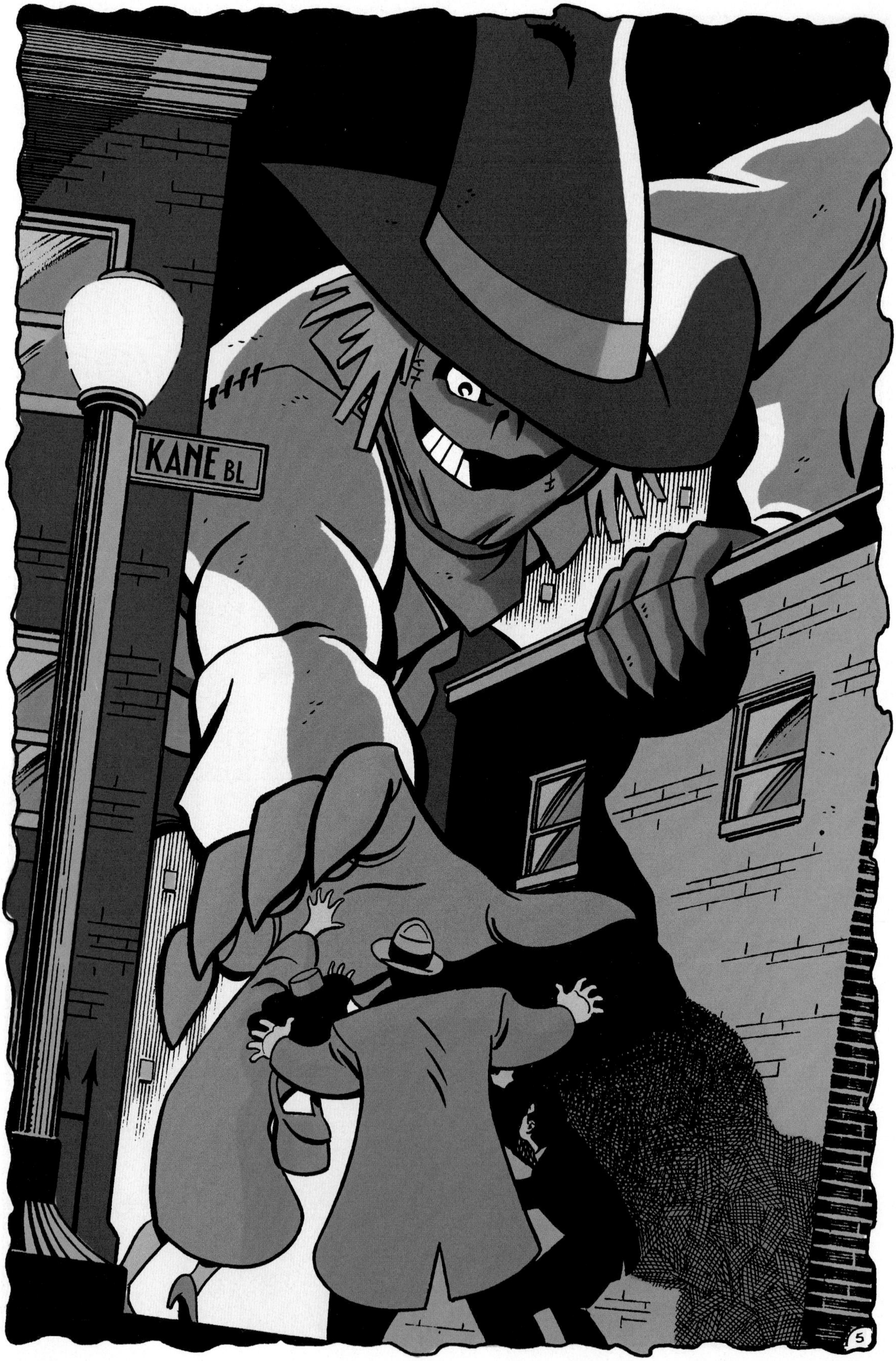
KANE BL

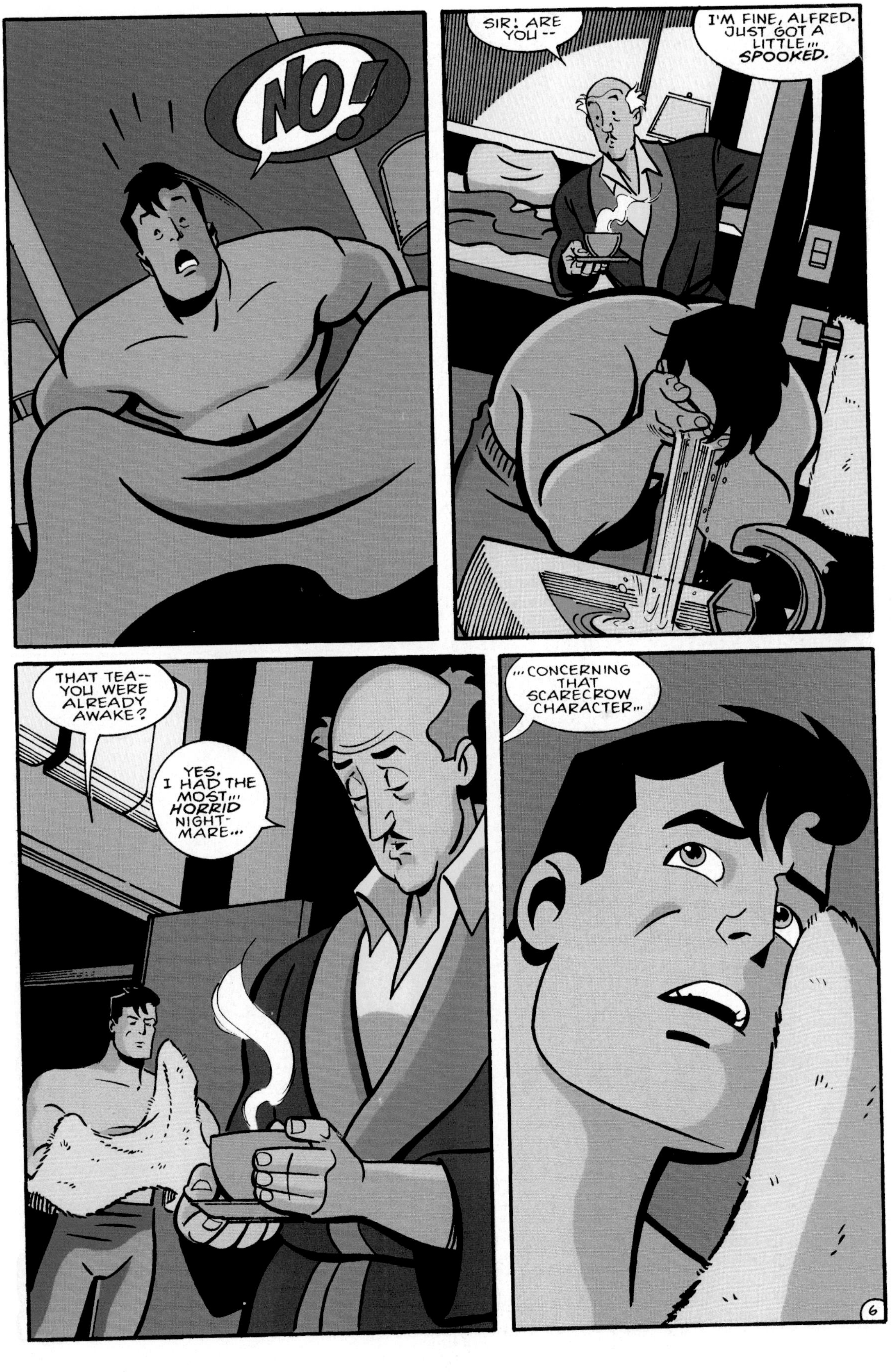
NO!
SIR! ARE YOU --
I'M FINE, ALFRED. JUST GOT A LITTLE... SPOOKED.
THAT TEA-- YOU WERE ALREADY AWAKE?
YES. I HAD THE MOST... HORRID NIGHT-MARE...
...CONCERNING THAT SCARECROW CHARACTER...

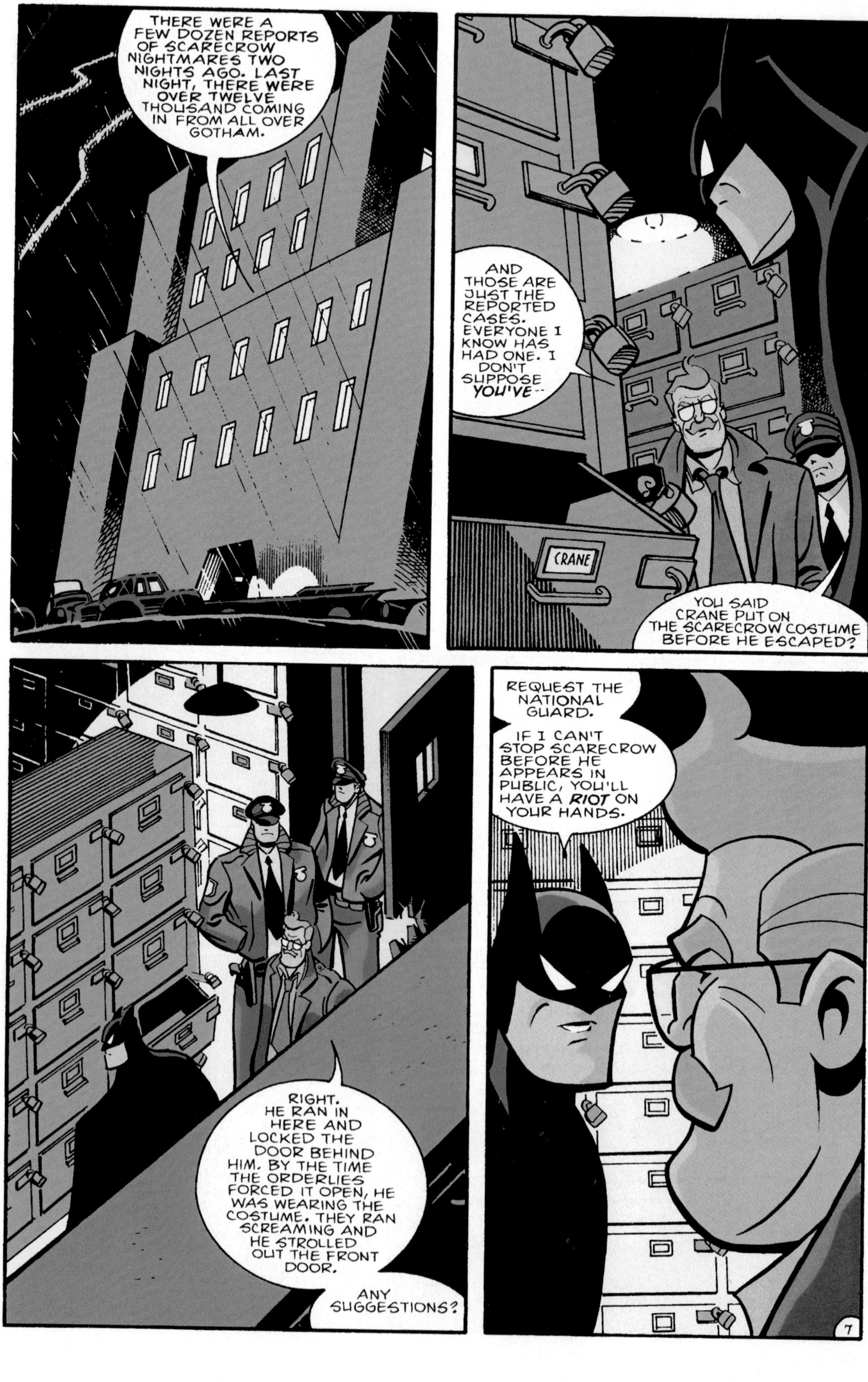
THERE WERE A FEW DOZEN REPORTS OF SCARECROW NIGHTMARES TWO NIGHTS AGO. LAST NIGHT, THERE WERE OVER TWELVE THOUSAND COMING IN FROM ALL OVER GOTHAM.
AND THOSE ARE JUST THE REPORTED CASES. EVERYONE I KNOW HAS HAD ONE. I DON'T SUPPOSE *YOU'VE*--
CRANE
YOU SAID CRANE PUT ON THE SCARECROW COSTUME BEFORE HE ESCAPED?
RIGHT. HE RAN IN HERE AND LOCKED THE DOOR BEHIND HIM. BY THE TIME THE ORDERLIES FORCED IT OPEN, HE WAS WEARING THE COSTUME. THEY RAN SCREAMING AND HE STROLLED OUT THE FRONT DOOR.
ANY SUGGESTIONS?
REQUEST THE NATIONAL GUARD.
IF I CAN'T STOP SCARECROW BEFORE HE APPEARS IN PUBLIC, YOU'LL HAVE A *RIOT* ON YOUR HANDS.

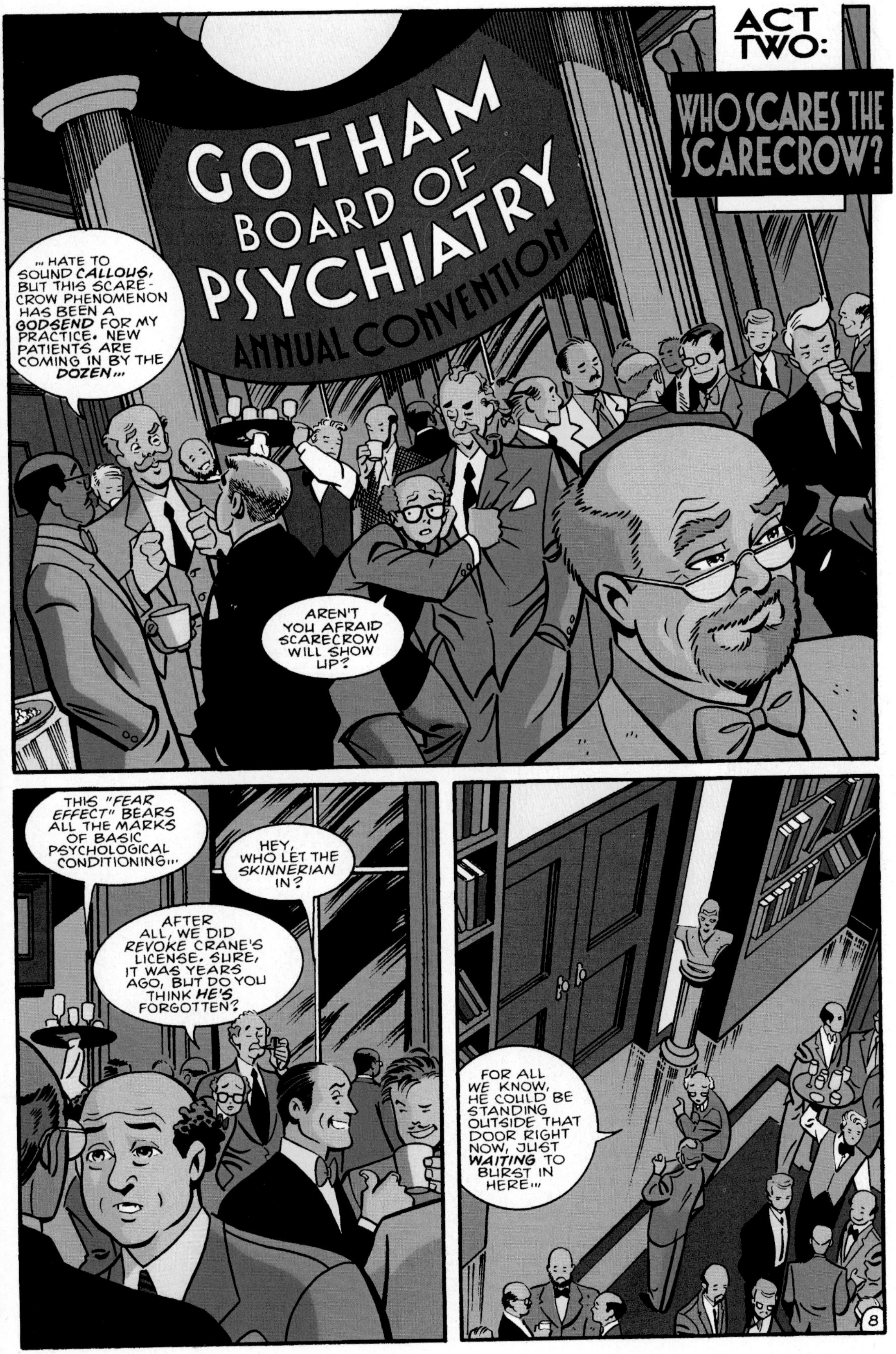
ACT TWO:
WHO SCARES THE SCARECROW?
GOTHAM BOARD OF PSYCHIATRY ANNUAL CONVENTION
...HATE TO SOUND CALLOUS, BUT THIS SCARE-CROW PHENOMENON HAS BEEN A GODSEND FOR MY PRACTICE. NEW PATIENTS ARE COMING IN BY THE DOZEN...
AREN'T YOU AFRAID SCARECROW WILL SHOW UP?
THIS "FEAR EFFECT" BEARS ALL THE MARKS OF BASIC PSYCHOLOGICAL CONDITIONING...
HEY, WHO LET THE SKINNERIAN IN?
AFTER ALL, WE DID REVOKE CRANE'S LICENSE. SURE, IT WAS YEARS AGO, BUT DO YOU THINK HE'S FORGOTTEN?
FOR ALL WE KNOW, HE COULD BE STANDING OUTSIDE THAT DOOR RIGHT NOW, JUST WAITING TO BURST IN HERE...

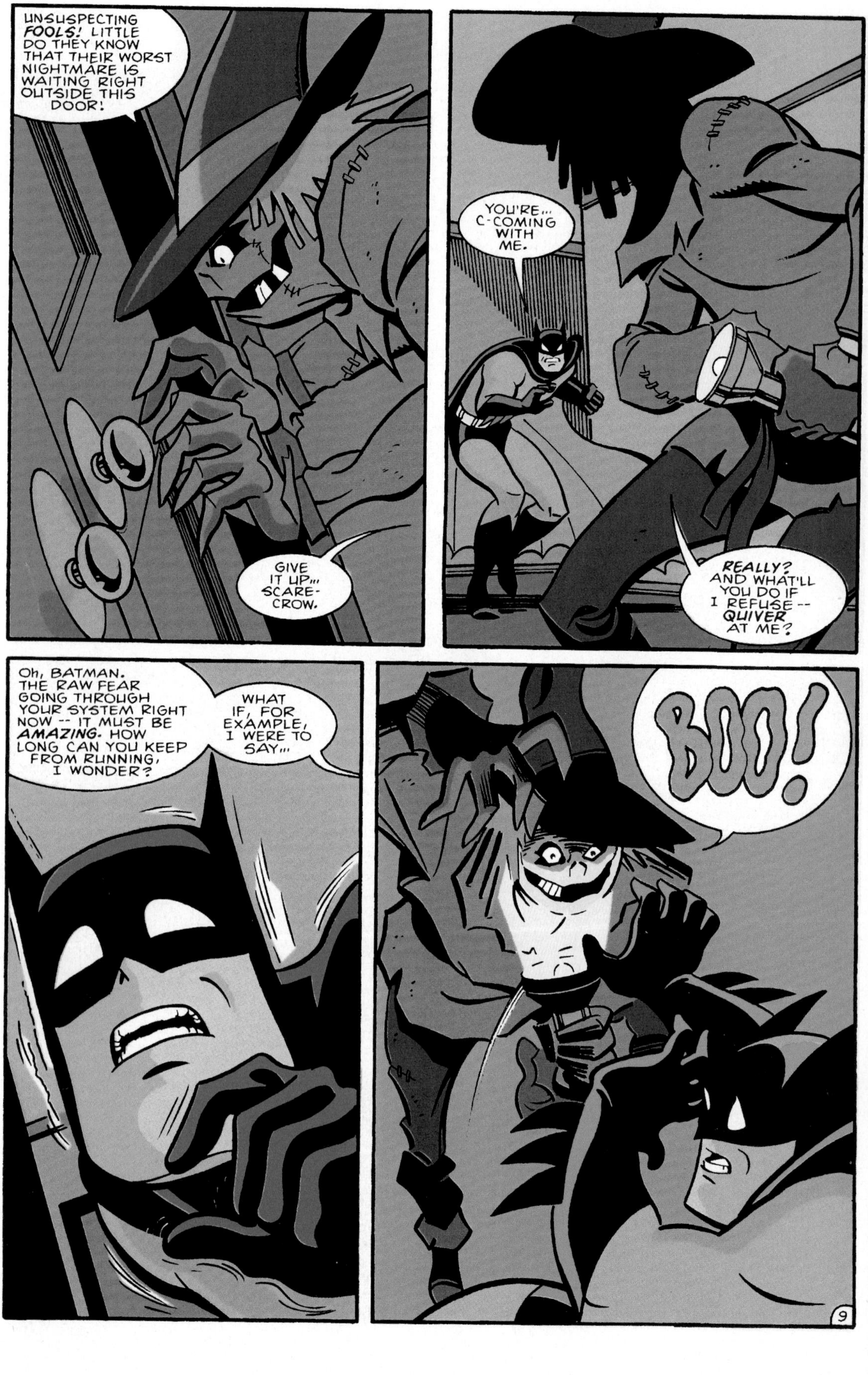

UNSUSPECTING FOOLS! LITTLE DO THEY KNOW THAT THEIR WORST NIGHTMARE IS WAITING RIGHT OUTSIDE THIS DOOR!
GIVE IT UP... SCARE-CROW.
YOU'RE... C-COMING WITH ME.
REALLY? AND WHAT'LL YOU DO IF I REFUSE -- QUIVER AT ME?
Oh, BATMAN. THE RAW FEAR GOING THROUGH YOUR SYSTEM RIGHT NOW -- IT MUST BE AMAZING. HOW LONG CAN YOU KEEP FROM RUNNING, I WONDER?
WHAT IF, FOR EXAMPLE, I WERE TO SAY...
BOO!
9

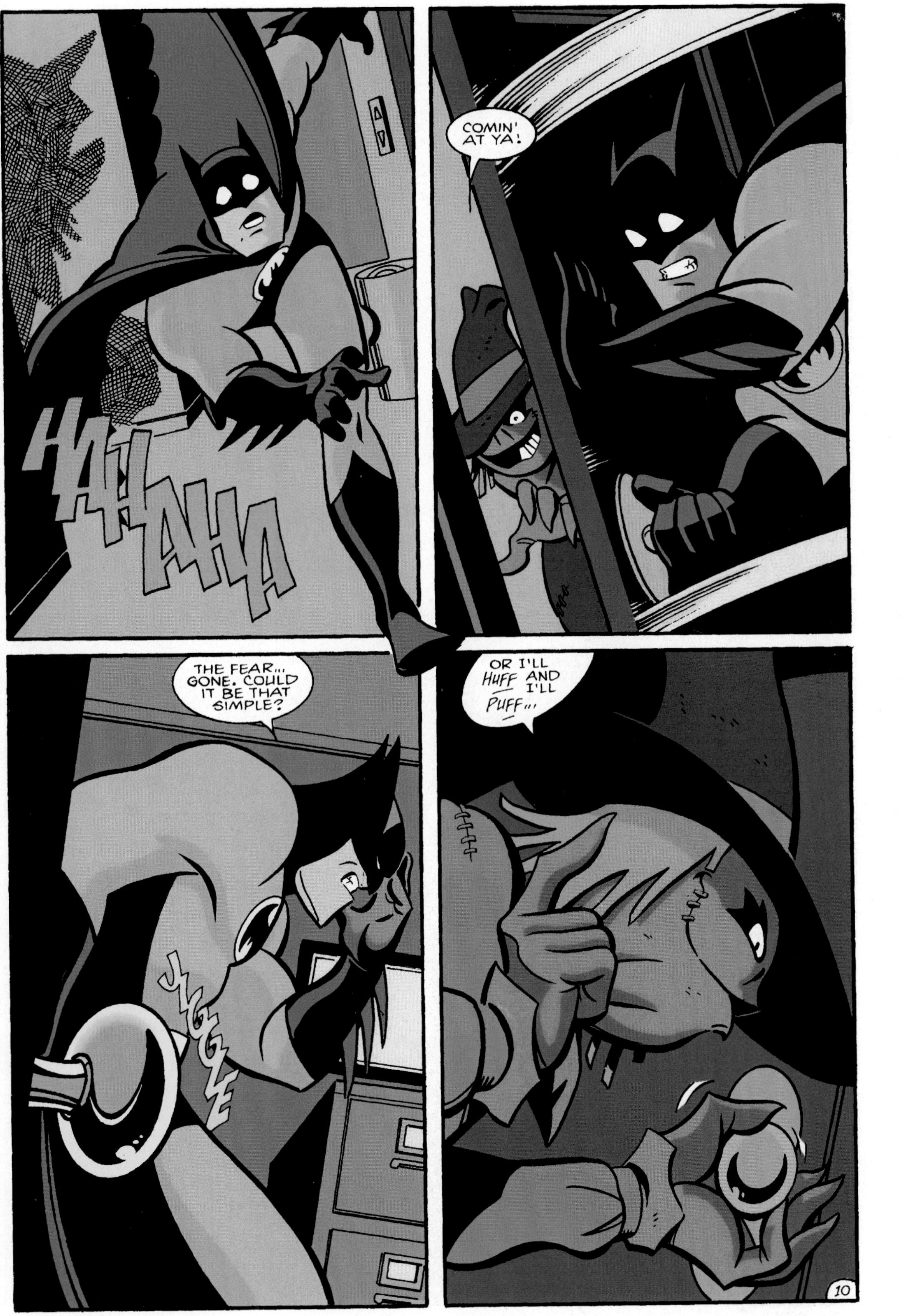
HAHAHAHA
COMIN' AT YA!
THE FEAR... GONE. COULD IT BE THAT SIMPLE?
OR I'LL HUFF AND I'LL PUFF...

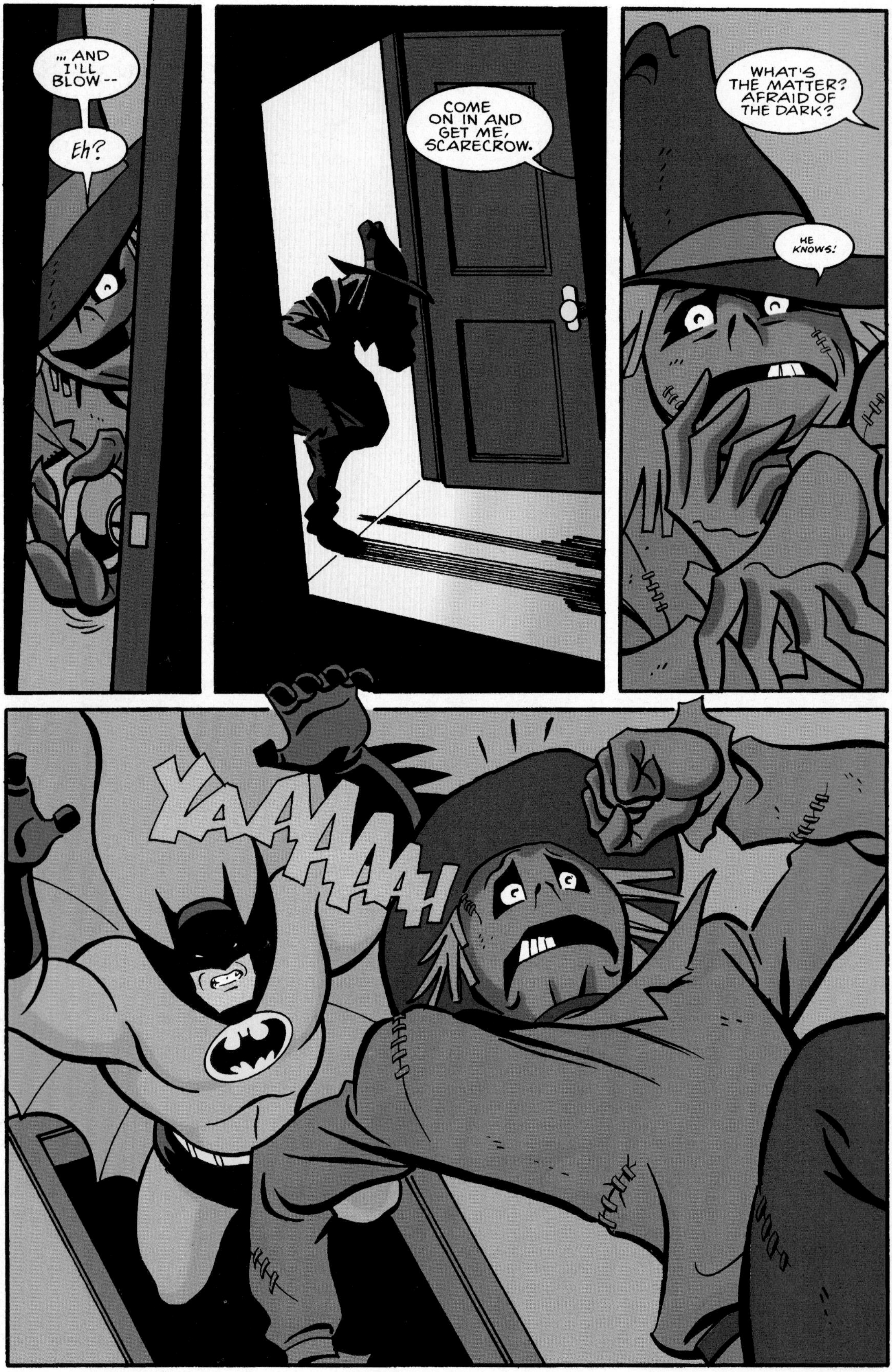

... AND I'LL BLOW --
Eh?
COME ON IN AND GET ME, SCARECROW.
WHAT'S THE MATTER? AFRAID OF THE DARK?
HE KNOWS!
YAAAAAAH

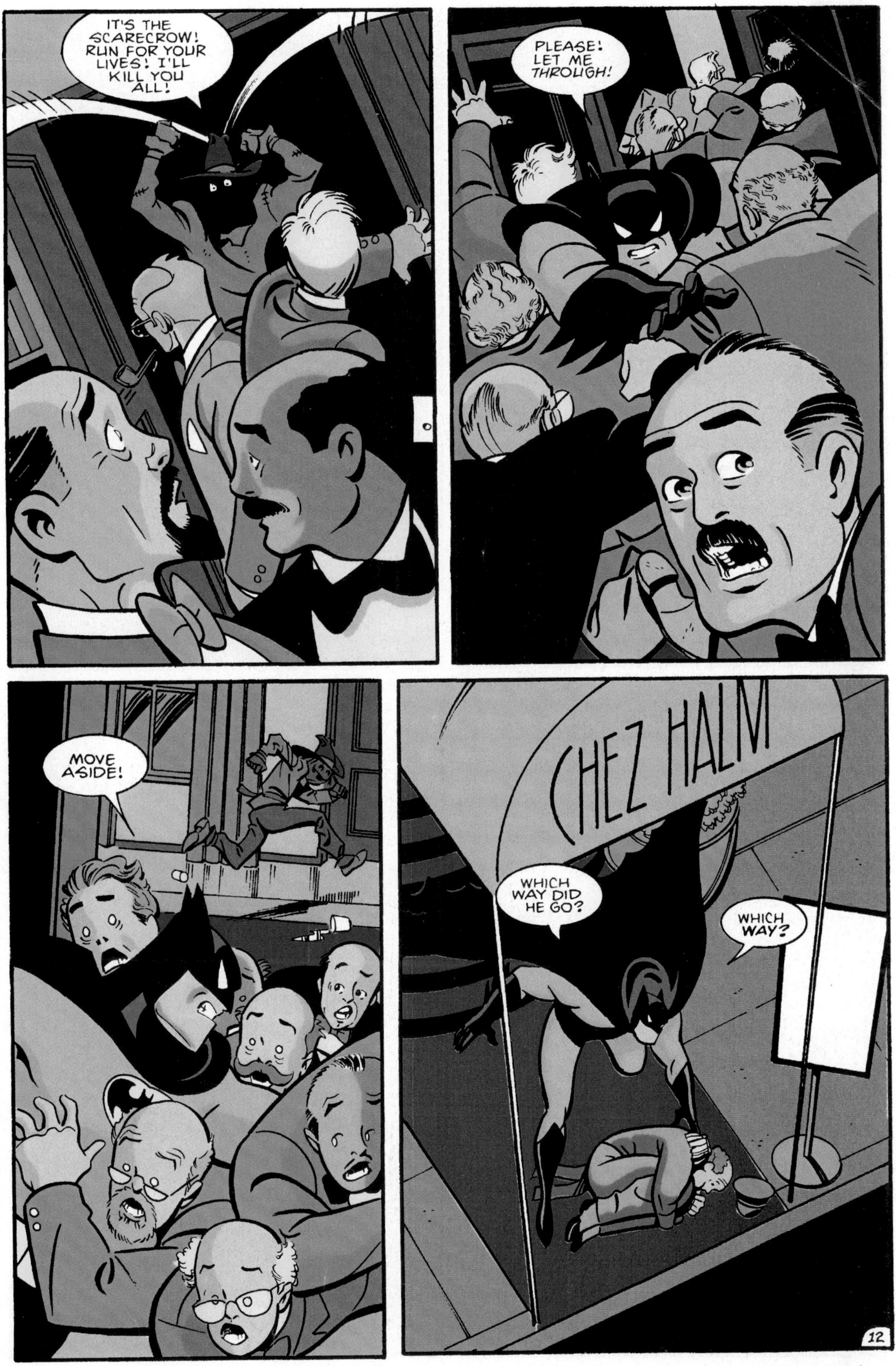
IT'S THE SCARECROW! RUN FOR YOUR LIVES! I'LL KILL YOU ALL!
PLEASE! LET ME THROUGH!
MOVE ASIDE!
CHEZ HALM
WHICH WAY DID HE GO?
WHICH WAY?

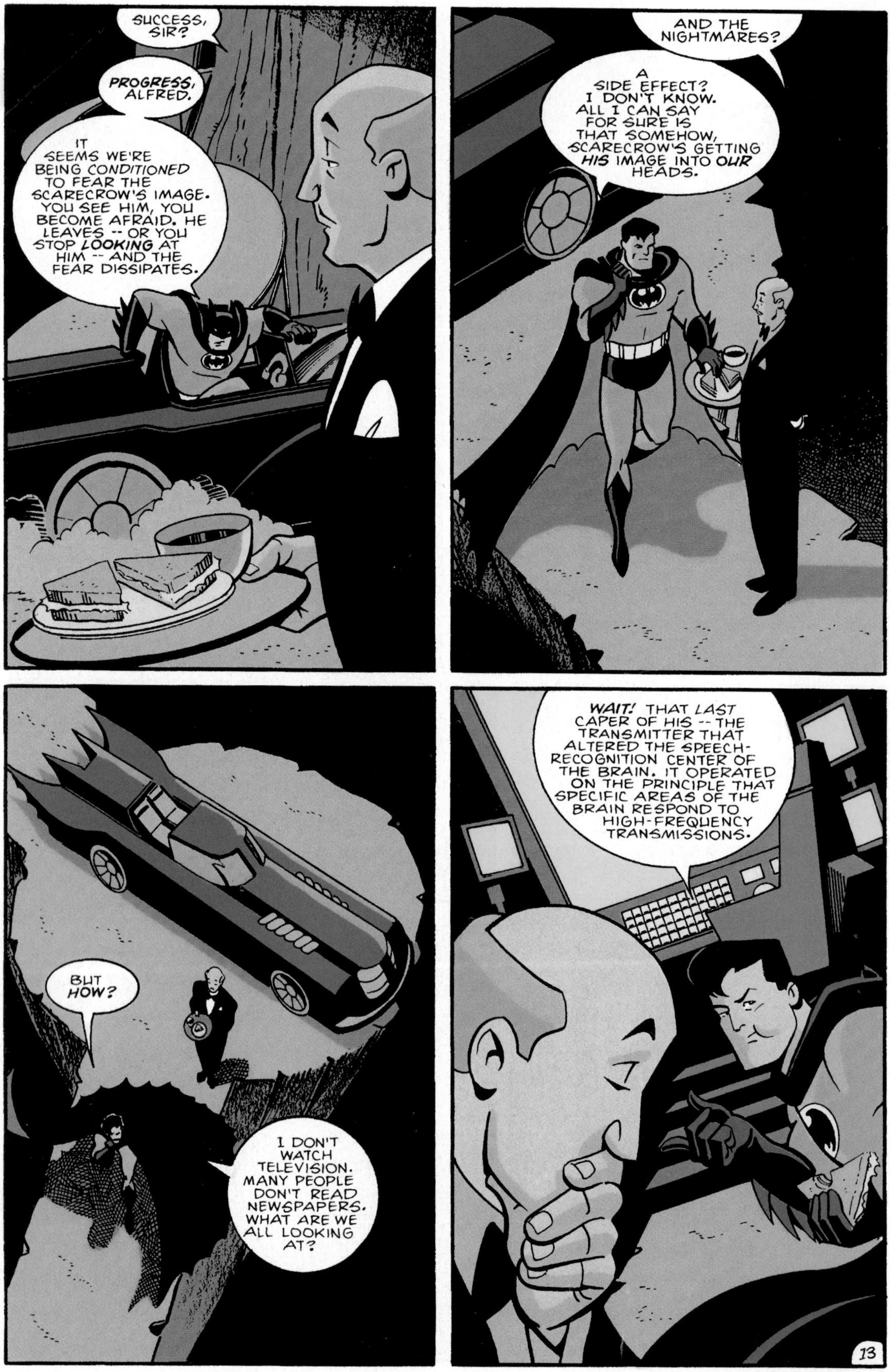
SUCCESS, SIR?
PROGRESS, ALFRED.
IT SEEMS WE'RE BEING CONDITIONED TO FEAR THE SCARECROW'S IMAGE. YOU SEE HIM, YOU BECOME AFRAID. HE LEAVES -- OR YOU STOP LOOKING AT HIM -- AND THE FEAR DISSIPATES.
AND THE NIGHTMARES?
A SIDE EFFECT? I DON'T KNOW. ALL I CAN SAY FOR SURE IS THAT SOMEHOW, SCARECROW'S GETTING HIS IMAGE INTO OUR HEADS.
BUT HOW?
I DON'T WATCH TELEVISION. MANY PEOPLE DON'T READ NEWSPAPERS. WHAT ARE WE ALL LOOKING AT?
WAIT! THAT LAST CAPER OF HIS -- THE TRANSMITTER THAT ALTERED THE SPEECH-RECOGNITION CENTER OF THE BRAIN. IT OPERATED ON THE PRINCIPLE THAT SPECIFIC AREAS OF THE BRAIN RESPOND TO HIGH-FREQUENCY TRANSMISSIONS.

COULD IT POSSIBLY HAVE BEEN REDESIGNED TO BEAM A SPECIFIC IMAGE *DIRECTLY* INTO OUR VISUAL CORTICES?

A SIGNAL OF THAT STRENGTH *SHOULD* BE EASILY DETECTABLE...

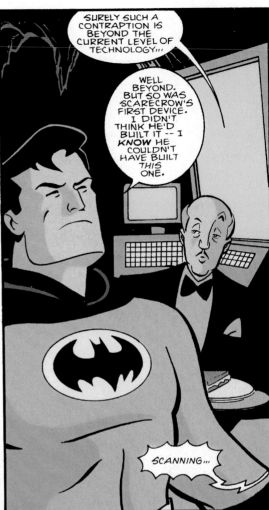

SURELY SUCH A CONTRAPTION IS BEYOND THE CURRENT LEVEL OF TECHNOLOGY...

WELL BEYOND. BUT SO WAS SCARECROW'S FIRST DEVICE. I DIDN'T THINK HE'D BUILT IT -- I *KNOW* HE COULDN'T HAVE BUILT *THIS* ONE.

SCANNING...

TRANSMISSION FOUND. TRACKING POINT OF ORIGIN...

GOT IT.

THANKS FOR DINNER, ALFRED.

->Ahem<- YOU'RE WELCOME, SIR.

14

ACT THREE: BENEATH THE MASK

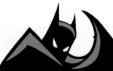

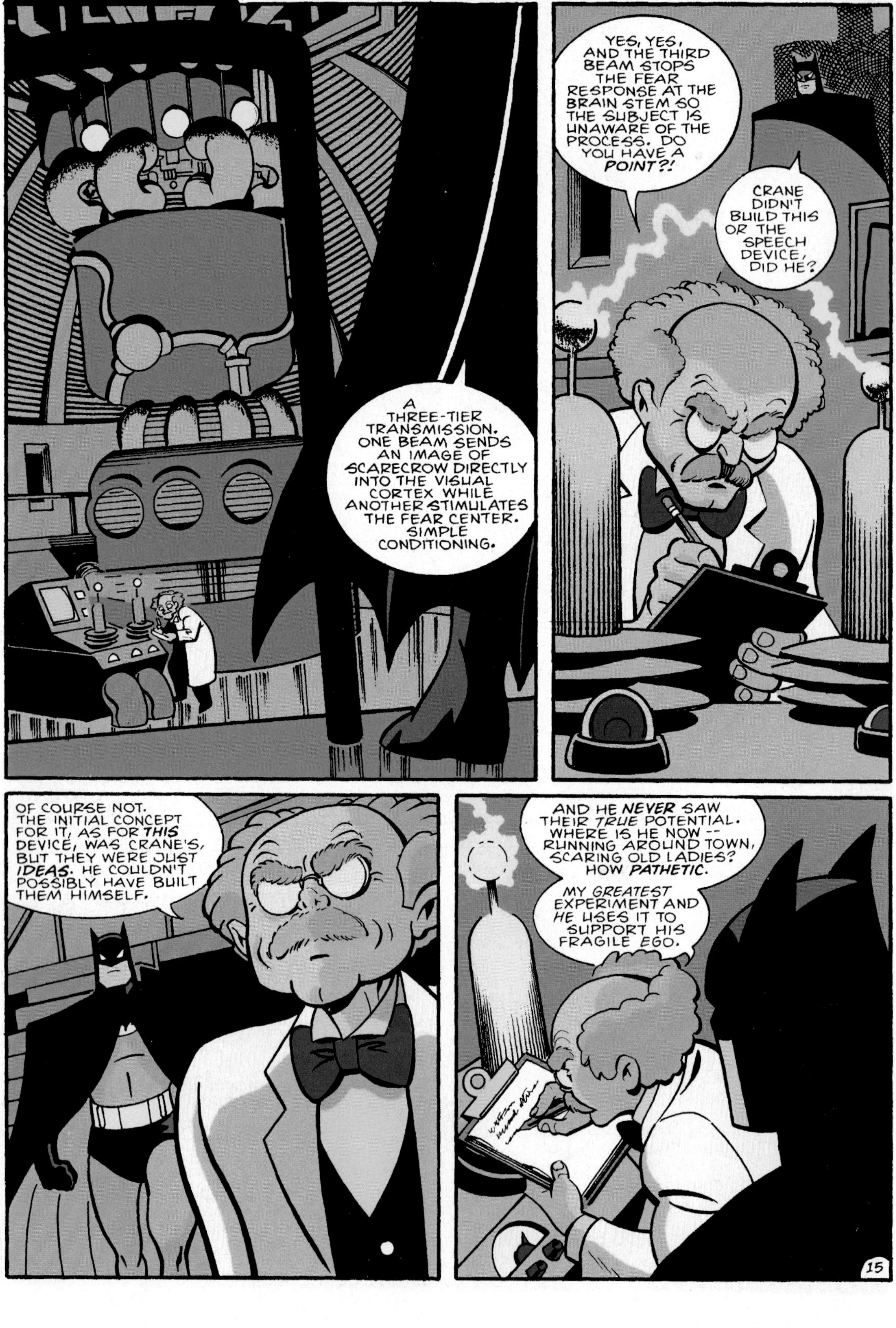
A THREE-TIER TRANSMISSION. ONE BEAM SENDS AN IMAGE OF SCARECROW DIRECTLY INTO THE VISUAL CORTEX WHILE ANOTHER STIMULATES THE FEAR CENTER. SIMPLE CONDITIONING.
YES, YES, AND THE THIRD BEAM STOPS THE FEAR RESPONSE AT THE BRAIN STEM SO THE SUBJECT IS UNAWARE OF THE PROCESS. DO YOU HAVE A POINT?!
CRANE DIDN'T BUILD THIS OR THE SPEECH DEVICE, DID HE?
OF COURSE NOT. THE INITIAL CONCEPT FOR IT, AS FOR THIS DEVICE, WAS CRANE'S, BUT THEY WERE JUST IDEAS. HE COULDN'T POSSIBLY HAVE BUILT THEM HIMSELF.
AND HE NEVER SAW THEIR TRUE POTENTIAL. WHERE IS HE NOW -- RUNNING AROUND TOWN, SCARING OLD LADIES? HOW PATHETIC.
MY GREATEST EXPERIMENT AND HE USES IT TO SUPPORT HIS FRAGILE EGO.

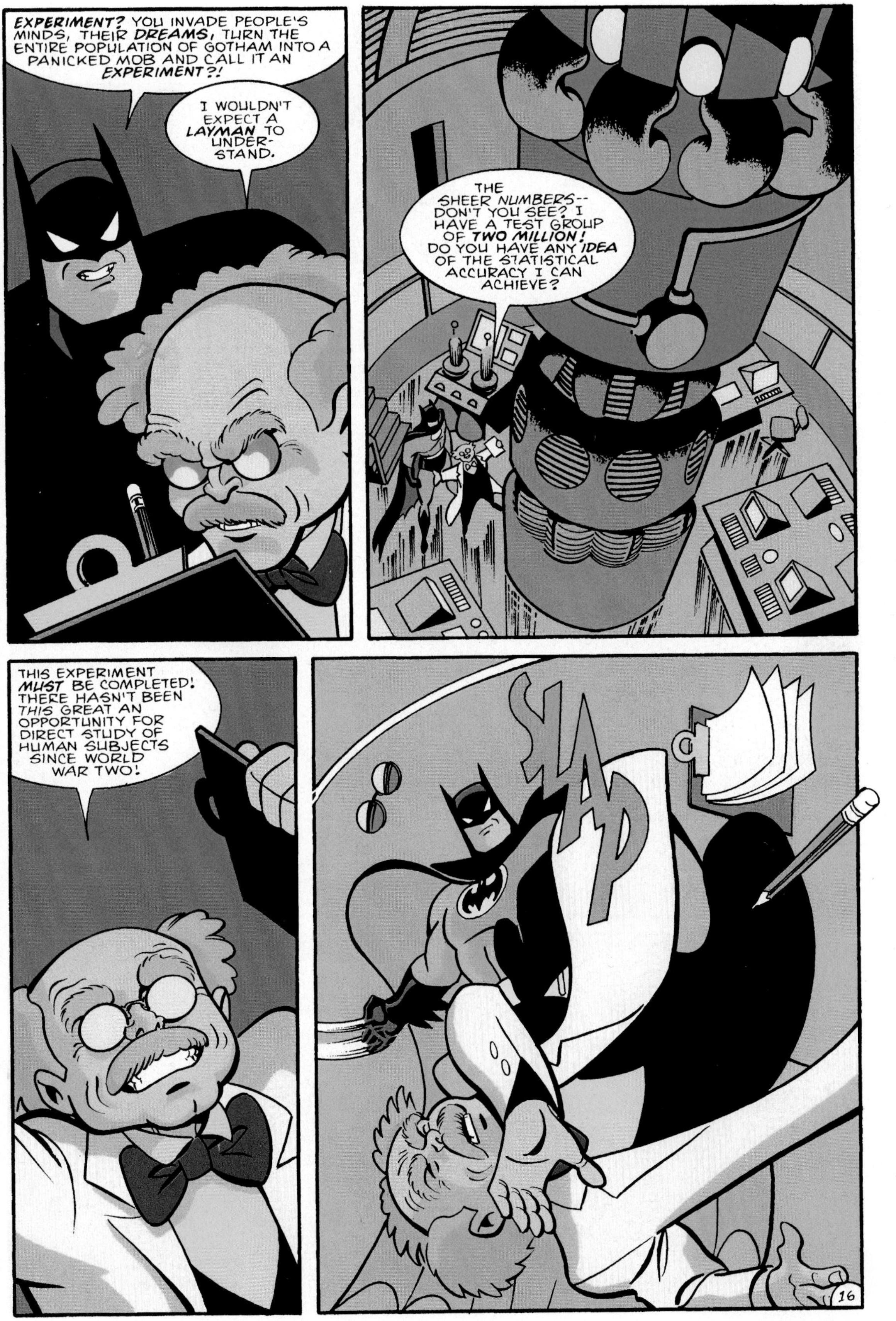
EXPERIMENT? YOU INVADE PEOPLE'S MINDS, THEIR DREAMS, TURN THE ENTIRE POPULATION OF GOTHAM INTO A PANICKED MOB AND CALL IT AN EXPERIMENT?!
I WOULDN'T EXPECT A LAYMAN TO UNDER-STAND.
THE SHEER NUMBERS-- DON'T YOU SEE? I HAVE A TEST GROUP OF TWO MILLION! DO YOU HAVE ANY IDEA OF THE STATISTICAL ACCURACY I CAN ACHIEVE?
THIS EXPERIMENT MUST BE COMPLETED! THERE HASN'T BEEN THIS GREAT AN OPPORTUNITY FOR DIRECT STUDY OF HUMAN SUBJECTS SINCE WORLD WAR TWO!
SLAP

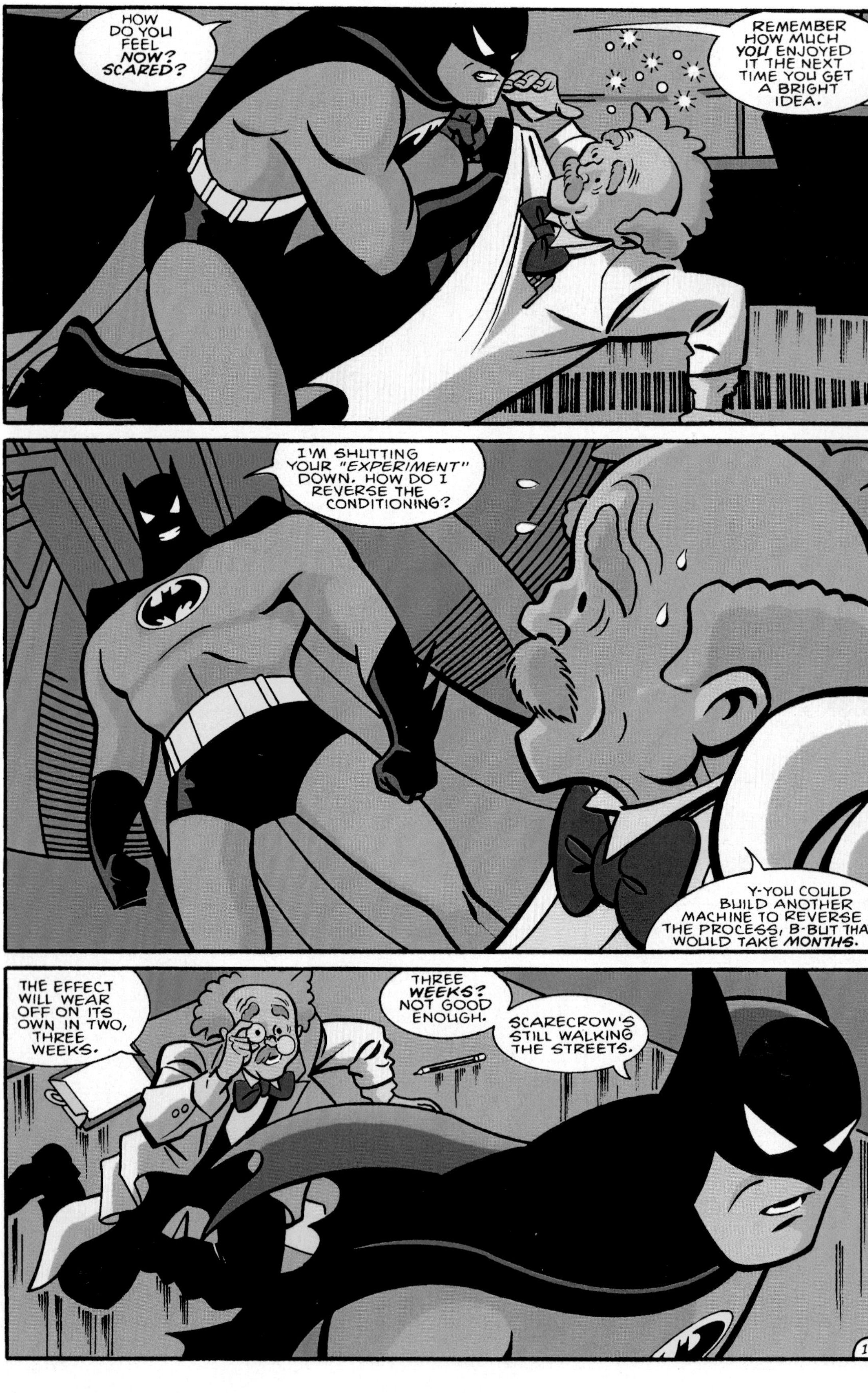
HOW DO YOU FEEL NOW? SCARED?
REMEMBER HOW MUCH YOU ENJOYED IT THE NEXT TIME YOU GET A BRIGHT IDEA.
I'M SHUTTING YOUR "EXPERIMENT" DOWN. HOW DO I REVERSE THE CONDITIONING?
Y-YOU COULD BUILD ANOTHER MACHINE TO REVERSE THE PROCESS, B-BUT THAT WOULD TAKE MONTHS.
THE EFFECT WILL WEAR OFF ON ITS OWN IN TWO, THREE WEEKS.
THREE WEEKS? NOT GOOD ENOUGH.
SCARECROW'S STILL WALKING THE STREETS.

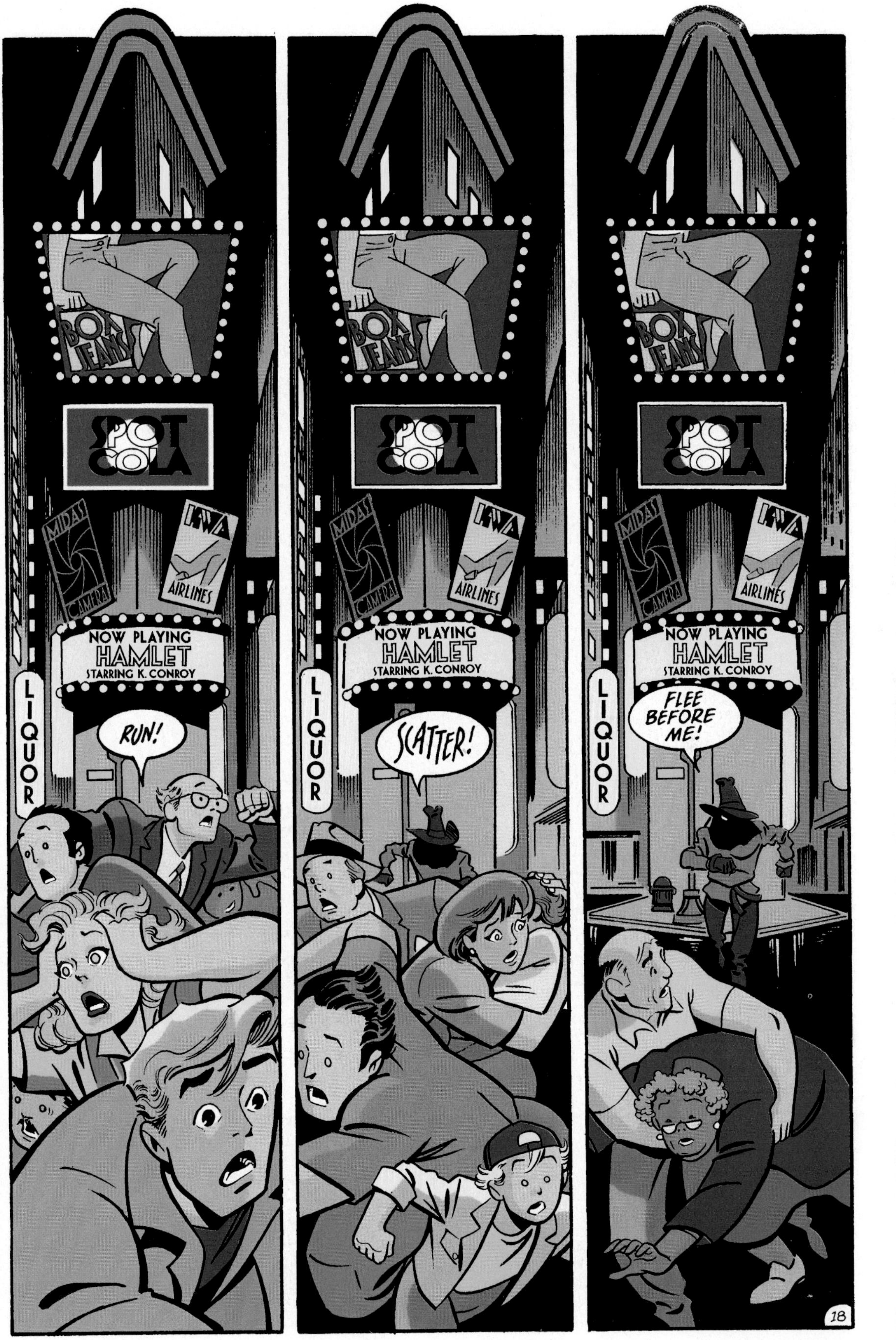
BOX JEANS
SPOT COLA
MIDAS CAMERA
LWA AIRLINES
NOW PLAYING HAMLET STARRING K. CONROY
LIQUOR
RUN!
SCATTER!
FLEE BEFORE ME!

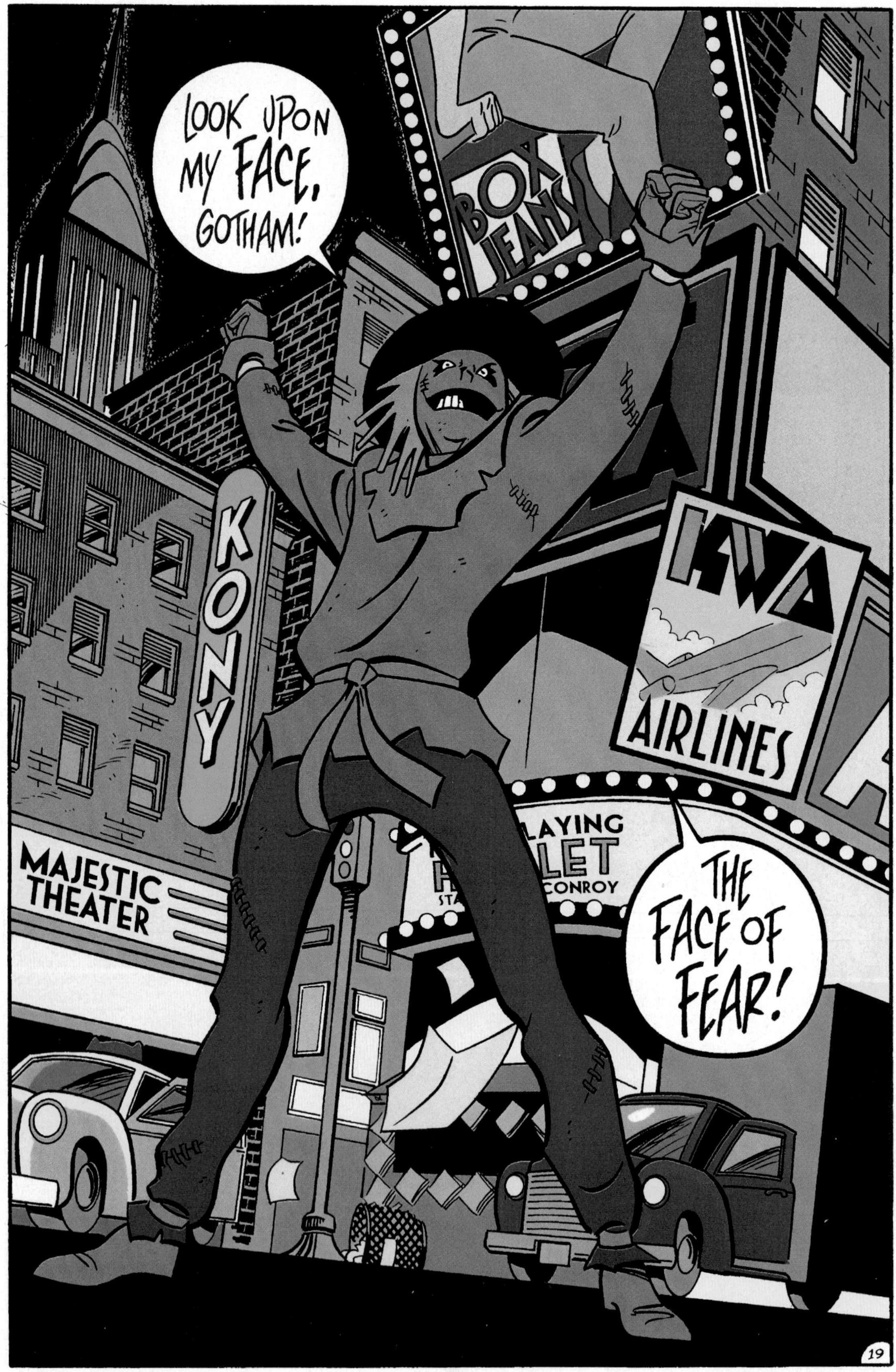
LOOK UPON MY FACE, GOTHAM!
BOX JEANS
KONY
KWA
AIRLINES
MAJESTIC THEATER
THE FACE OF FEAR!

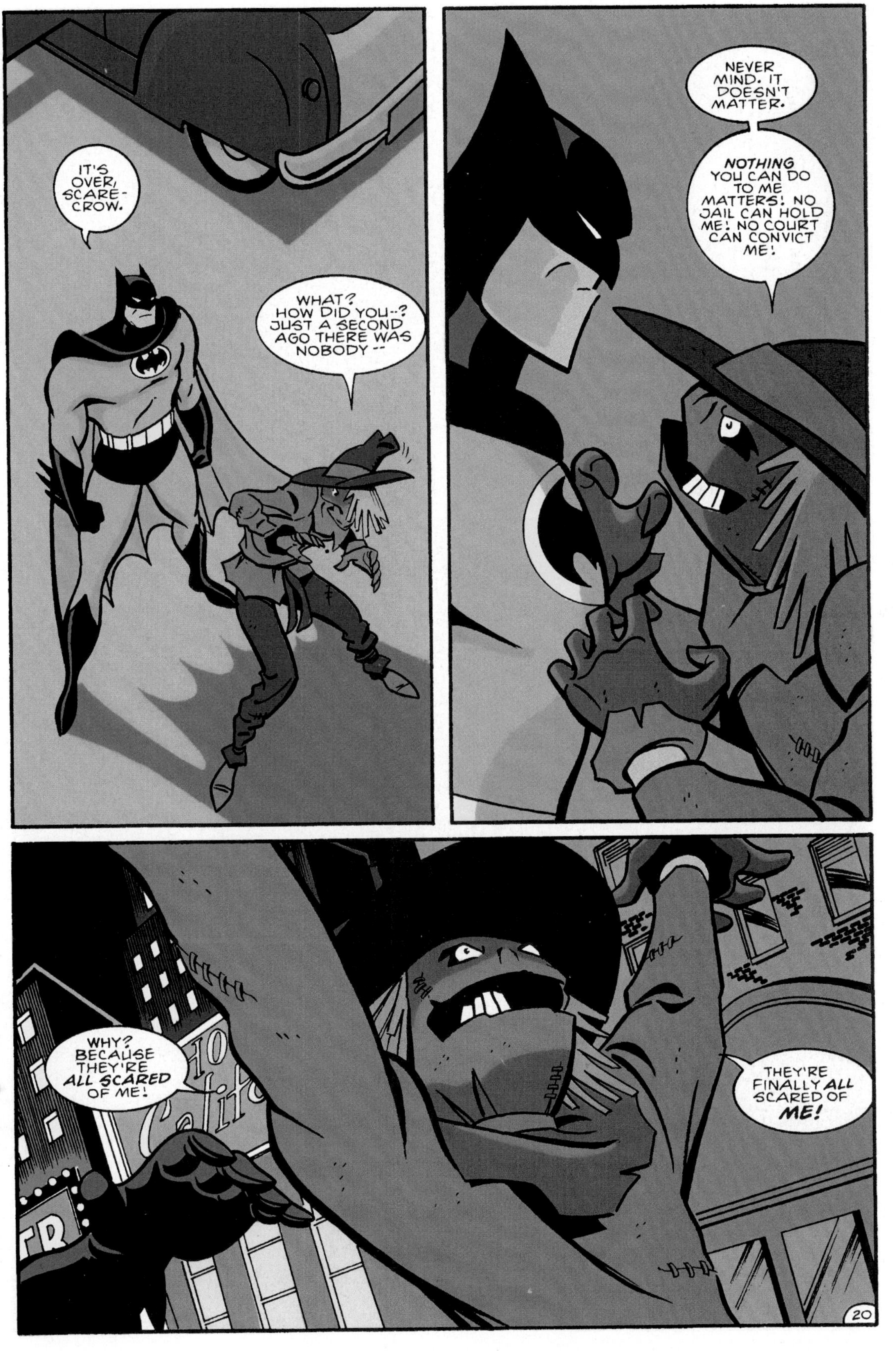
IT'S OVER, SCARE-CROW.
WHAT? HOW DID YOU--? JUST A SECOND AGO THERE WAS NOBODY --
NEVER MIND. IT DOESN'T MATTER.
NOTHING YOU CAN DO TO ME MATTERS! NO JAIL CAN HOLD ME! NO COURT CAN CONVICT ME!
WHY? BECAUSE THEY'RE ALL SCARED OF ME!
THEY'RE FINALLY ALL SCARED OF ME!
20

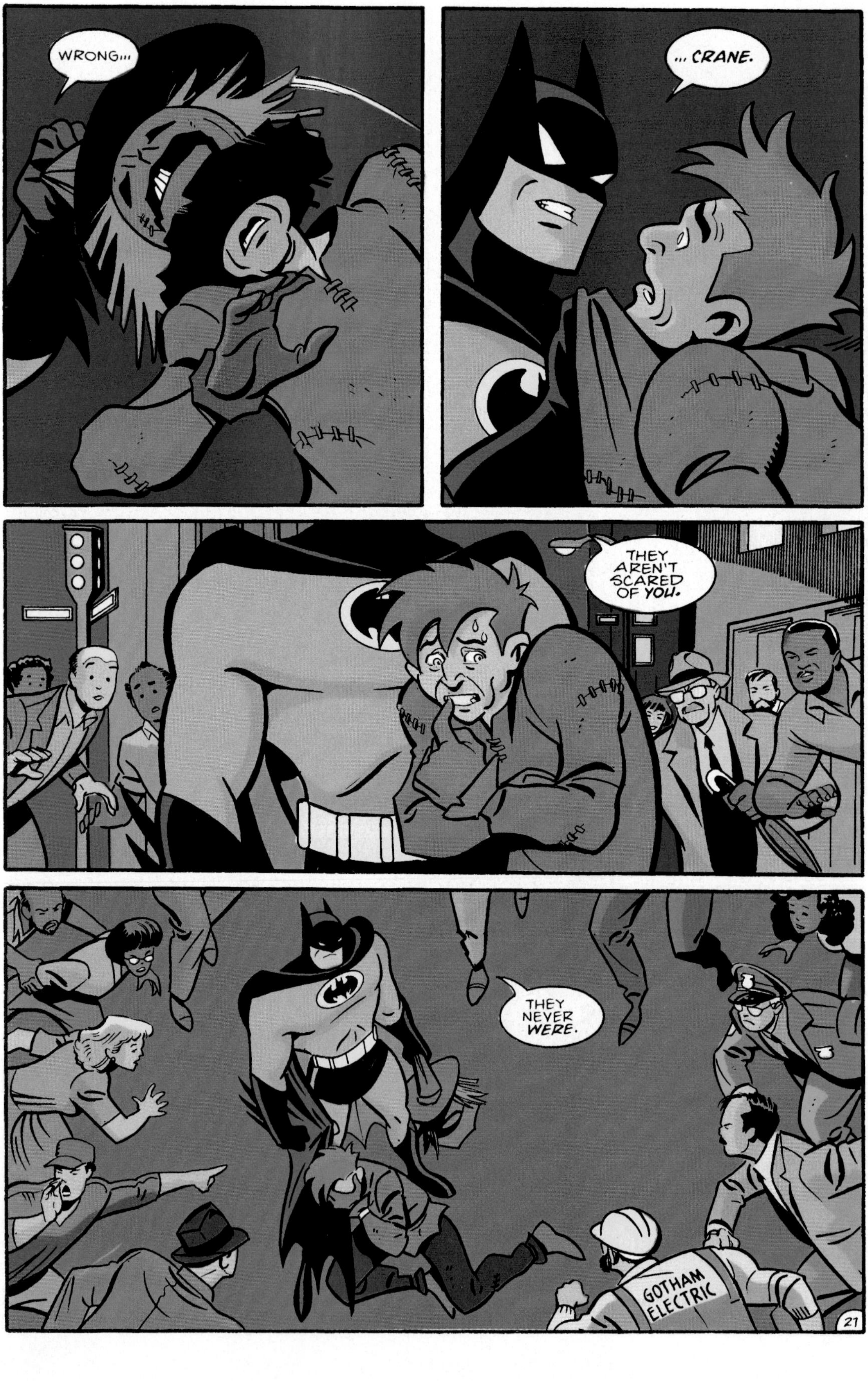
WRONG...
...CRANE.
THEY AREN'T SCARED OF *YOU*.
THEY NEVER *WERE*.
GOTHAM ELECTRIC

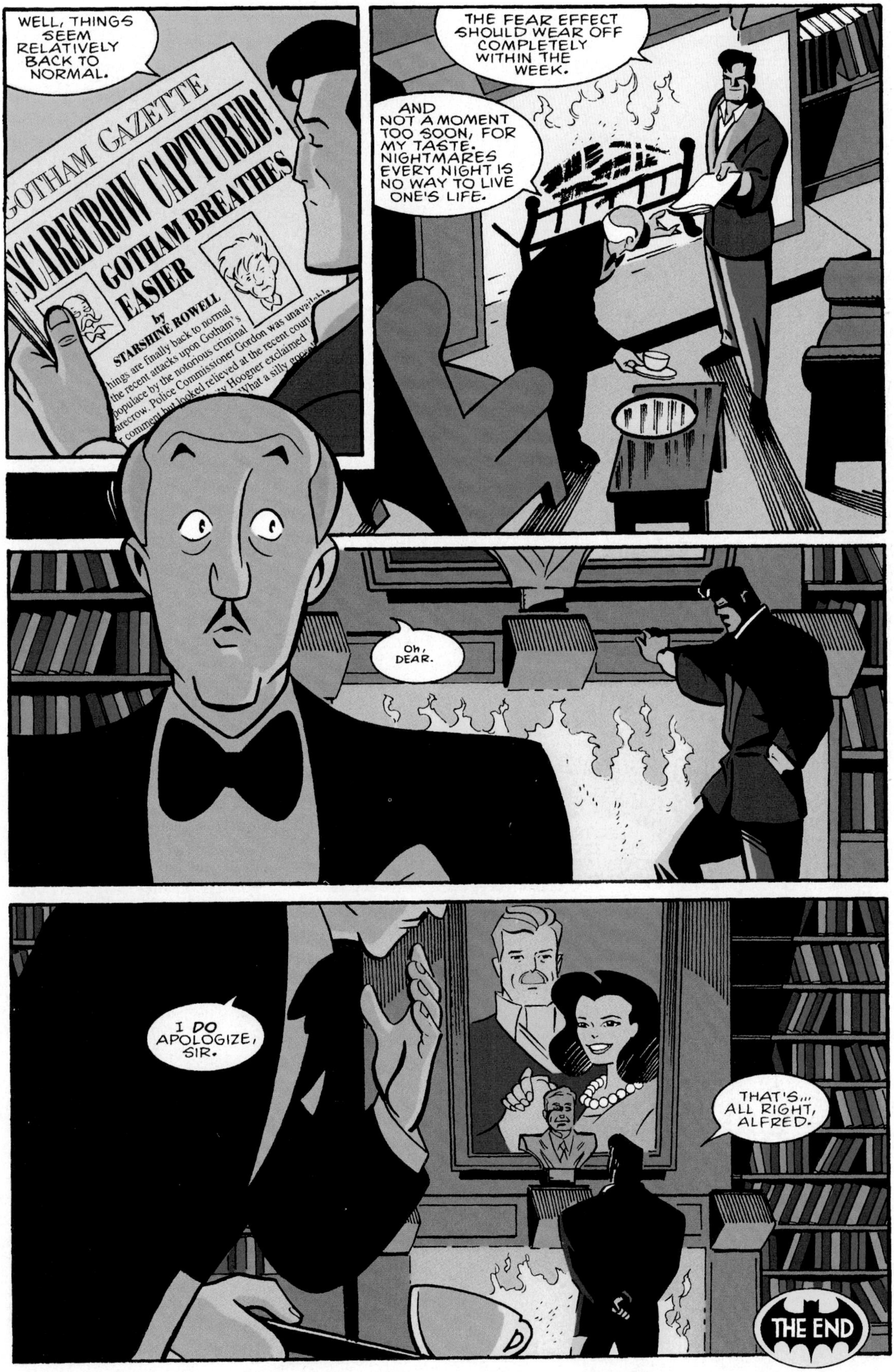
WELL, THINGS SEEM RELATIVELY BACK TO NORMAL.
GOTHAM GAZETTE
SCARECROW CAPTURED!
GOTHAM BREATHES EASIER
by STARSHINE ROWELL
THE FEAR EFFECT SHOULD WEAR OFF COMPLETELY WITHIN THE WEEK.
AND NOT A MOMENT TOO SOON, FOR MY TASTE. NIGHTMARES EVERY NIGHT IS NO WAY TO LIVE ONE'S LIFE.
Oh, DEAR.
I DO APOLOGIZE, SIR.
THAT'S... ALL RIGHT, ALFRED.
THE END

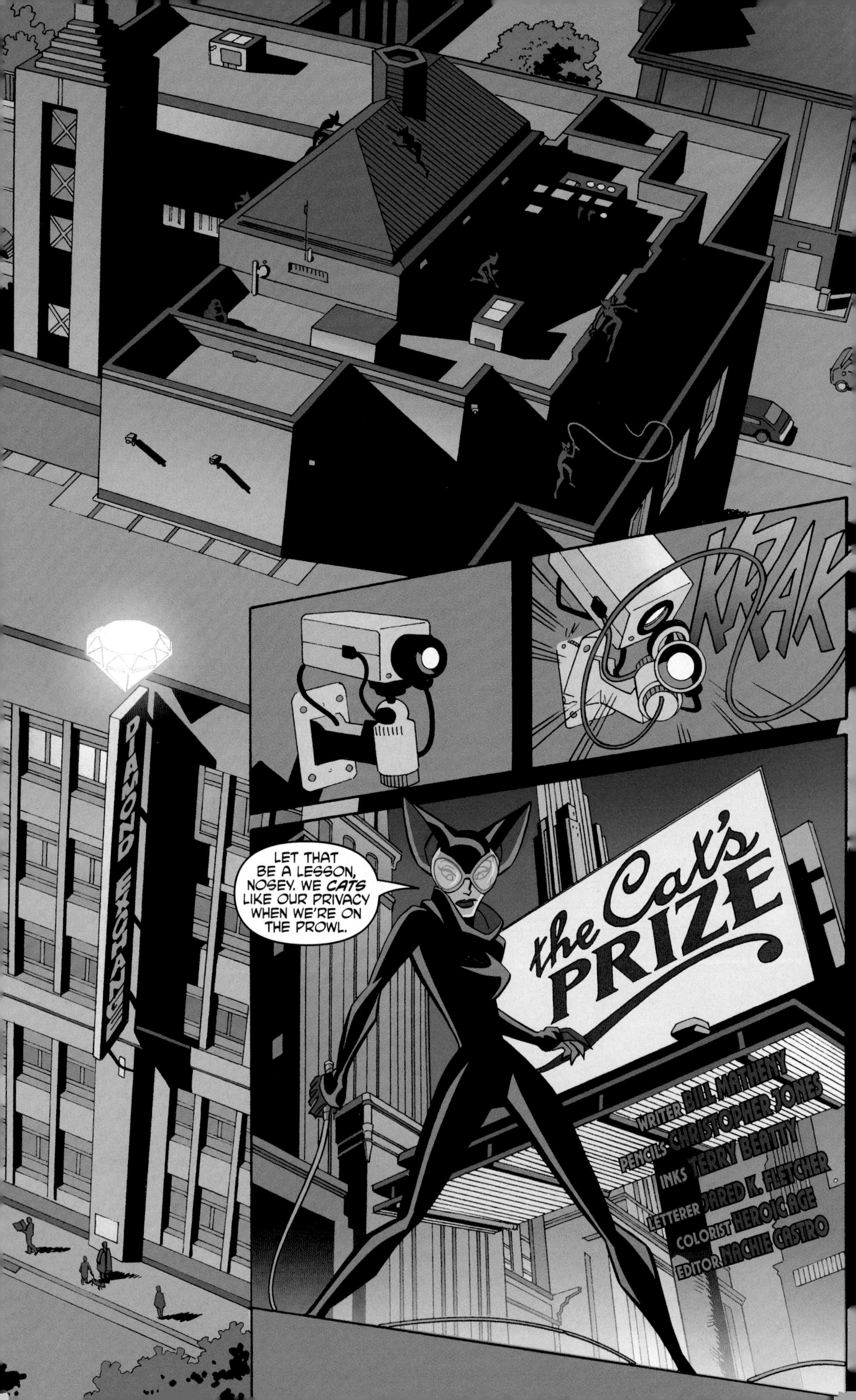
DIAMOND EXCHANGE
KKRAK
LET THAT BE A LESSON, NOSEY. WE CATS LIKE OUR PRIVACY WHEN WE'RE ON THE PROWL.
the Cat's PRIZE
WRITER BILL MATHENY
PENCILS CHRISTOPHER JONES
INKS TERRY BEATTY
LETTERER JARED K. FLETCHER
COLORIST HEROIC AGE
EDITOR NACHIE CASTRO

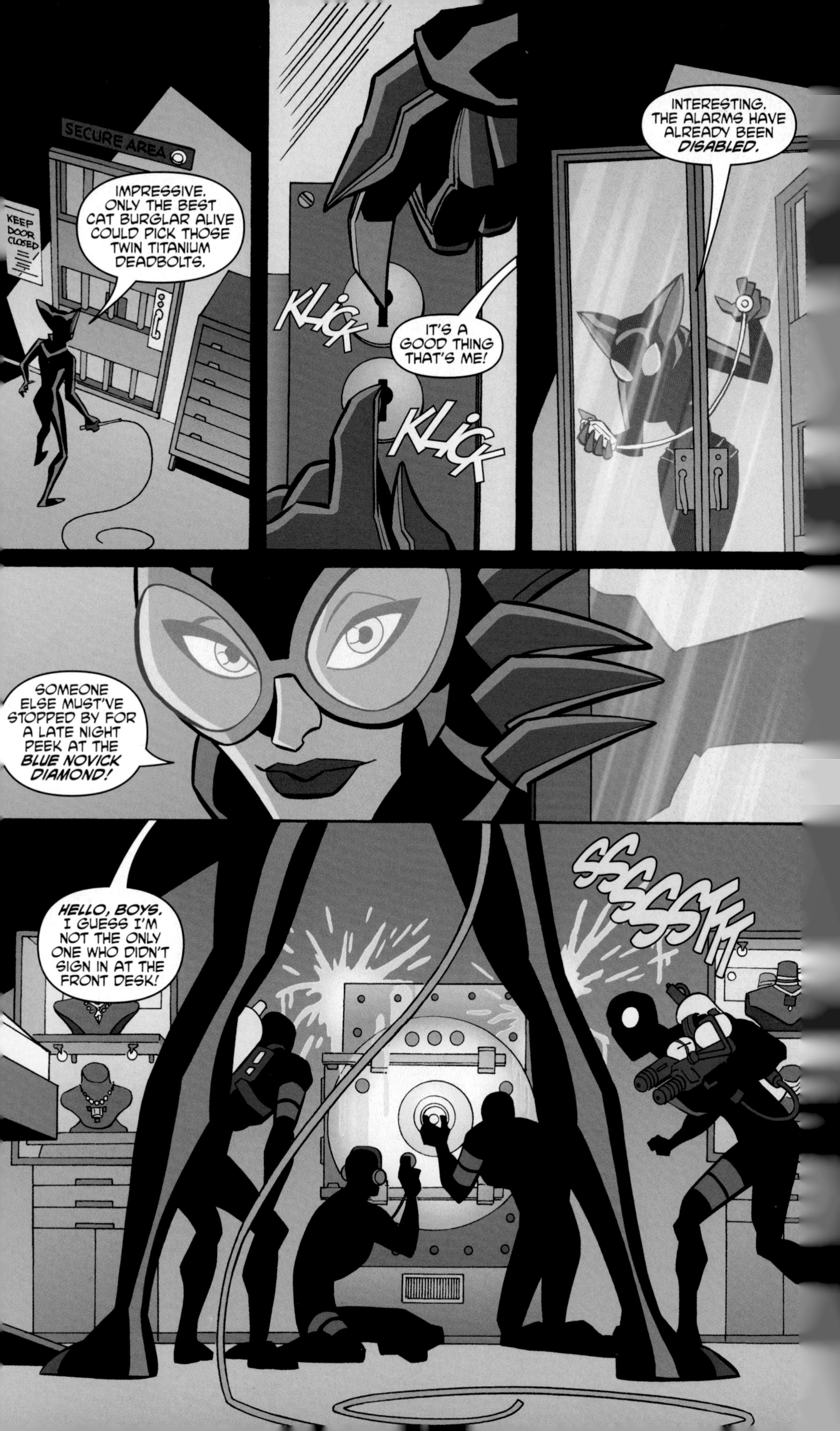
SECURE AREA
KEEP DOOR CLOSED
IMPRESSIVE. ONLY THE BEST CAT BURGLAR ALIVE COULD PICK THOSE TWIN TITANIUM DEADBOLTS.
KLICK
IT'S A GOOD THING THAT'S ME!
KLICK
INTERESTING. THE ALARMS HAVE ALREADY BEEN *DISABLED.*
SOMEONE ELSE MUST'VE STOPPED BY FOR A LATE NIGHT PEEK AT THE *BLUE NOVICK DIAMOND!*
HELLO, BOYS. I GUESS I'M NOT THE ONLY ONE WHO DIDN'T SIGN IN AT THE FRONT DESK!
SSSSSKKT

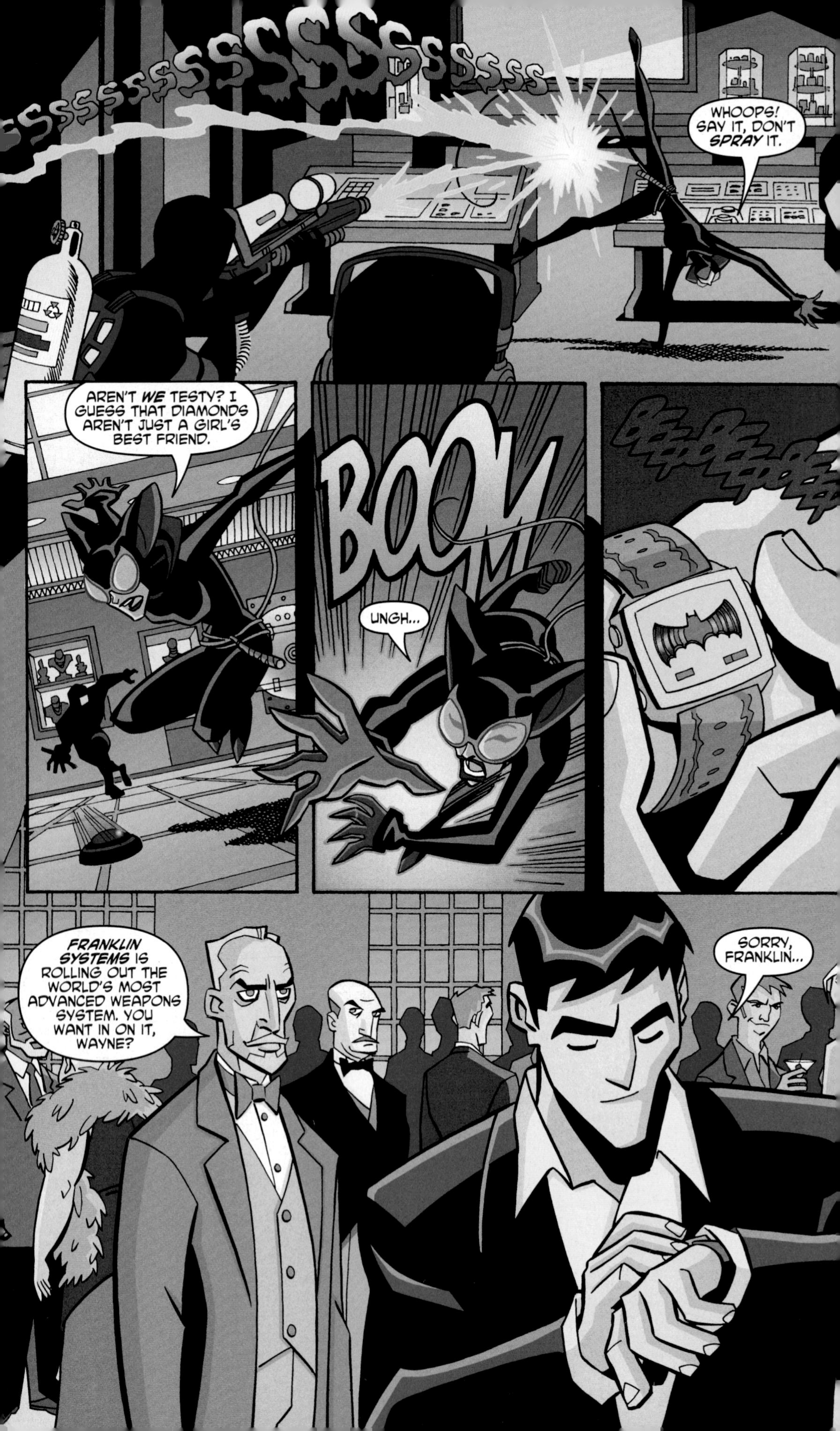
SSSSSSSSSSSSSSSSSS
WHOOPS! SAY IT, DON'T SPRAY IT.
AREN'T WE TESTY? I GUESS THAT DIAMONDS AREN'T JUST A GIRL'S BEST FRIEND.
BOOM
UNGH...
FRANKLIN SYSTEMS IS ROLLING OUT THE WORLD'S MOST ADVANCED WEAPONS SYSTEM. YOU WANT IN ON IT, WAYNE?
SORRY, FRANKLIN...

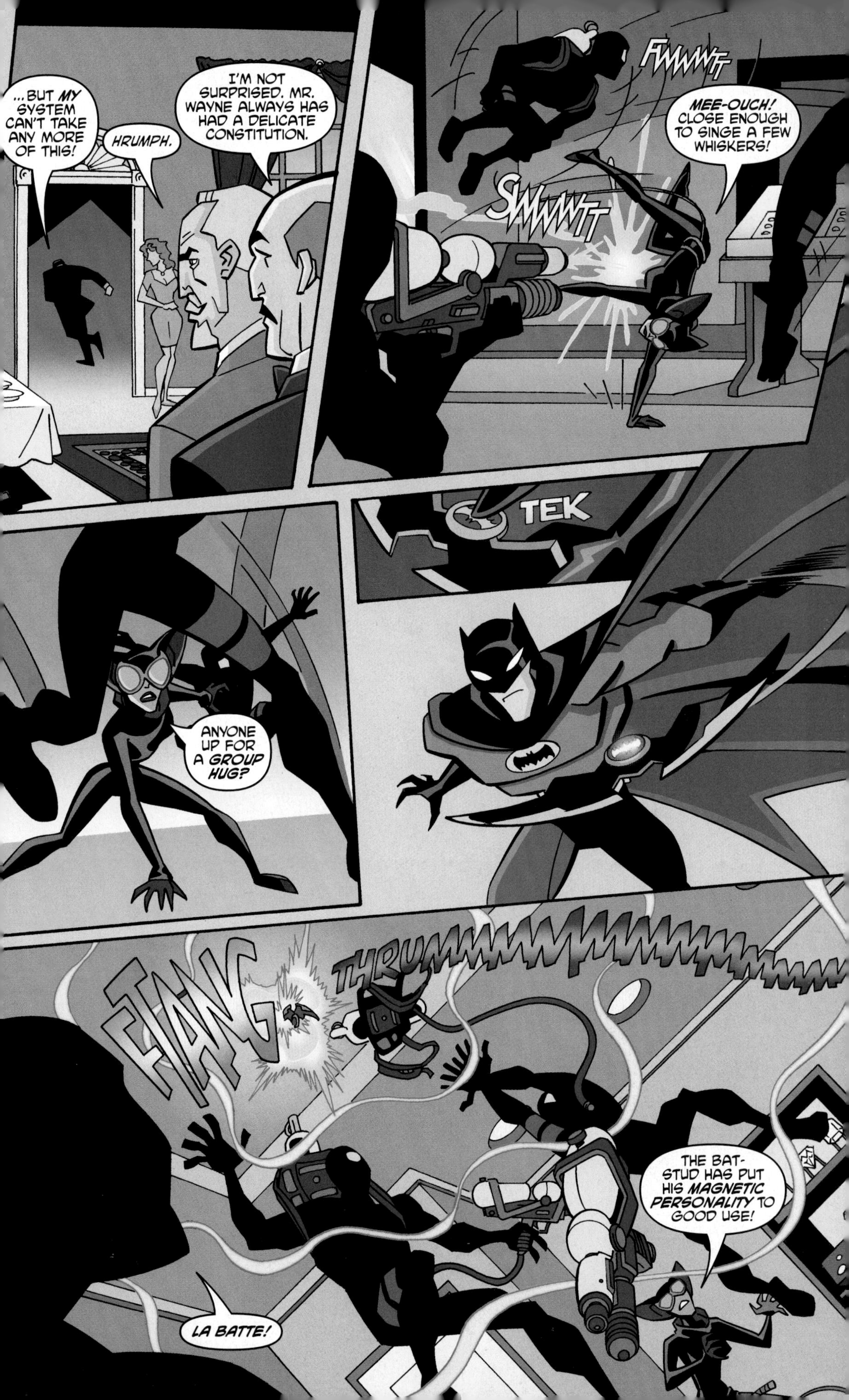
...BUT MY SYSTEM CAN'T TAKE ANY MORE OF THIS!
HRUMPH.
I'M NOT SURPRISED. MR. WAYNE ALWAYS HAS HAD A DELICATE CONSTITUTION.
FWWWTT
SWWWTT
MEE-OUCH! CLOSE ENOUGH TO SINGE A FEW WHISKERS!
ANYONE UP FOR A GROUP HUG?
TEK
FTANG
THRUMMMMMMMMMMMMMMM
THE BAT-STUD HAS PUT HIS MAGNETIC PERSONALITY TO GOOD USE!
LA BATTE!

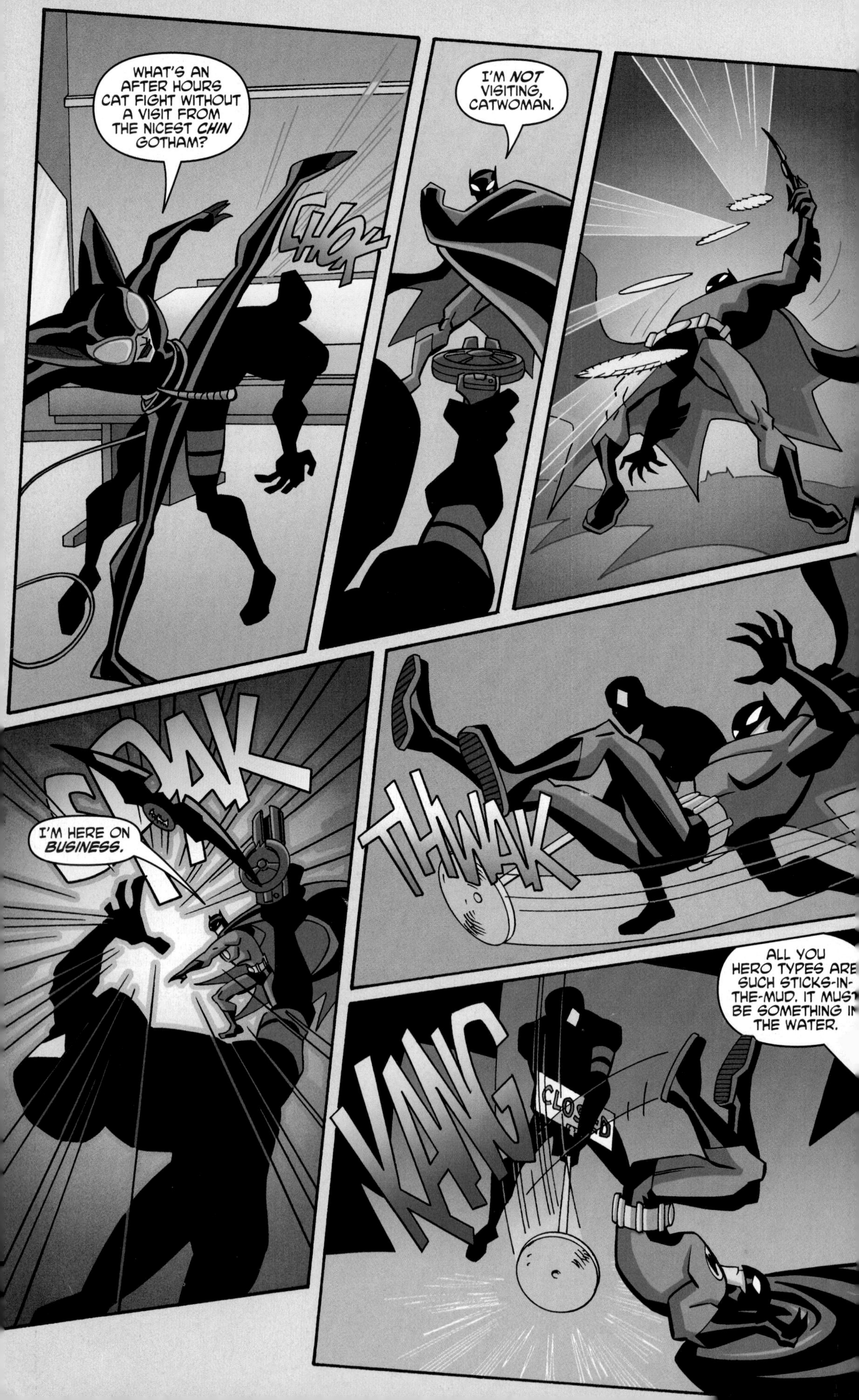
WHAT'S AN AFTER HOURS CAT FIGHT WITHOUT A VISIT FROM THE NICEST CHIN GOTHAM?
CHOK
I'M NOT VISITING, CATWOMAN.
SPOAK
I'M HERE ON BUSINESS.
THWAK
ALL YOU HERO TYPES ARE SUCH STICKS-IN-THE-MUD. IT MUST BE SOMETHING IN THE WATER.
KANG
CLOSED

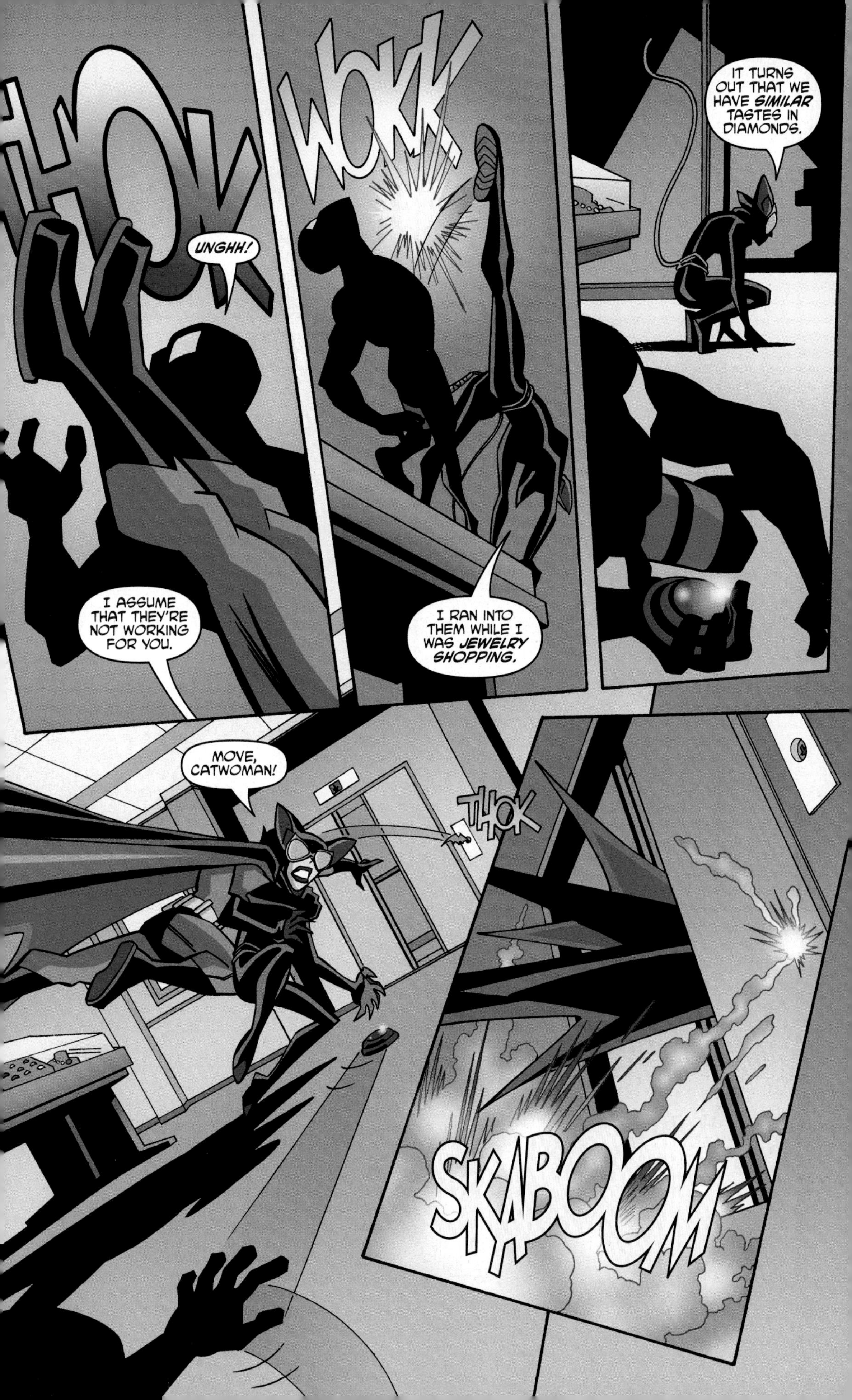
THOK
UNGHH!
I ASSUME THAT THEY'RE NOT WORKING FOR YOU.
WOKK
I RAN INTO THEM WHILE I WAS JEWELRY SHOPPING.
IT TURNS OUT THAT WE HAVE SIMILAR TASTES IN DIAMONDS.
MOVE, CATWOMAN!
THOK
SKABOOM

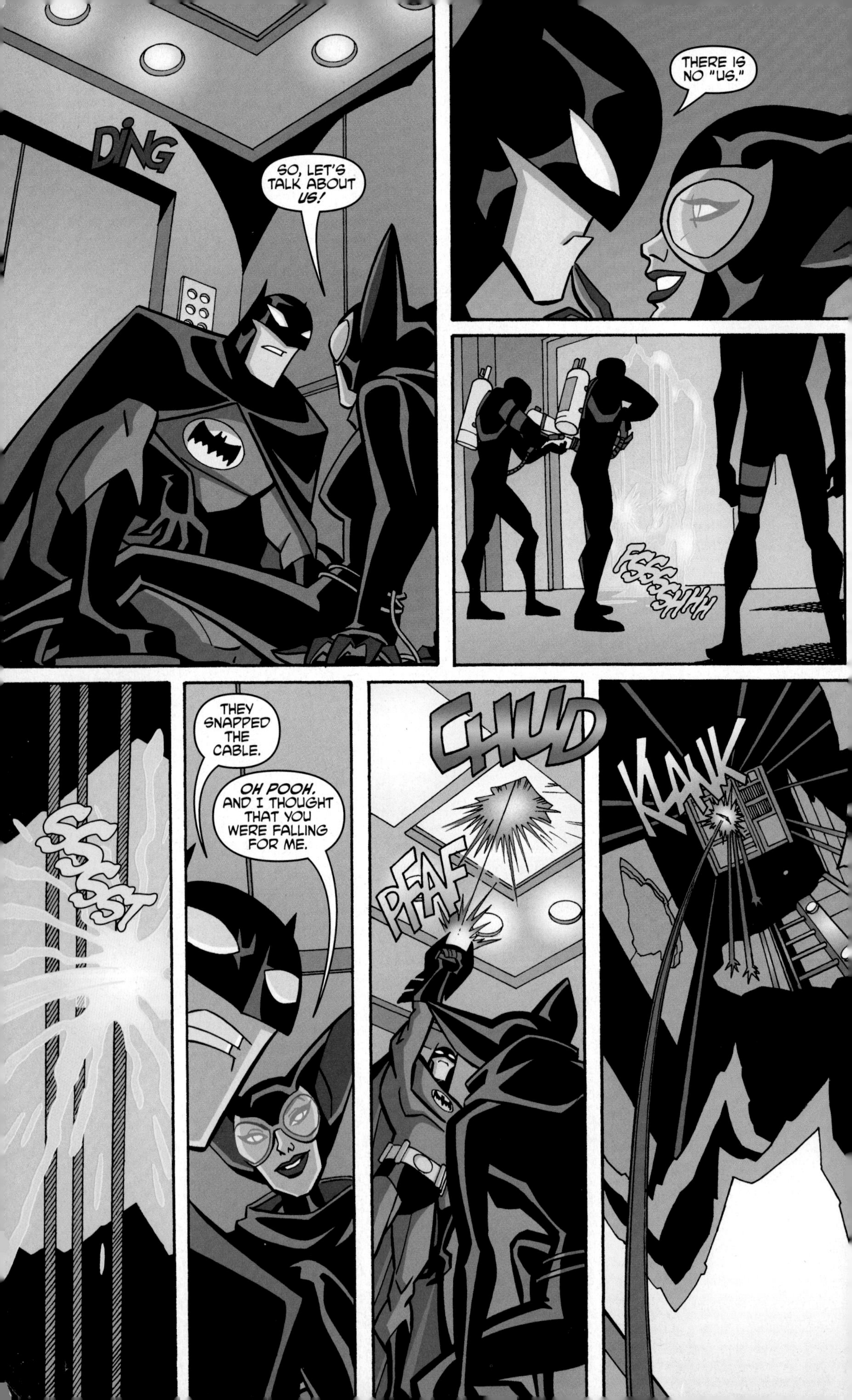
DING
SO, LET'S TALK ABOUT *US!*
THERE IS NO "US."
FSSSHHH
SSSST
THEY SNAPPED THE CABLE.
OH POOH. AND I THOUGHT THAT YOU WERE FALLING FOR ME.
CHUD
PFAF
KLANK

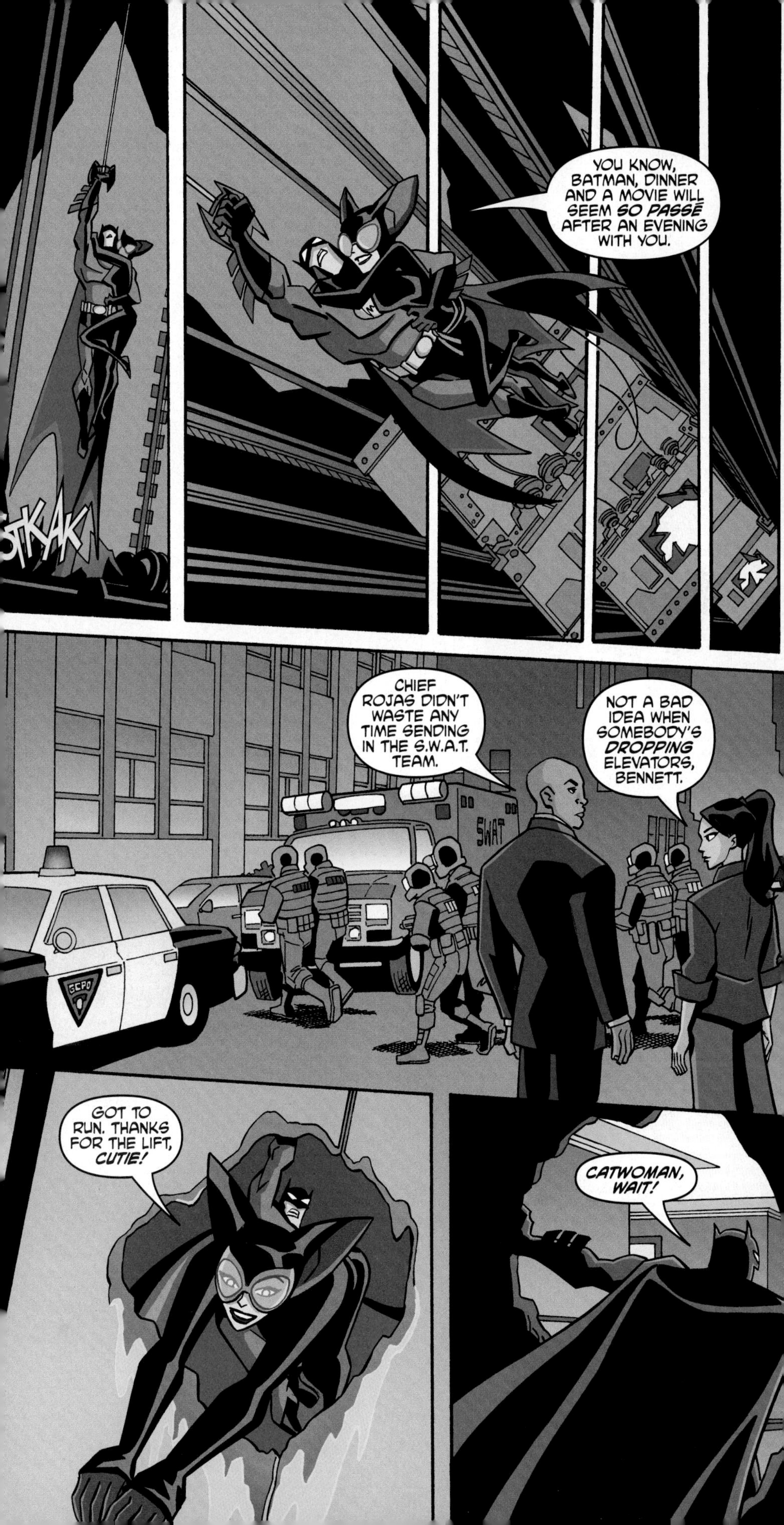
STKAK
YOU KNOW, BATMAN, DINNER AND A MOVIE WILL SEEM *SO PASSÉ* AFTER AN EVENING WITH YOU.
CHIEF ROJAS DIDN'T WASTE ANY TIME SENDING IN THE S.W.A.T. TEAM.
NOT A BAD IDEA WHEN SOMEBODY'S *DROPPING* ELEVATORS, BENNETT.
SWAT
GCPD
GOT TO RUN. THANKS FOR THE LIFT, *CUTIE!*
CATWOMAN, WAIT!

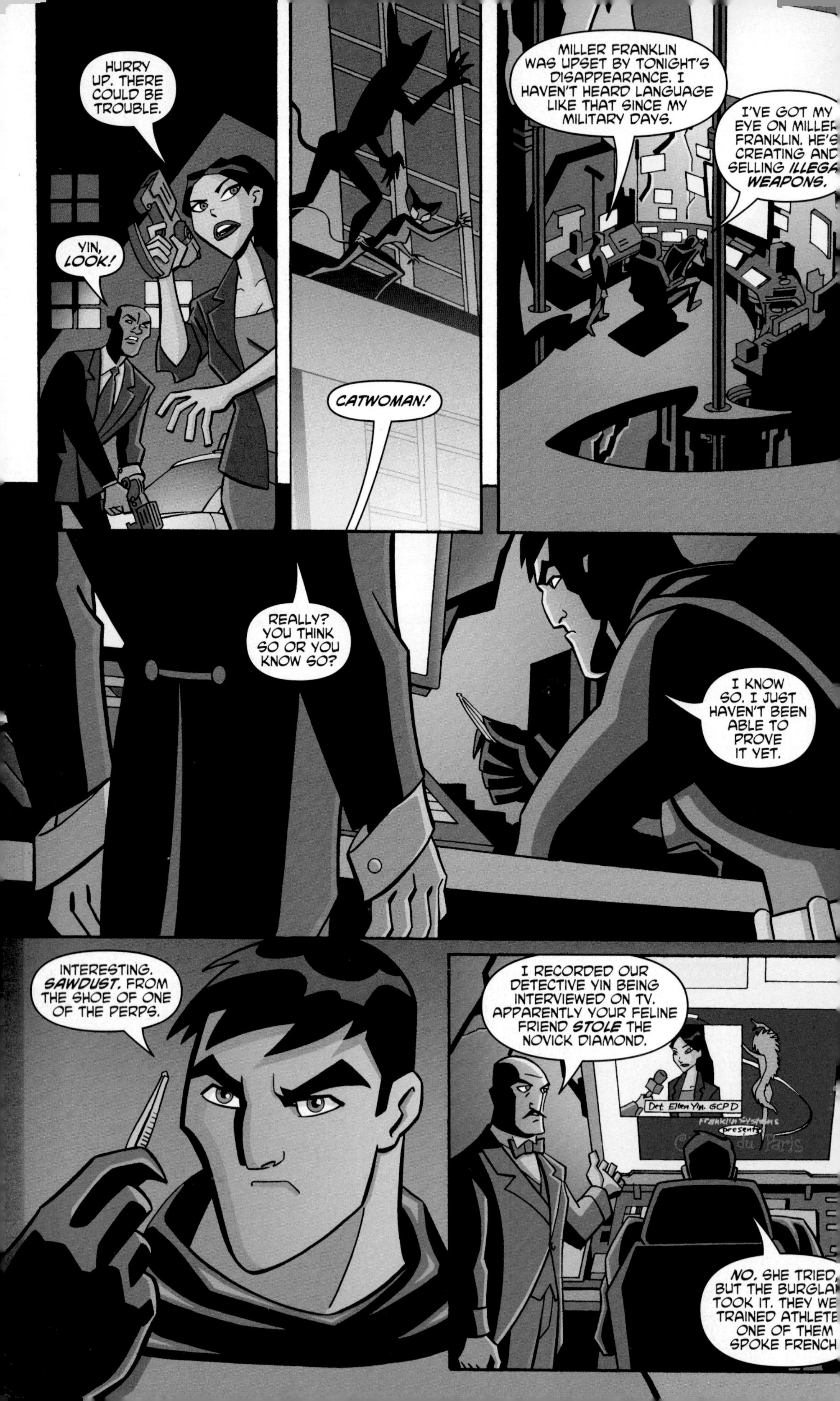
HURRY UP. THERE COULD BE TROUBLE.
YIN, LOOK!
CATWOMAN!
MILLER FRANKLIN WAS UPSET BY TONIGHT'S DISAPPEARANCE. I HAVEN'T HEARD LANGUAGE LIKE THAT SINCE MY MILITARY DAYS.
I'VE GOT MY EYE ON MILLER FRANKLIN. HE'S CREATING AND SELLING ILLEGA WEAPONS.
REALLY? YOU THINK SO OR YOU KNOW SO?
I KNOW SO. I JUST HAVEN'T BEEN ABLE TO PROVE IT YET.
INTERESTING. SAWDUST. FROM THE SHOE OF ONE OF THE PERPS.
I RECORDED OUR DETECTIVE YIN BEING INTERVIEWED ON TV. APPARENTLY YOUR FELINE FRIEND STOLE THE NOVICK DIAMOND.
Det. Ellen Yin. GCPD
NO. SHE TRIED, BUT THE BURGLA TOOK IT. THEY WE TRAINED ATHLETE ONE OF THEM SPOKE FRENCH

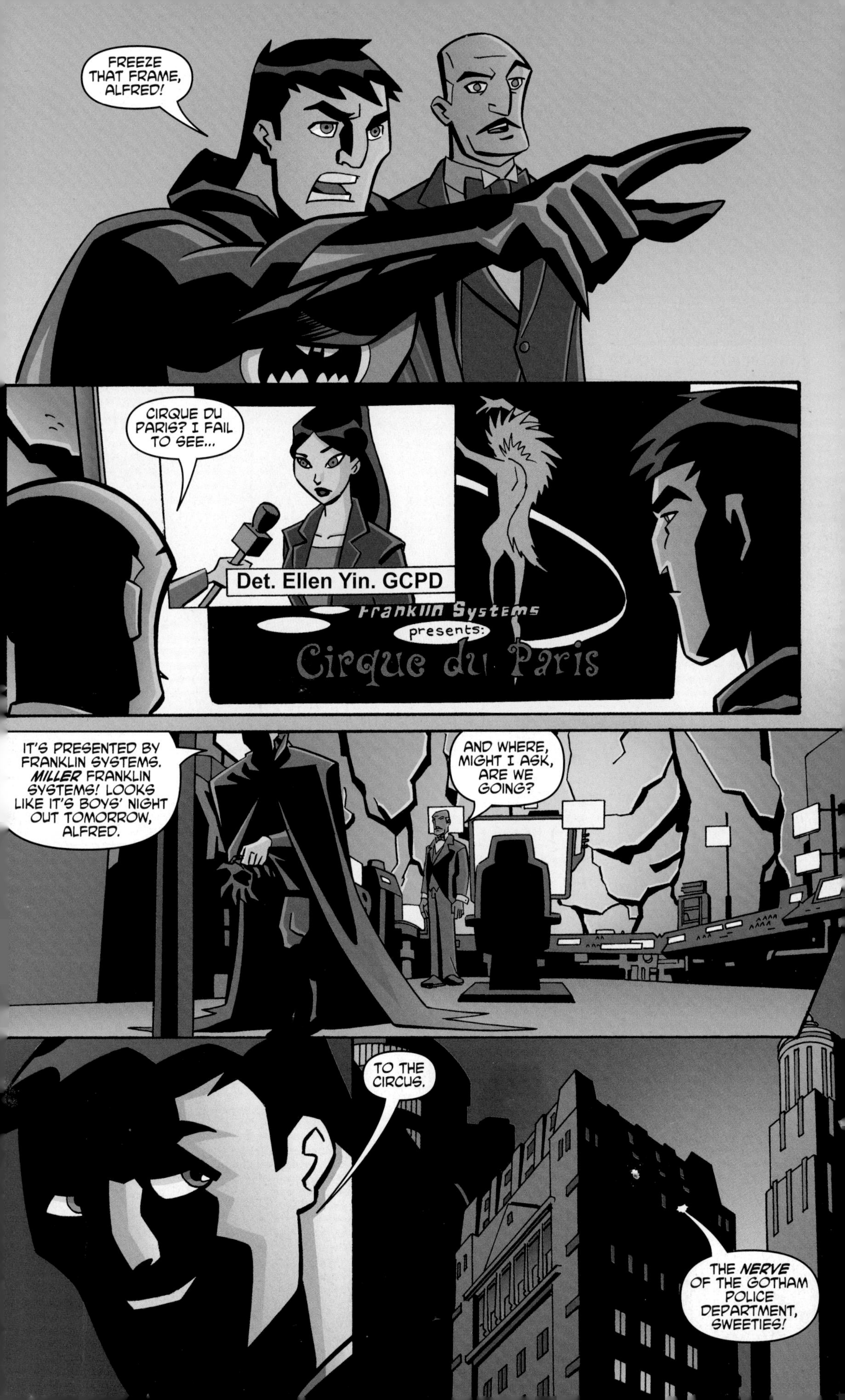
FREEZE THAT FRAME, ALFRED!
CIRQUE DU PARIS? I FAIL TO SEE...
Det. Ellen Yin. GCPD
Franklin Systems presents:
Cirque du Paris
IT'S PRESENTED BY FRANKLIN SYSTEMS. *MILLER* FRANKLIN SYSTEMS! LOOKS LIKE IT'S BOYS' NIGHT OUT TOMORROW, ALFRED.
AND WHERE, MIGHT I ASK, ARE WE GOING?
TO THE CIRCUS.
THE *NERVE* OF THE GOTHAM POLICE DEPARTMENT, SWEETIES!

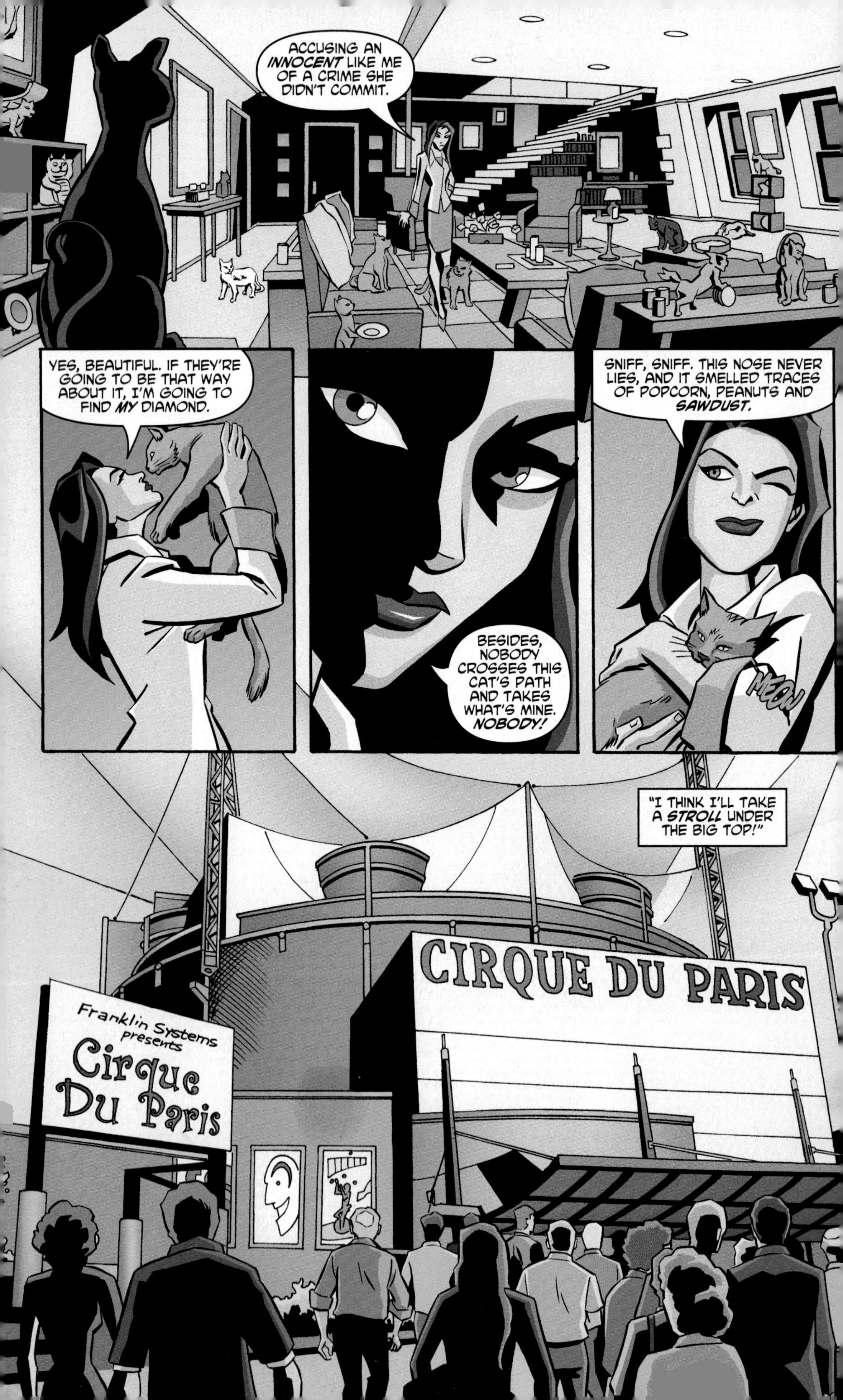

ACCUSING AN INNOCENT LIKE ME OF A CRIME SHE DIDN'T COMMIT.
YES, BEAUTIFUL. IF THEY'RE GOING TO BE THAT WAY ABOUT IT, I'M GOING TO FIND MY DIAMOND.
BESIDES, NOBODY CROSSES THIS CAT'S PATH AND TAKES WHAT'S MINE. NOBODY!
SNIFF, SNIFF. THIS NOSE NEVER LIES, AND IT SMELLED TRACES OF POPCORN, PEANUTS AND SAWDUST.
MEOW
"I THINK I'LL TAKE A STROLL UNDER THE BIG TOP!"
CIRQUE DU PARIS
Franklin Systems presents
Cirque Du Paris

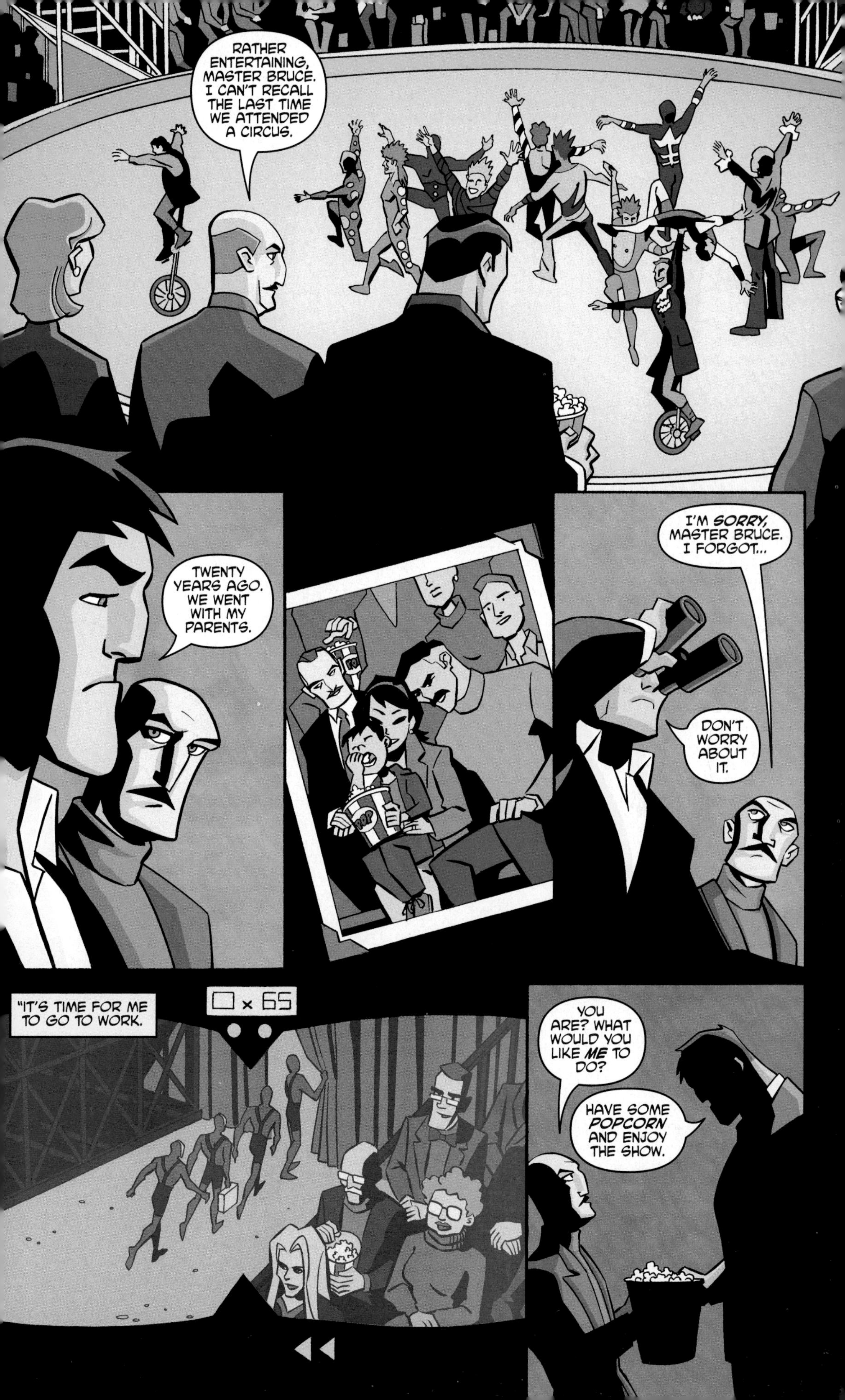
RATHER ENTERTAINING, MASTER BRUCE. I CAN'T RECALL THE LAST TIME WE ATTENDED A CIRCUS.
TWENTY YEARS AGO. WE WENT WITH MY PARENTS.
I'M SORRY, MASTER BRUCE. I FORGOT...
DON'T WORRY ABOUT IT.
"IT'S TIME FOR ME TO GO TO WORK.
YOU ARE? WHAT WOULD YOU LIKE ME TO DO?
HAVE SOME POPCORN AND ENJOY THE SHOW.

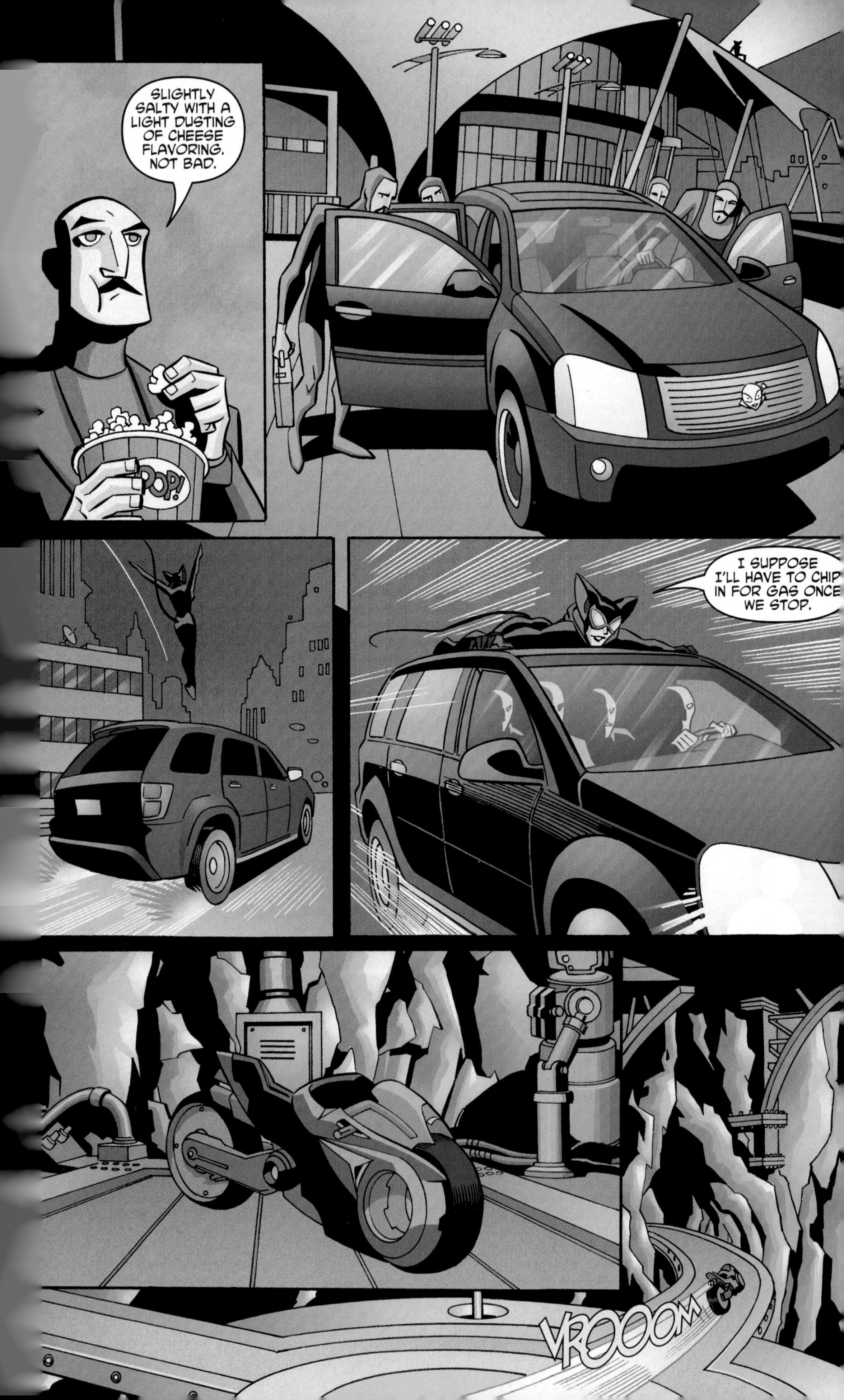
SLIGHTLY SALTY WITH A LIGHT DUSTING OF CHEESE FLAVORING. NOT BAD.
POP!
I SUPPOSE I'LL HAVE TO CHIP IN FOR GAS ONCE WE STOP.
VROOOM

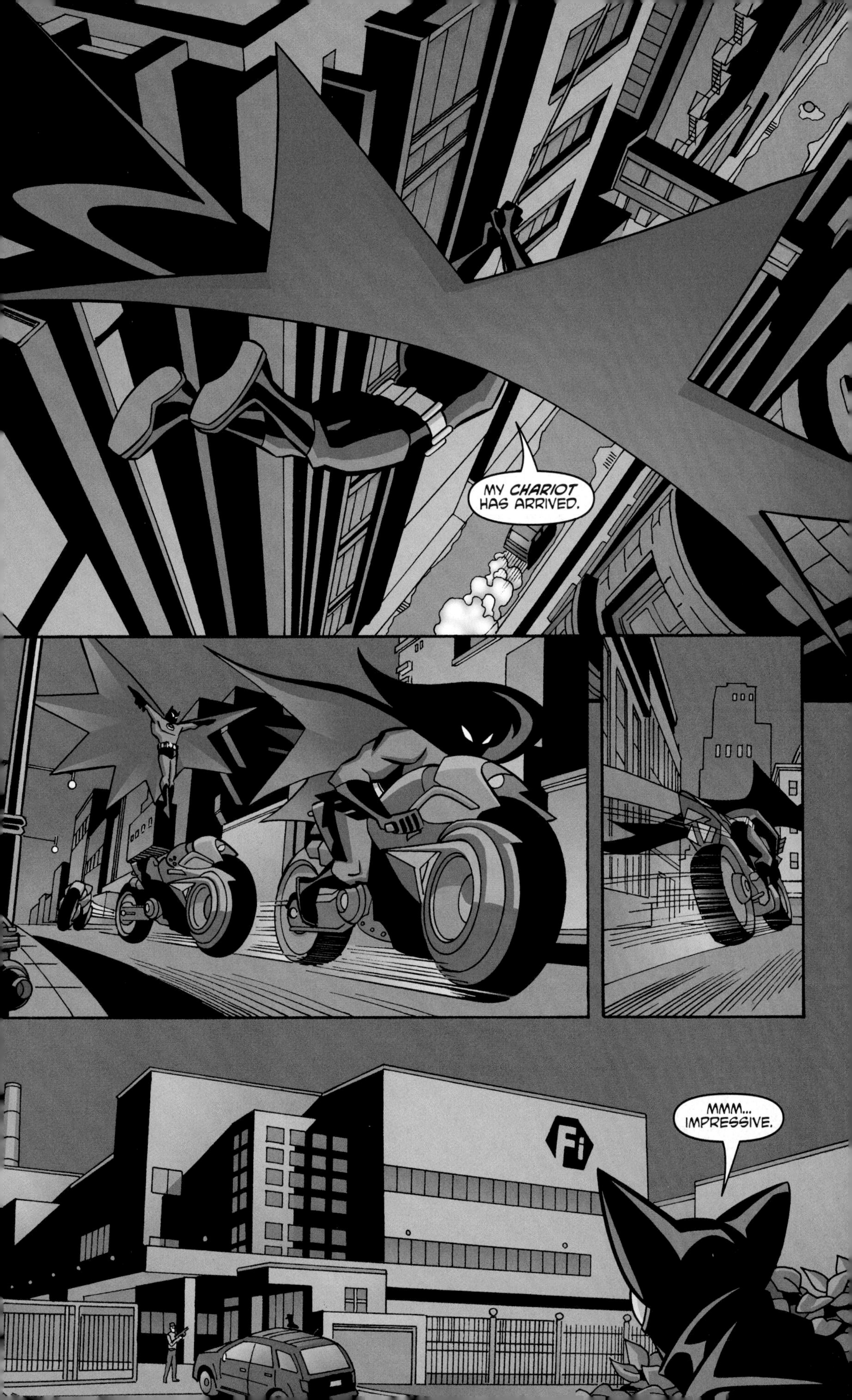
MY CHARIOT HAS ARRIVED.
MMM... IMPRESSIVE.

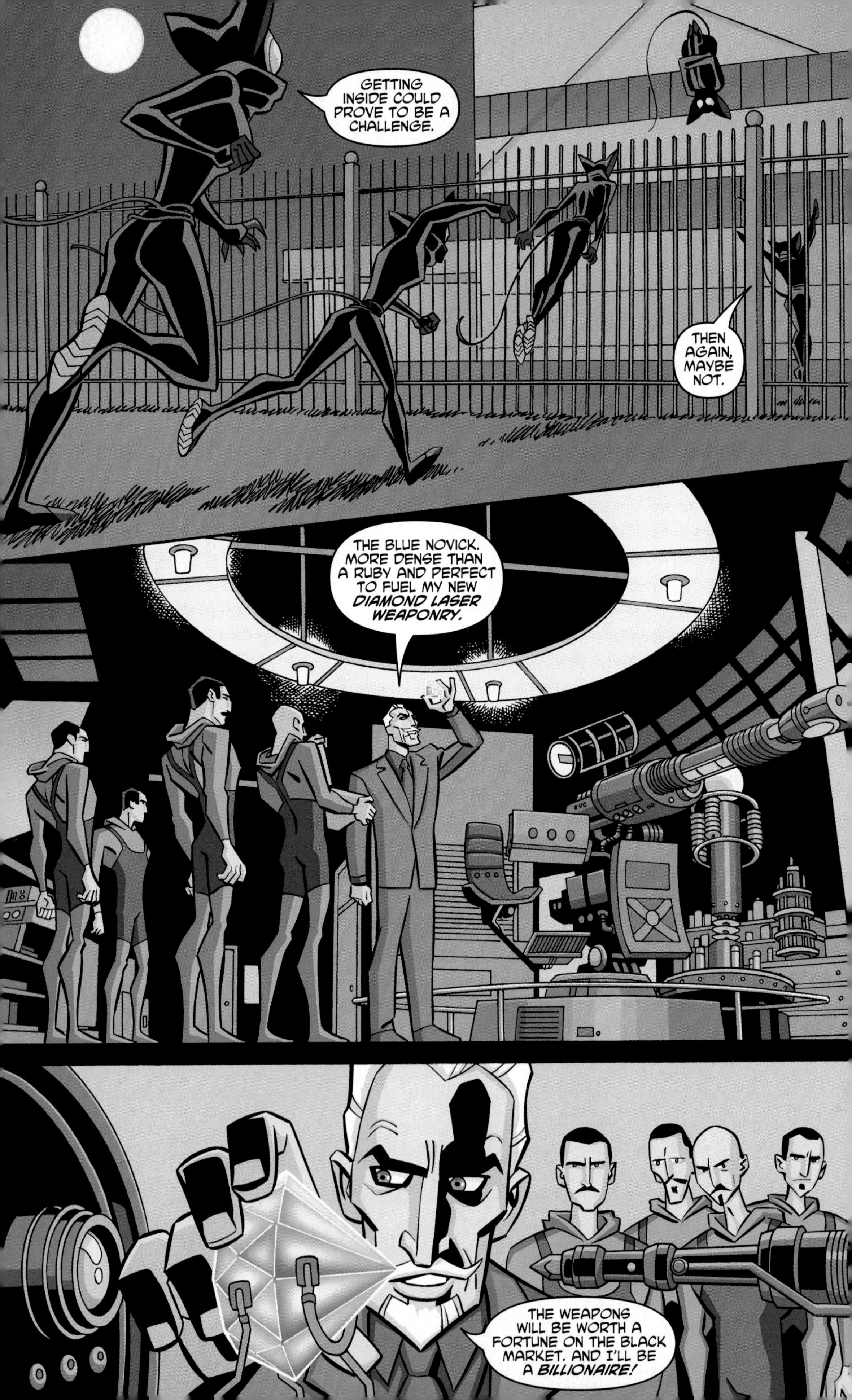
GETTING INSIDE COULD PROVE TO BE A CHALLENGE.
THEN AGAIN, MAYBE NOT.
THE BLUE NOVICK. MORE DENSE THAN A RUBY AND PERFECT TO FUEL MY NEW *DIAMOND LASER WEAPONRY.*
THE WEAPONS WILL BE WORTH A FORTUNE ON THE BLACK MARKET. AND I'LL BE A *BILLIONAIRE!*

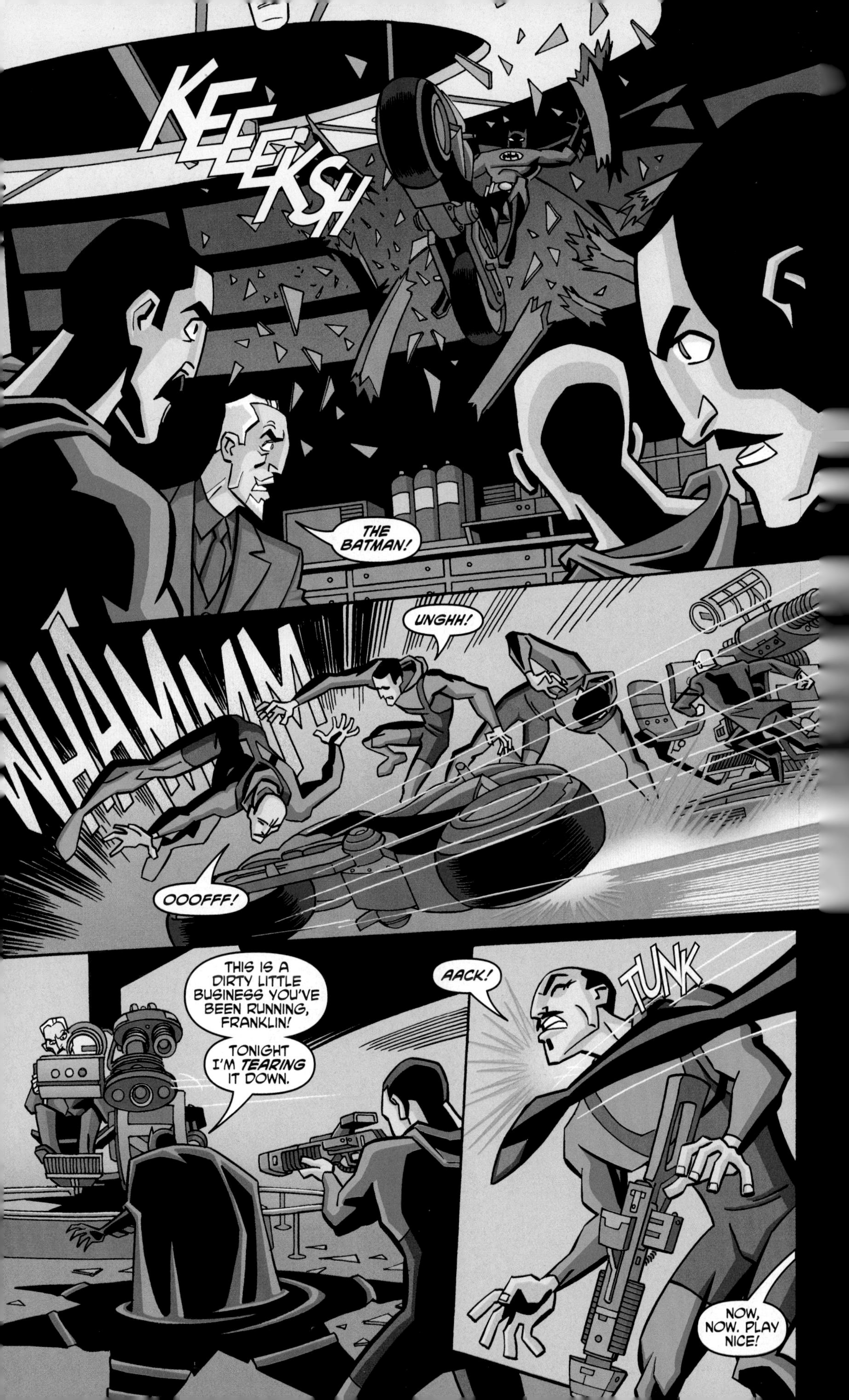
KEEEKSH
THE BATMAN!
WHAMMM
UNGHH!
OOOFFF!
THIS IS A DIRTY LITTLE BUSINESS YOU'VE BEEN RUNNING, FRANKLIN!
TONIGHT I'M *TEARING* IT DOWN.
AACK!
TUNK
NOW, NOW. PLAY NICE!

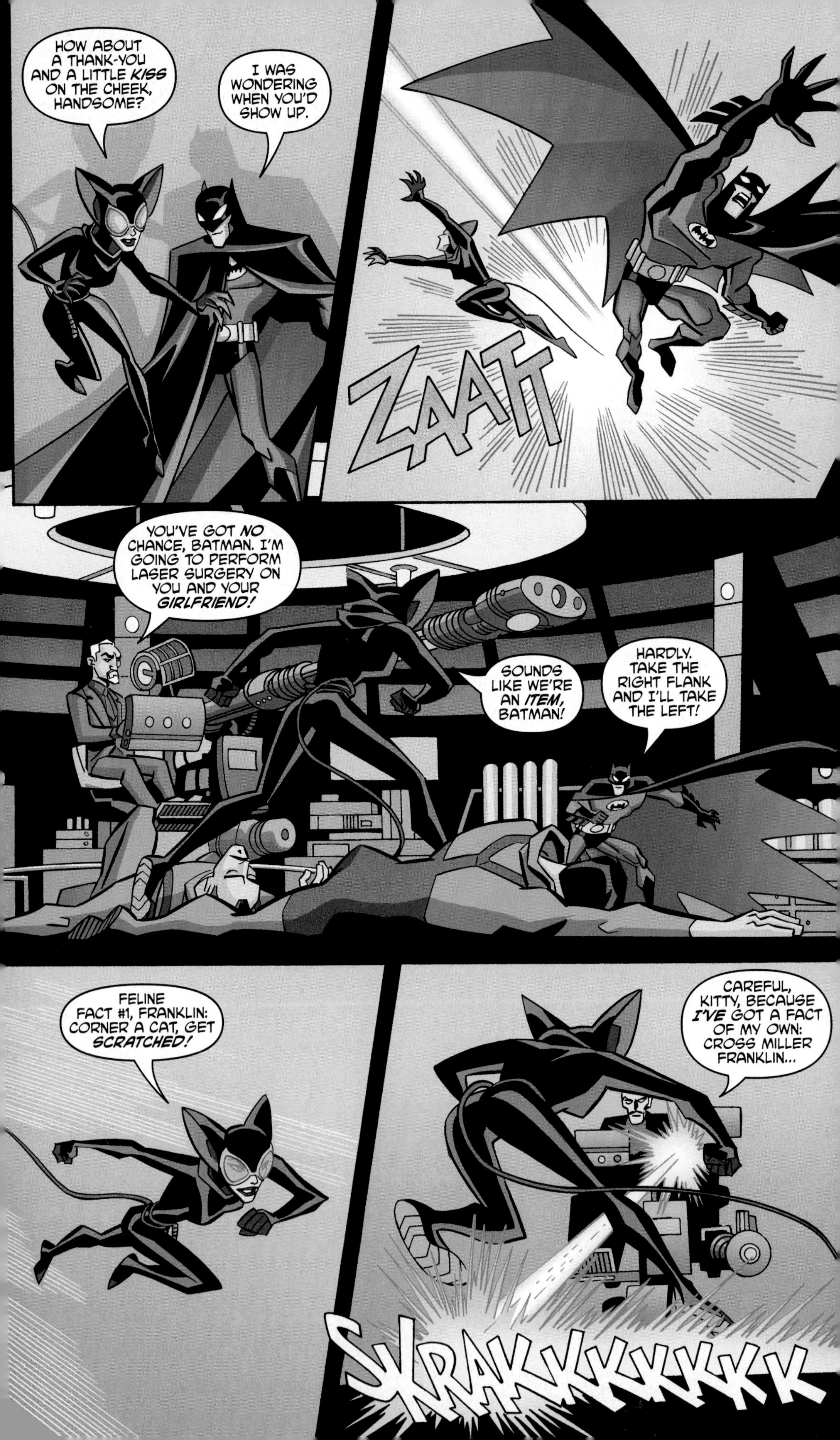

HOW ABOUT A THANK-YOU AND A LITTLE KISS ON THE CHEEK, HANDSOME?
I WAS WONDERING WHEN YOU'D SHOW UP.
ZAATT
YOU'VE GOT NO CHANCE, BATMAN. I'M GOING TO PERFORM LASER SURGERY ON YOU AND YOUR GIRLFRIEND!
SOUNDS LIKE WE'RE AN ITEM, BATMAN!
HARDLY. TAKE THE RIGHT FLANK AND I'LL TAKE THE LEFT!
FELINE FACT #1, FRANKLIN: CORNER A CAT, GET SCRATCHED!
CAREFUL, KITTY, BECAUSE I'VE GOT A FACT OF MY OWN: CROSS MILLER FRANKLIN...
SKRAKKKKKKKK

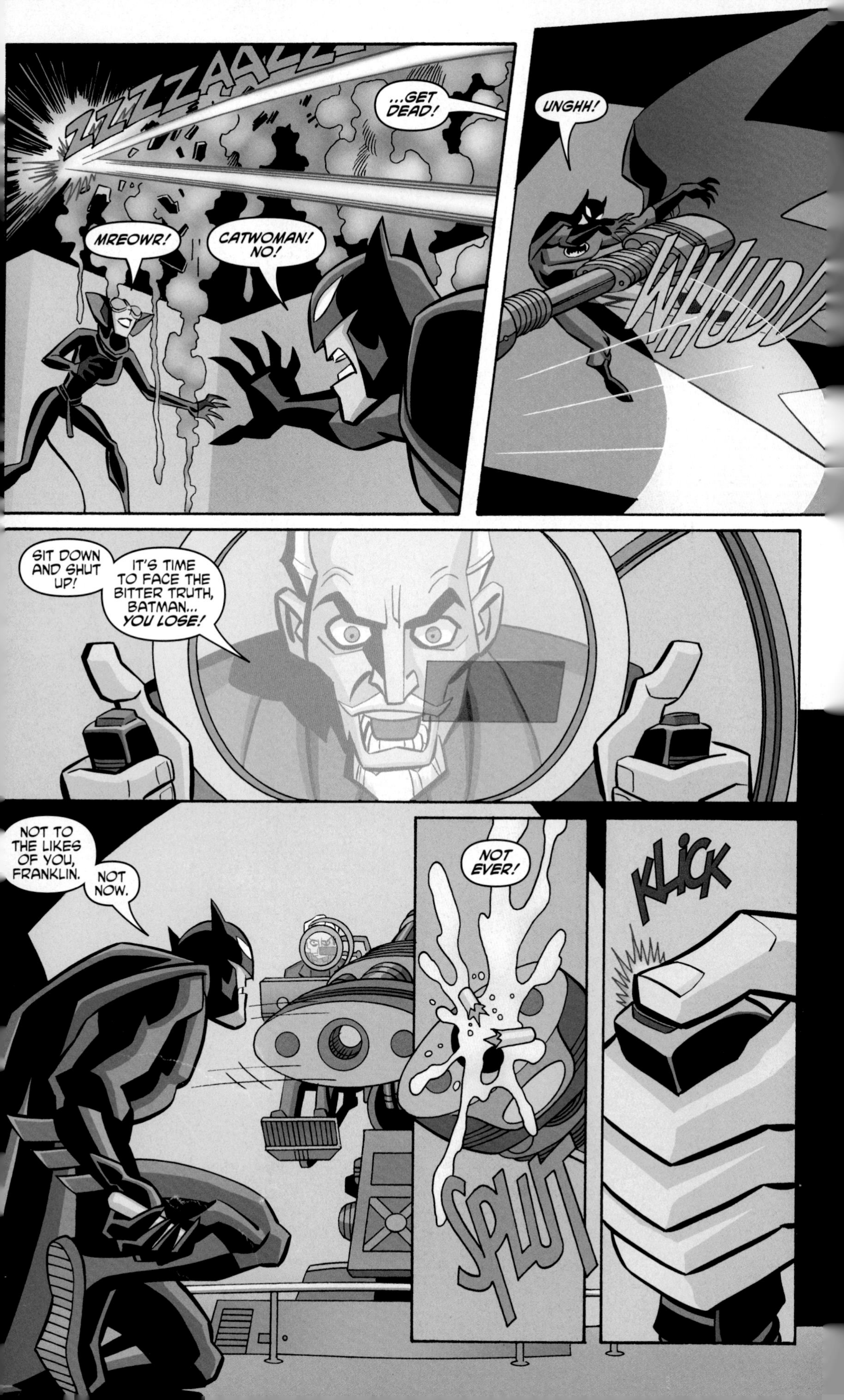
...GET DEAD!
MREOWR!
CATWOMAN! NO!
UNGHH!
SIT DOWN AND SHUT UP!
IT'S TIME TO FACE THE BITTER TRUTH, BATMAN... *YOU LOSE!*
NOT TO THE LIKES OF YOU, FRANKLIN.
NOT NOW.
NOT EVER!
SPLUT
KLICK

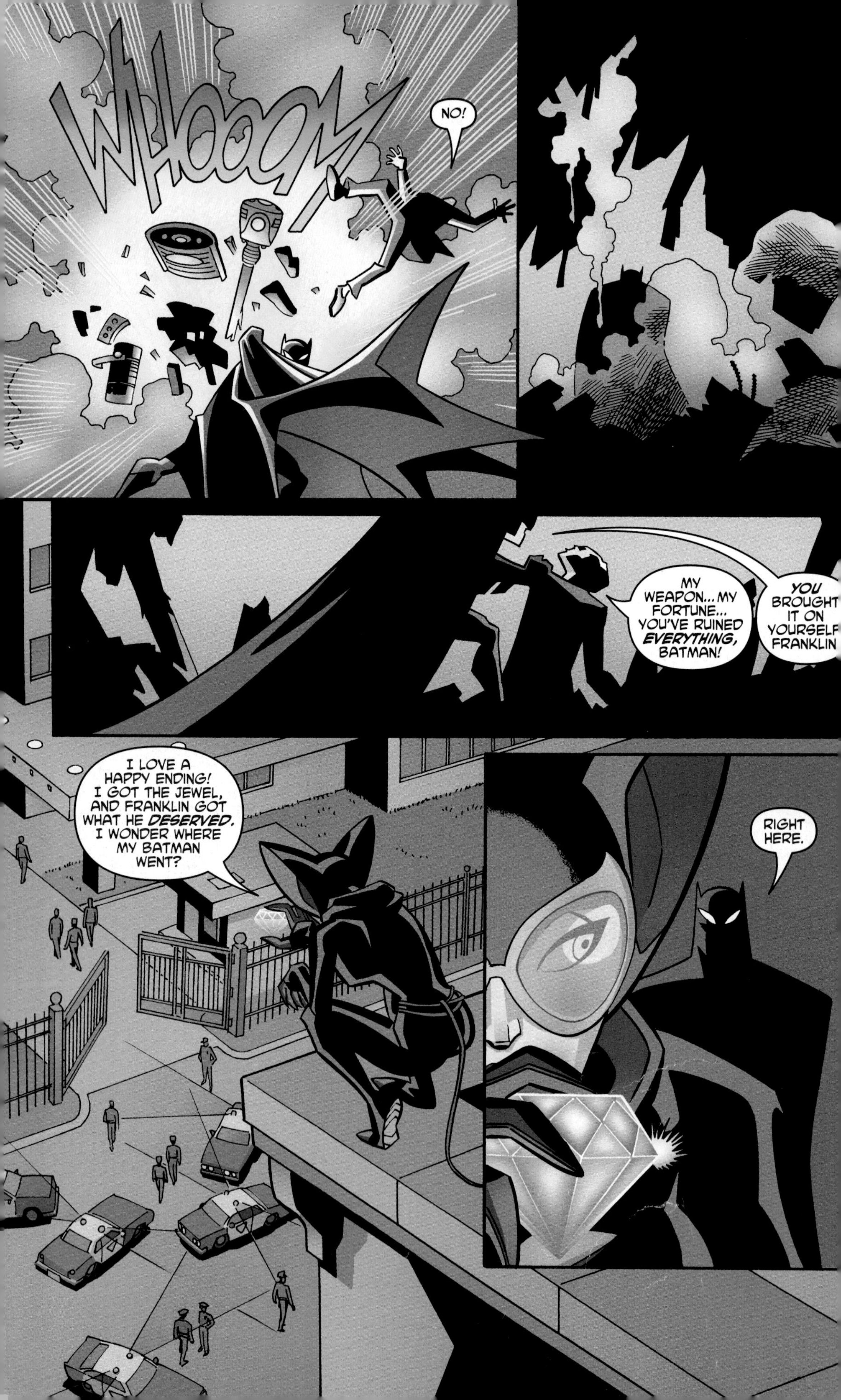
WHOOOM
NO!
MY WEAPON... MY FORTUNE... YOU'VE RUINED *EVERYTHING*, BATMAN!
YOU BROUGHT IT ON YOURSELF FRANKLIN
I LOVE A HAPPY ENDING! I GOT THE JEWEL, AND FRANKLIN GOT WHAT HE *DESERVED*. I WONDER WHERE MY BATMAN WENT?
RIGHT HERE.

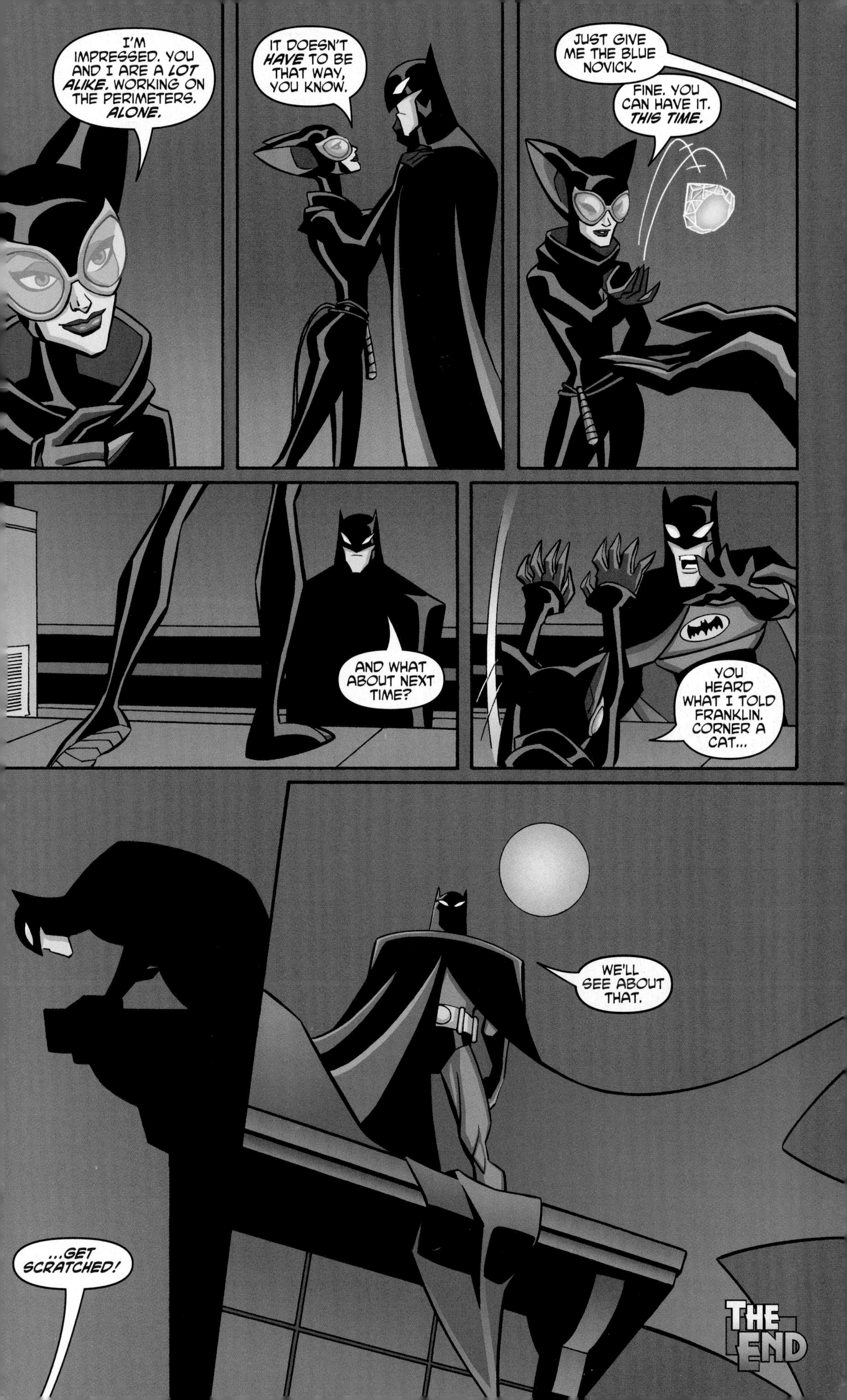
I'M IMPRESSED. YOU AND I ARE A *LOT ALIKE.* WORKING ON THE PERIMETERS. *ALONE.*
IT DOESN'T *HAVE* TO BE THAT WAY, YOU KNOW.
JUST GIVE ME THE BLUE NOVICK.
FINE. YOU CAN HAVE IT. *THIS TIME.*
AND WHAT ABOUT NEXT TIME?
YOU HEARD WHAT I TOLD FRANKLIN. CORNER A CAT...
WE'LL SEE ABOUT THAT.
...GET SCRATCHED!
THE END

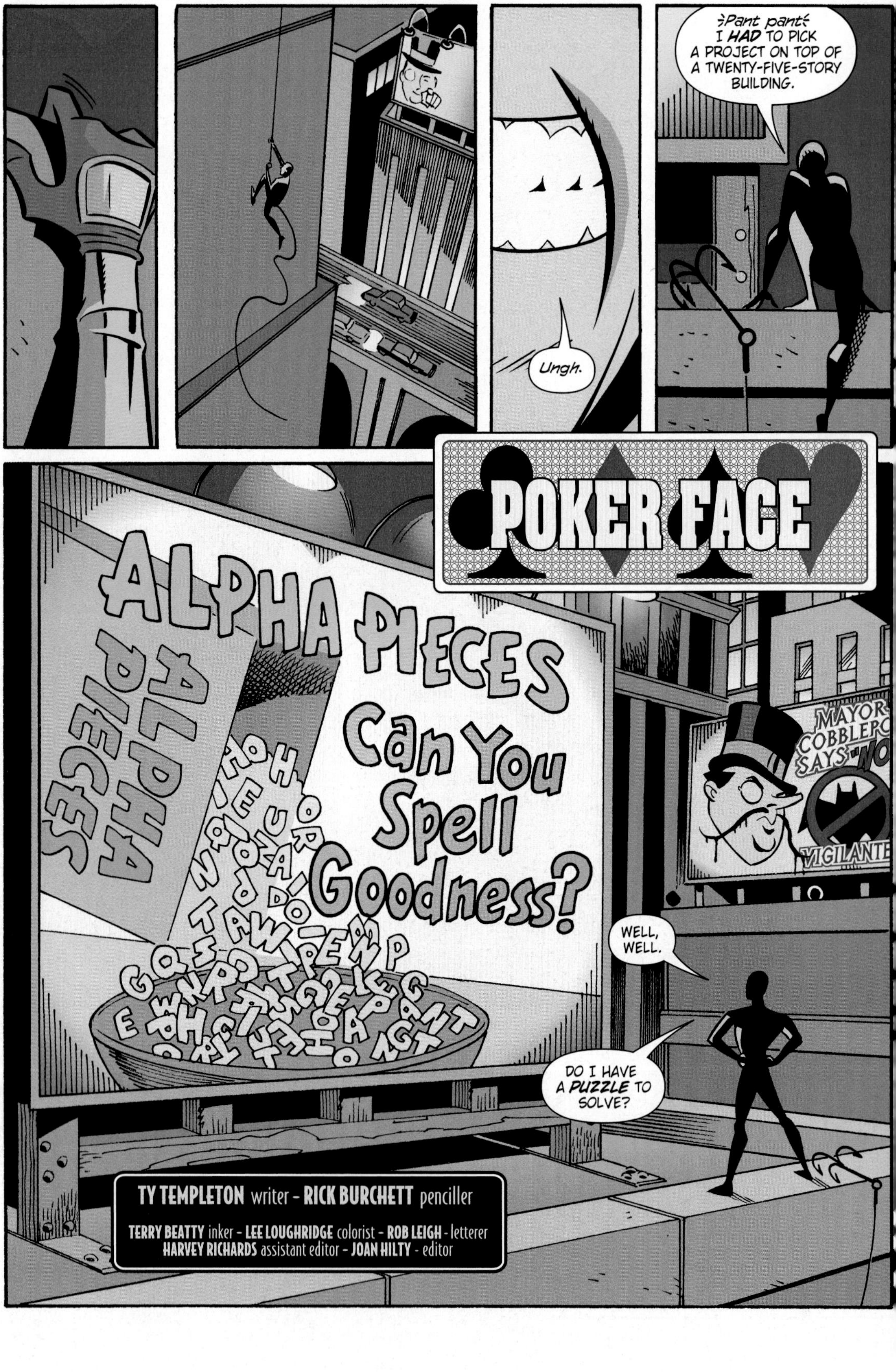
Ungh.
⁐Pant pant⁐ I HAD TO PICK A PROJECT ON TOP OF A TWENTY-FIVE-STORY BUILDING.
POKER FACE
ALPHA PIECES
ALPHA PIECES
Can You Spell Goodness?
MAYOR COBBLEPO SAYS "NO"
VIGILANTE
WELL, WELL.
DO I HAVE A PUZZLE TO SOLVE?
TY TEMPLETON writer - RICK BURCHETT penciller
TERRY BEATTY inker - LEE LOUGHRIDGE colorist - ROB LEIGH - letterer
HARVEY RICHARDS assistant editor - JOAN HILTY - editor

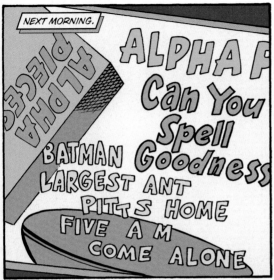

NEXT MORNING.

ALPHA PIECE

Can You Spell Goodness

BATMAN

LARGEST ANT

PITTS HOME

FIVE A M

COME ALONE

I SAID THIS SORT OF THING WAS GOING TO *STOP!!*

GOTHAM GAZE

RIDDLER'S BACK!

HAS EDWARD NYGMA RETURNED TO A LIFE OF CRIME?

WHAT DO *YOU* CARE IF THE RIDDLER HAS A LITTLE FUN, MR. MAYOR? IT AIN'T ONE A' *YOUR* BILLBOARDS HE WAS DEFACING.

THE CITIZENS BEEN DOIN' ENOUGH OF *THAT* ON THEIR OWN.

I GAVE MY *WORD* TO THE PEOPLE OF THIS CITY I WOULD PUT AN *END* TO THE LUNATICS IN MASKS AND THEIR DANGEROUS GAMES.

MY INCOMPETENT POLICE FORCE MAY NOT BE ABLE TO BRING IN BATMAN, TO STAND TRIAL...

BUT WE *KNOW* WHERE NYGMA LIVES.

I GOT *BETTER* THAN KNOWING WHERE HE LIVES, BOSS.

I KNOW WHERE HE IS RIGHT *NOW...*

ON THE TV.

MR. NYGMA! MR. NYGMA! A *COMMENT*, PLEASE?

NYGMATECH

LIVE

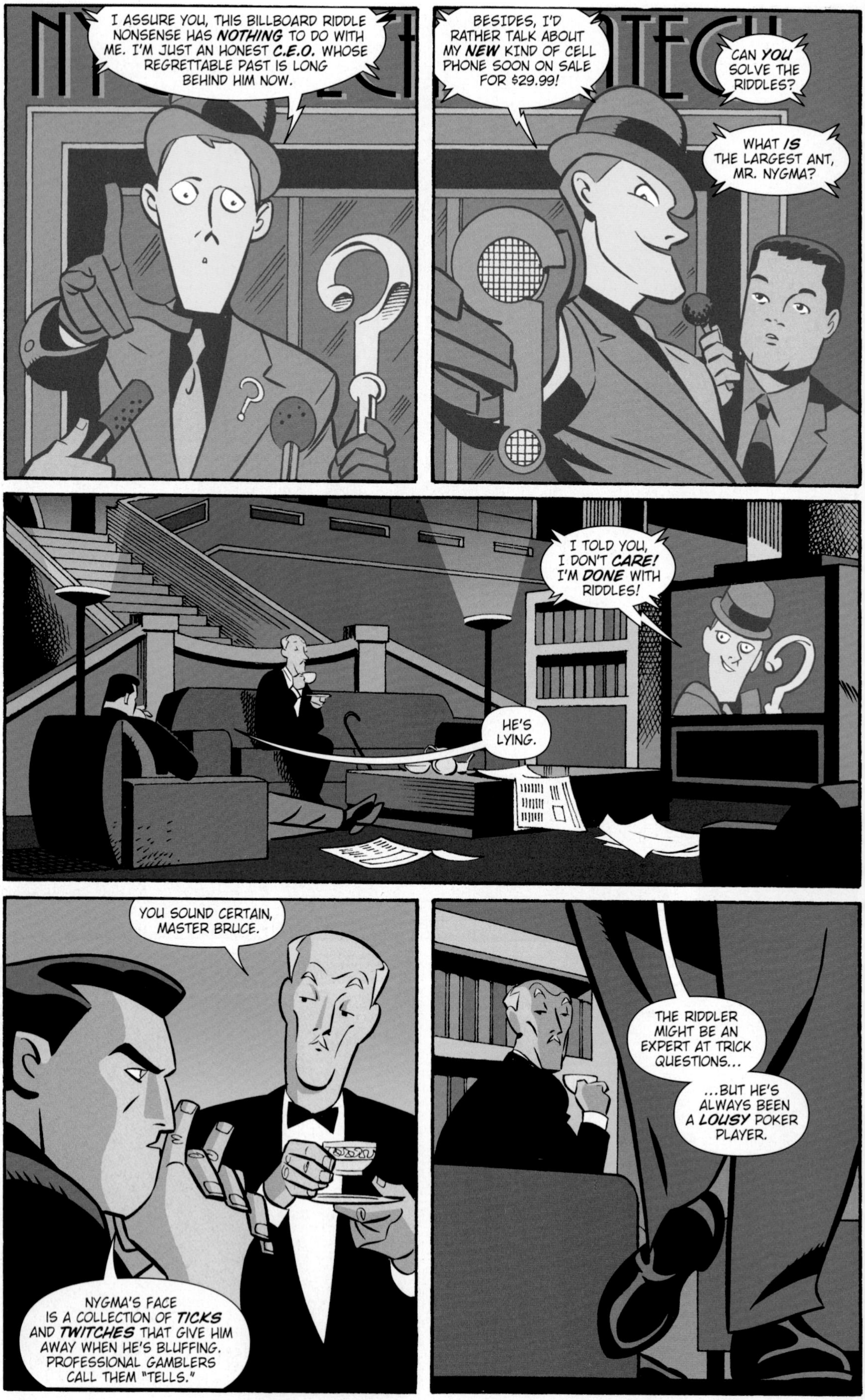
I ASSURE YOU, THIS BILLBOARD RIDDLE NONSENSE HAS NOTHING TO DO WITH ME. I'M JUST AN HONEST C.E.O. WHOSE REGRETTABLE PAST IS LONG BEHIND HIM NOW.
BESIDES, I'D RATHER TALK ABOUT MY NEW KIND OF CELL PHONE SOON ON SALE FOR $29.99!
CAN YOU SOLVE THE RIDDLES?
WHAT IS THE LARGEST ANT, MR. NYGMA?
I TOLD YOU, I DON'T CARE! I'M DONE WITH RIDDLES!
HE'S LYING.
YOU SOUND CERTAIN, MASTER BRUCE.
NYGMA'S FACE IS A COLLECTION OF TICKS AND TWITCHES THAT GIVE HIM AWAY WHEN HE'S BLUFFING. PROFESSIONAL GAMBLERS CALL THEM "TELLS."
THE RIDDLER MIGHT BE AN EXPERT AT TRICK QUESTIONS...
...BUT HE'S ALWAYS BEEN A LOUSY POKER PLAYER.

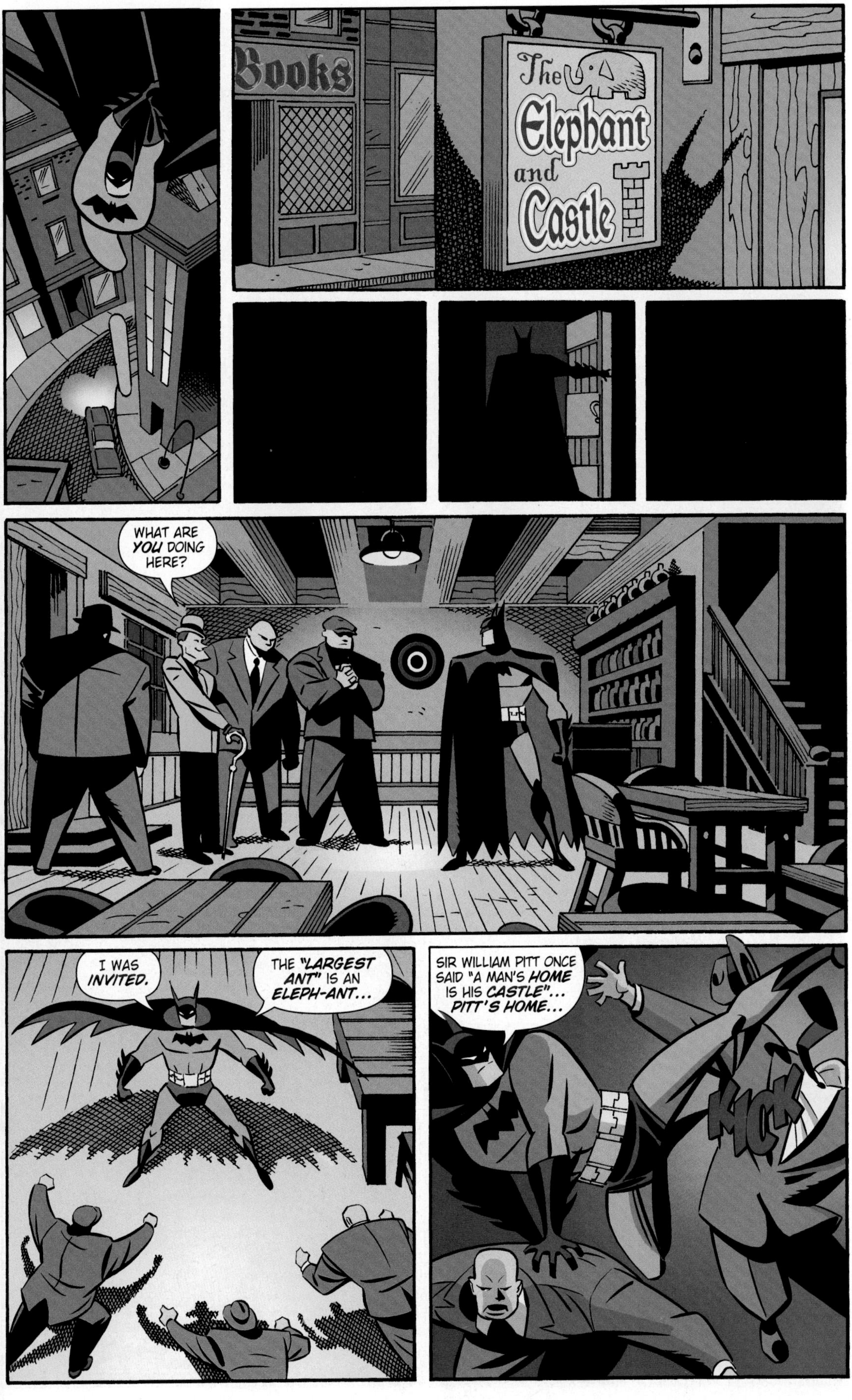
Books
The Elephant and Castle
WHAT ARE YOU DOING HERE?
I WAS INVITED.
THE "LARGEST ANT" IS AN ELEPH-ANT...
SIR WILLIAM PITT ONCE SAID "A MAN'S HOME IS HIS CASTLE"... PITT'S HOME...
KICK

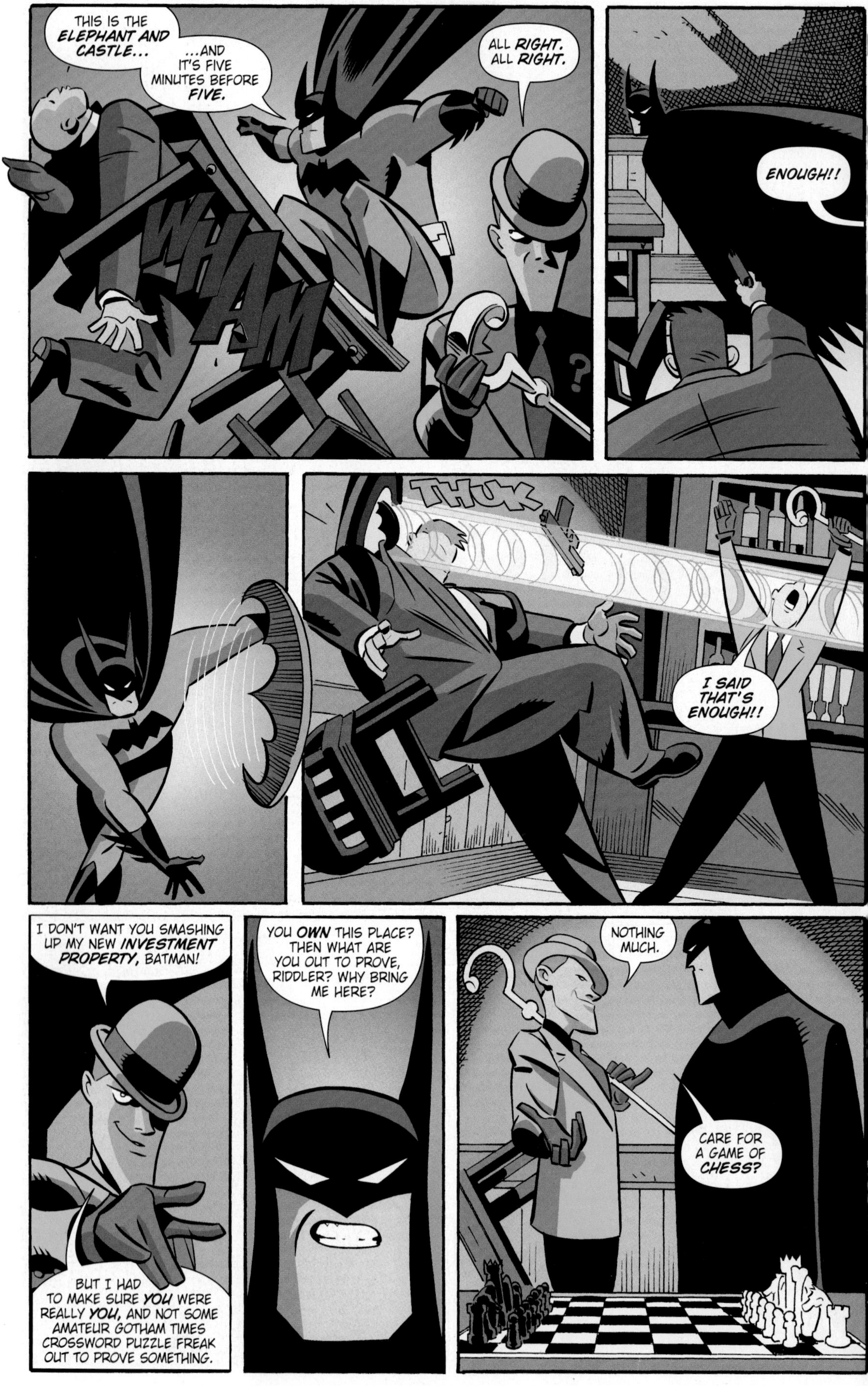
THIS IS THE ELEPHANT AND CASTLE...
...AND IT'S FIVE MINUTES BEFORE FIVE.
WHAM
ALL RIGHT. ALL RIGHT.
ENOUGH!!
THUK
I SAID THAT'S ENOUGH!!
I DON'T WANT YOU SMASHING UP MY NEW INVESTMENT PROPERTY, BATMAN!
BUT I HAD TO MAKE SURE YOU WERE REALLY YOU, AND NOT SOME AMATEUR GOTHAM TIMES CROSSWORD PUZZLE FREAK OUT TO PROVE SOMETHING.
YOU OWN THIS PLACE? THEN WHAT ARE YOU OUT TO PROVE, RIDDLER? WHY BRING ME HERE?
NOTHING MUCH.
CARE FOR A GAME OF CHESS?

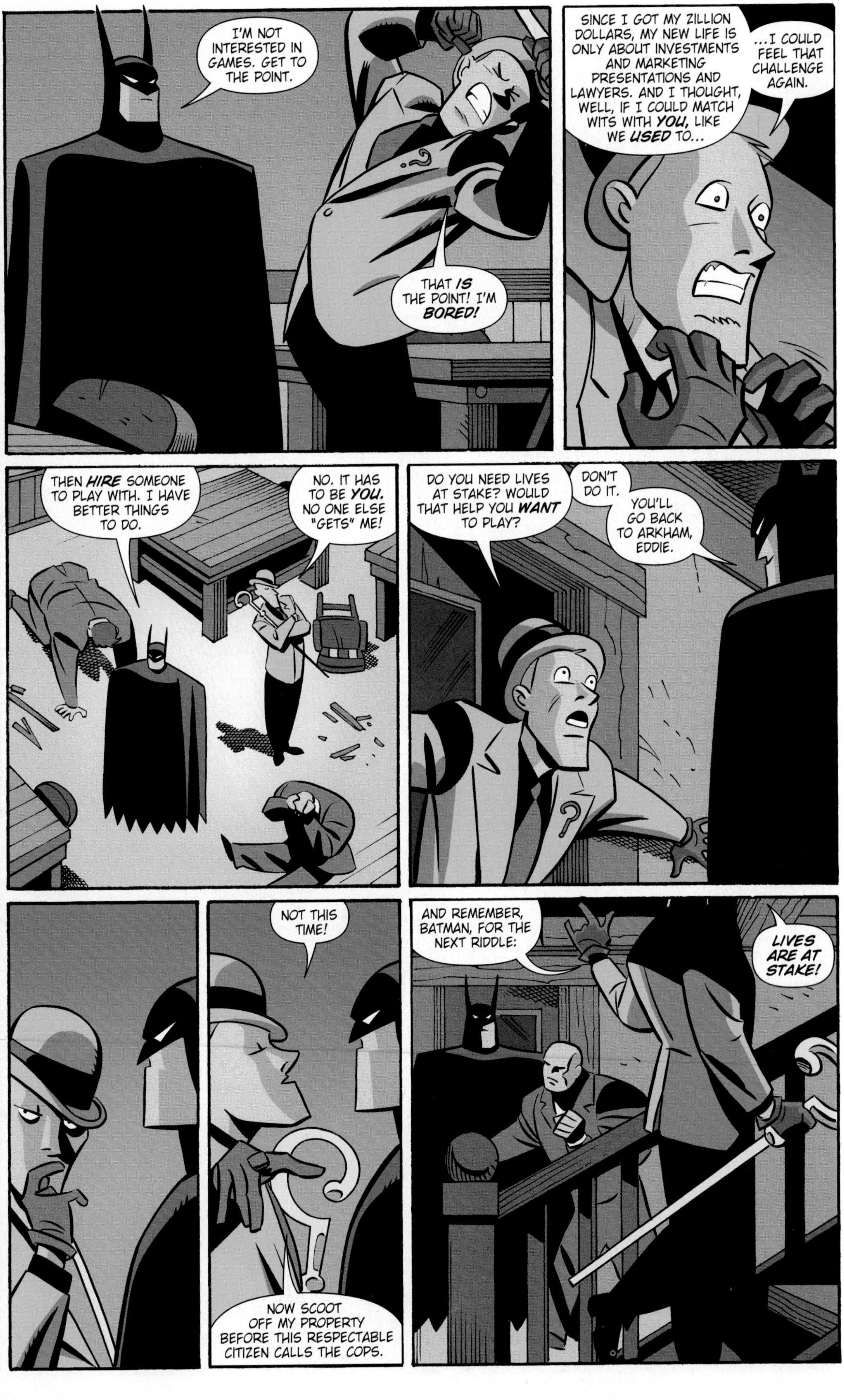
I'M NOT INTERESTED IN GAMES. GET TO THE POINT.
THAT IS THE POINT! I'M BORED!
SINCE I GOT MY ZILLION DOLLARS, MY NEW LIFE IS ONLY ABOUT INVESTMENTS AND MARKETING PRESENTATIONS AND LAWYERS. AND I THOUGHT, WELL, IF I COULD MATCH WITS WITH YOU, LIKE WE USED TO...
...I COULD FEEL THAT CHALLENGE AGAIN.
THEN HIRE SOMEONE TO PLAY WITH. I HAVE BETTER THINGS TO DO.
NO. IT HAS TO BE YOU. NO ONE ELSE "GETS" ME!
DO YOU NEED LIVES AT STAKE? WOULD THAT HELP YOU WANT TO PLAY?
DON'T DO IT.
YOU'LL GO BACK TO ARKHAM, EDDIE.
NOT THIS TIME!
NOW SCOOT OFF MY PROPERTY BEFORE THIS RESPECTABLE CITIZEN CALLS THE COPS.
AND REMEMBER, BATMAN, FOR THE NEXT RIDDLE:
LIVES ARE AT STAKE!

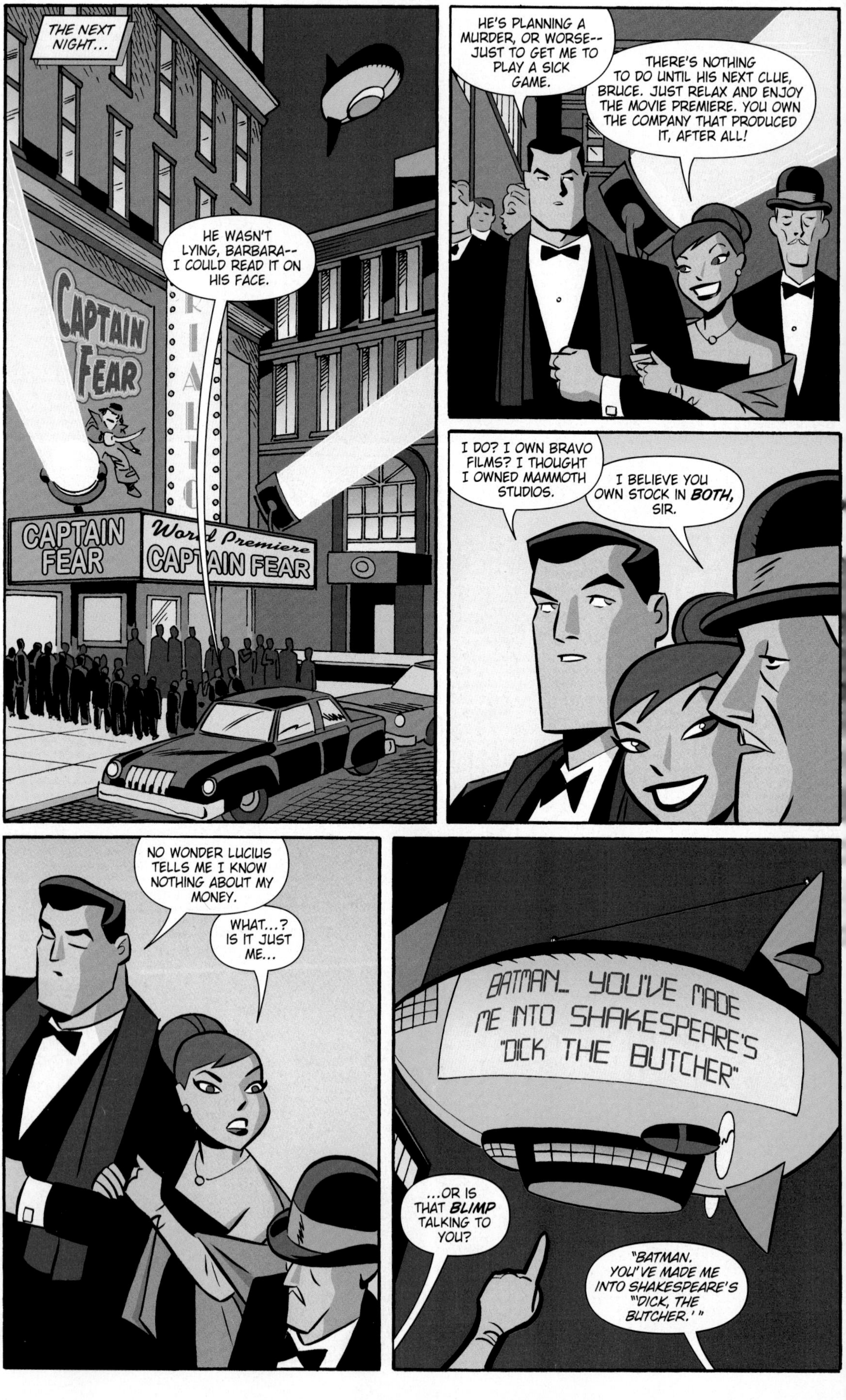
THE NEXT NIGHT...
CAPTAIN FEAR
RIALTO
CAPTAIN FEAR
World Premiere CAPTAIN FEAR
HE WASN'T LYING, BARBARA-- I COULD READ IT ON HIS FACE.
HE'S PLANNING A MURDER, OR WORSE-- JUST TO GET ME TO PLAY A SICK GAME.
THERE'S NOTHING TO DO UNTIL HIS NEXT CLUE, BRUCE. JUST RELAX AND ENJOY THE MOVIE PREMIERE. YOU OWN THE COMPANY THAT PRODUCED IT, AFTER ALL!
I DO? I OWN BRAVO FILMS? I THOUGHT I OWNED MAMMOTH STUDIOS.
I BELIEVE YOU OWN STOCK IN BOTH, SIR.
NO WONDER LUCIUS TELLS ME I KNOW NOTHING ABOUT MY MONEY.
WHAT...? IS IT JUST ME...
BATMAN... YOU'VE MADE ME INTO SHAKESPEARE'S "DICK THE BUTCHER"
...OR IS THAT BLIMP TALKING TO YOU?
"BATMAN. YOU'VE MADE ME INTO SHAKESPEARE'S "DICK, THE BUTCHER.' "

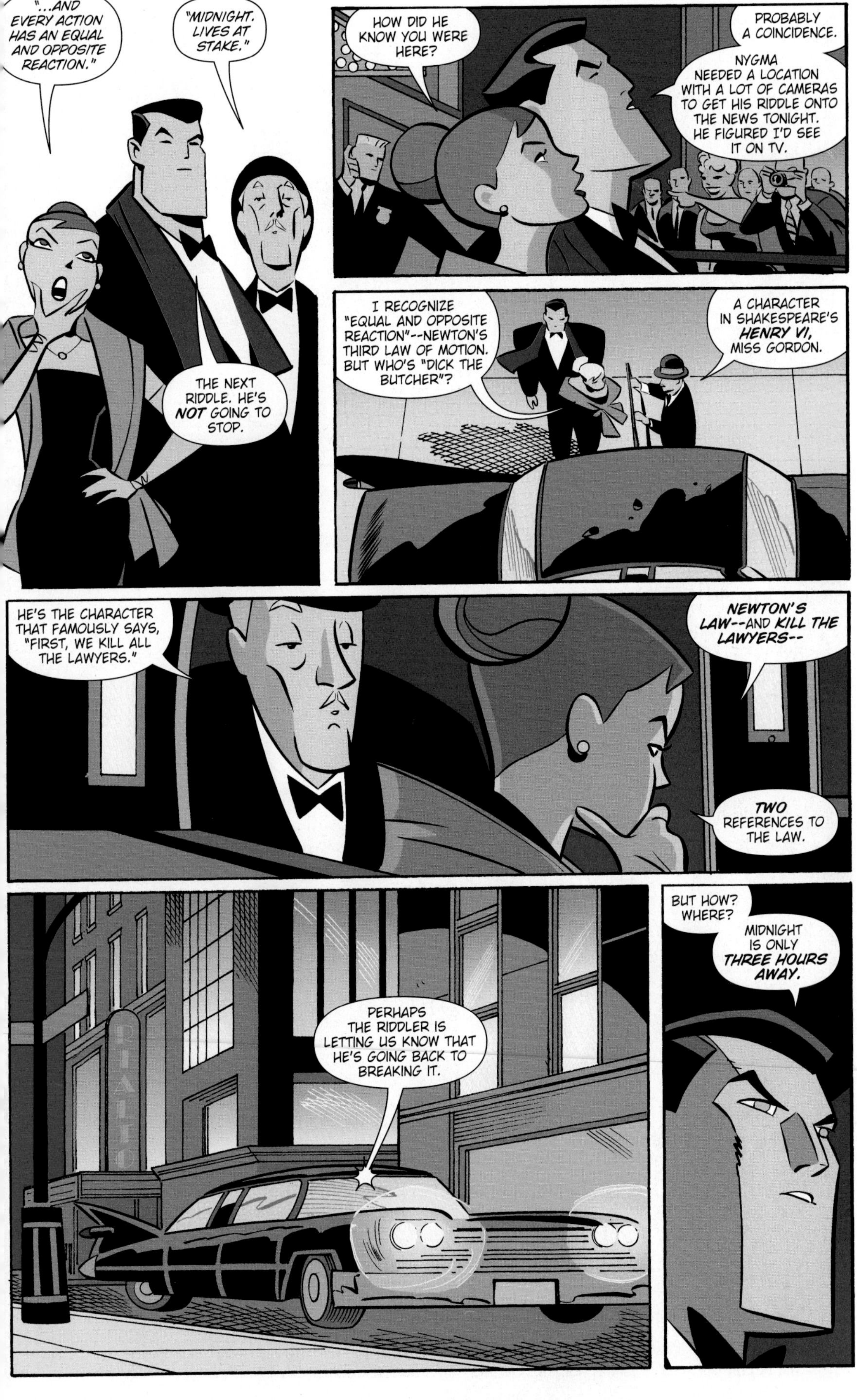
"...AND EVERY ACTION HAS AN EQUAL AND OPPOSITE REACTION."
"MIDNIGHT. LIVES AT STAKE."
THE NEXT RIDDLE. HE'S **NOT** GOING TO STOP.
HOW DID HE KNOW YOU WERE HERE?
PROBABLY A COINCIDENCE.
NYGMA NEEDED A LOCATION WITH A LOT OF CAMERAS TO GET HIS RIDDLE ONTO THE NEWS TONIGHT. HE FIGURED I'D SEE IT ON TV.
I RECOGNIZE "EQUAL AND OPPOSITE REACTION"--NEWTON'S THIRD LAW OF MOTION. BUT WHO'S "DICK THE BUTCHER"?
A CHARACTER IN SHAKESPEARE'S ***HENRY VI,*** MISS GORDON.
HE'S THE CHARACTER THAT FAMOUSLY SAYS, "FIRST, WE KILL ALL THE LAWYERS."
NEWTON'S LAW--AND ***KILL THE LAWYERS***--
TWO REFERENCES TO THE LAW.
RIALTO
PERHAPS THE RIDDLER IS LETTING US KNOW THAT HE'S GOING BACK TO BREAKING IT.
BUT HOW? WHERE?
MIDNIGHT IS ONLY ***THREE HOURS AWAY.***

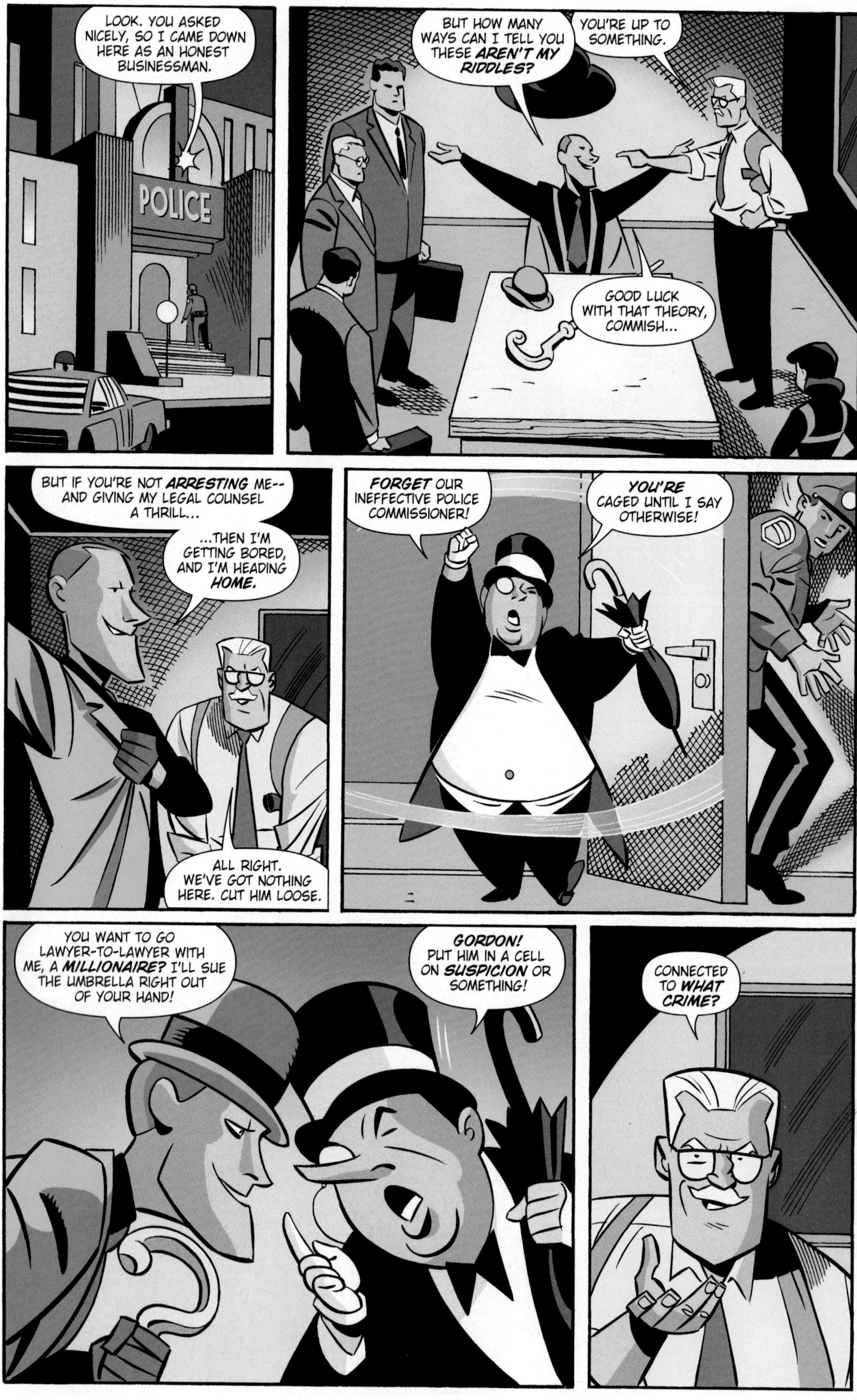
LOOK. YOU ASKED NICELY, SO I CAME DOWN HERE AS AN HONEST BUSINESSMAN.
POLICE
BUT HOW MANY WAYS CAN I TELL YOU THESE AREN'T MY RIDDLES?
YOU'RE UP TO SOMETHING.
GOOD LUCK WITH THAT THEORY, COMMISH...
BUT IF YOU'RE NOT ARRESTING ME-- AND GIVING MY LEGAL COUNSEL A THRILL...
...THEN I'M GETTING BORED, AND I'M HEADING HOME.
ALL RIGHT. WE'VE GOT NOTHING HERE. CUT HIM LOOSE.
FORGET OUR INEFFECTIVE POLICE COMMISSIONER!
YOU'RE CAGED UNTIL I SAY OTHERWISE!
YOU WANT TO GO LAWYER-TO-LAWYER WITH ME, A MILLIONAIRE? I'LL SUE THE UMBRELLA RIGHT OUT OF YOUR HAND!
GORDON! PUT HIM IN A CELL ON SUSPICION OR SOMETHING!
CONNECTED TO WHAT CRIME?

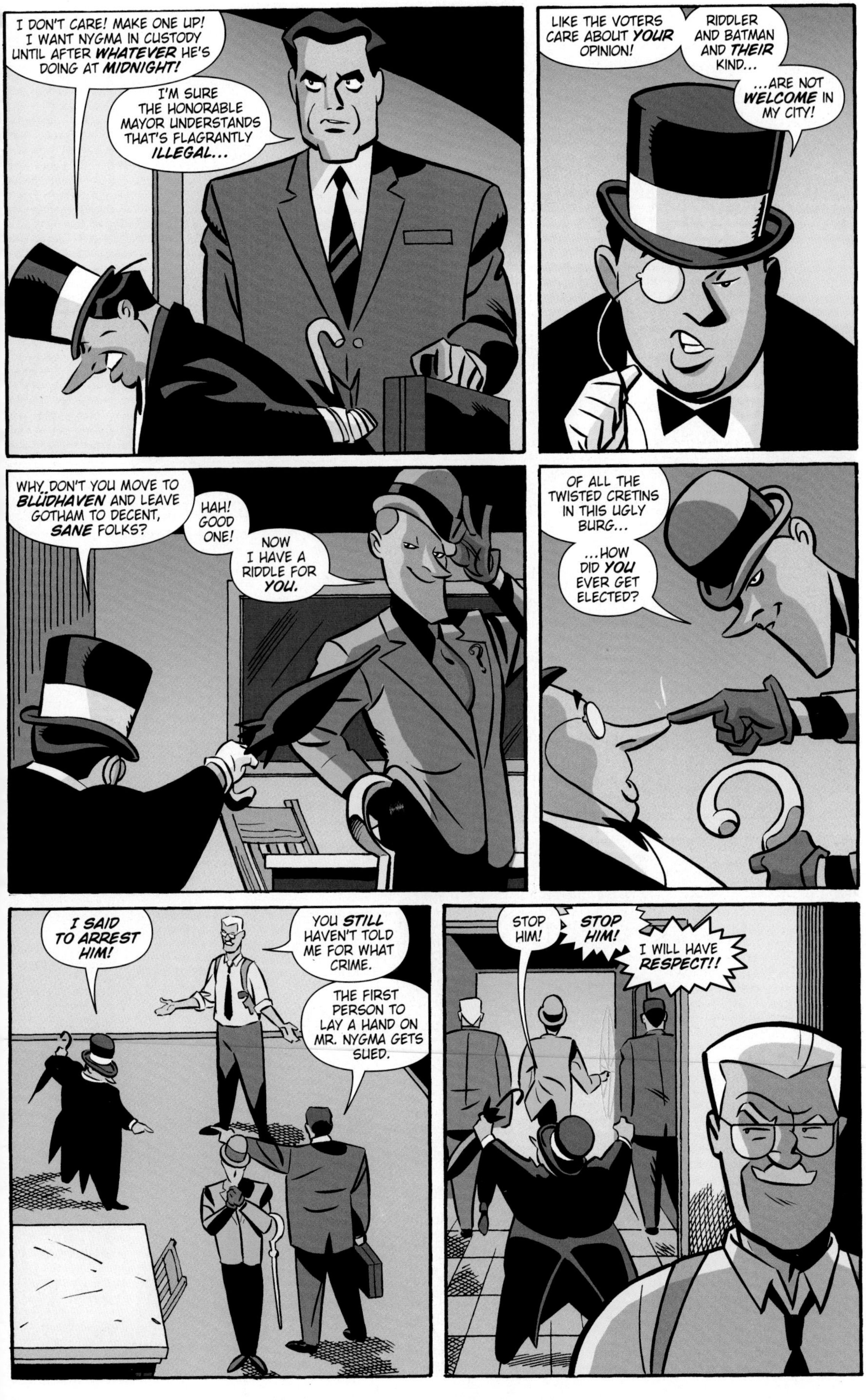
I DON'T CARE! MAKE ONE UP! I WANT NYGMA IN CUSTODY UNTIL AFTER WHATEVER HE'S DOING AT MIDNIGHT!
I'M SURE THE HONORABLE MAYOR UNDERSTANDS THAT'S FLAGRANTLY ILLEGAL...
LIKE THE VOTERS CARE ABOUT YOUR OPINION!
RIDDLER AND BATMAN AND THEIR KIND...
...ARE NOT WELCOME IN MY CITY!
WHY DON'T YOU MOVE TO BLÜDHAVEN AND LEAVE GOTHAM TO DECENT, SANE FOLKS?
HAH! GOOD ONE!
NOW I HAVE A RIDDLE FOR YOU.
OF ALL THE TWISTED CRETINS IN THIS UGLY BURG...
...HOW DID YOU EVER GET ELECTED?
I SAID TO ARREST HIM!
YOU STILL HAVEN'T TOLD ME FOR WHAT CRIME.
THE FIRST PERSON TO LAY A HAND ON MR. NYGMA GETS SUED.
STOP HIM!
STOP HIM!
I WILL HAVE RESPECT!!

I CAN LOSE THEM AROUND THE NEXT CORNER, BATMAN.

MAYBE WE SHOULD START THINKING OF THE BATMOBILE AS A LIABILITY?

WEEOWEEOWEEOWEE

YOU MAY BE RIGHT, ROBIN. THE POLICE SPOT IT FAR TOO EASILY.

BUT FOR RIGHT NOW, STAY ON THIS ROAD.

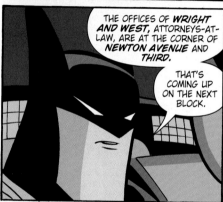

THE OFFICES OF **WRIGHT AND WEST**, ATTORNEYS-AT-LAW, ARE AT THE CORNER OF **NEWTON AVENUE** AND **THIRD**.

THAT'S COMING UP ON THE NEXT BLOCK.

"RIGHT" AND "WEST" ARE **EQUAL** BUT **OPPOSITE** DIRECTIONS ON A MAP.

THIS IS WHERE NYGMA WILL BE.

FOOF

NEWTON
THIRD

ALL THE PIECES FIT.

WEEO WEEO WEEOO

EEEEEEEEE

WRIGHT & WEST

A **SCREAM!**

I'M **TOO LATE!**

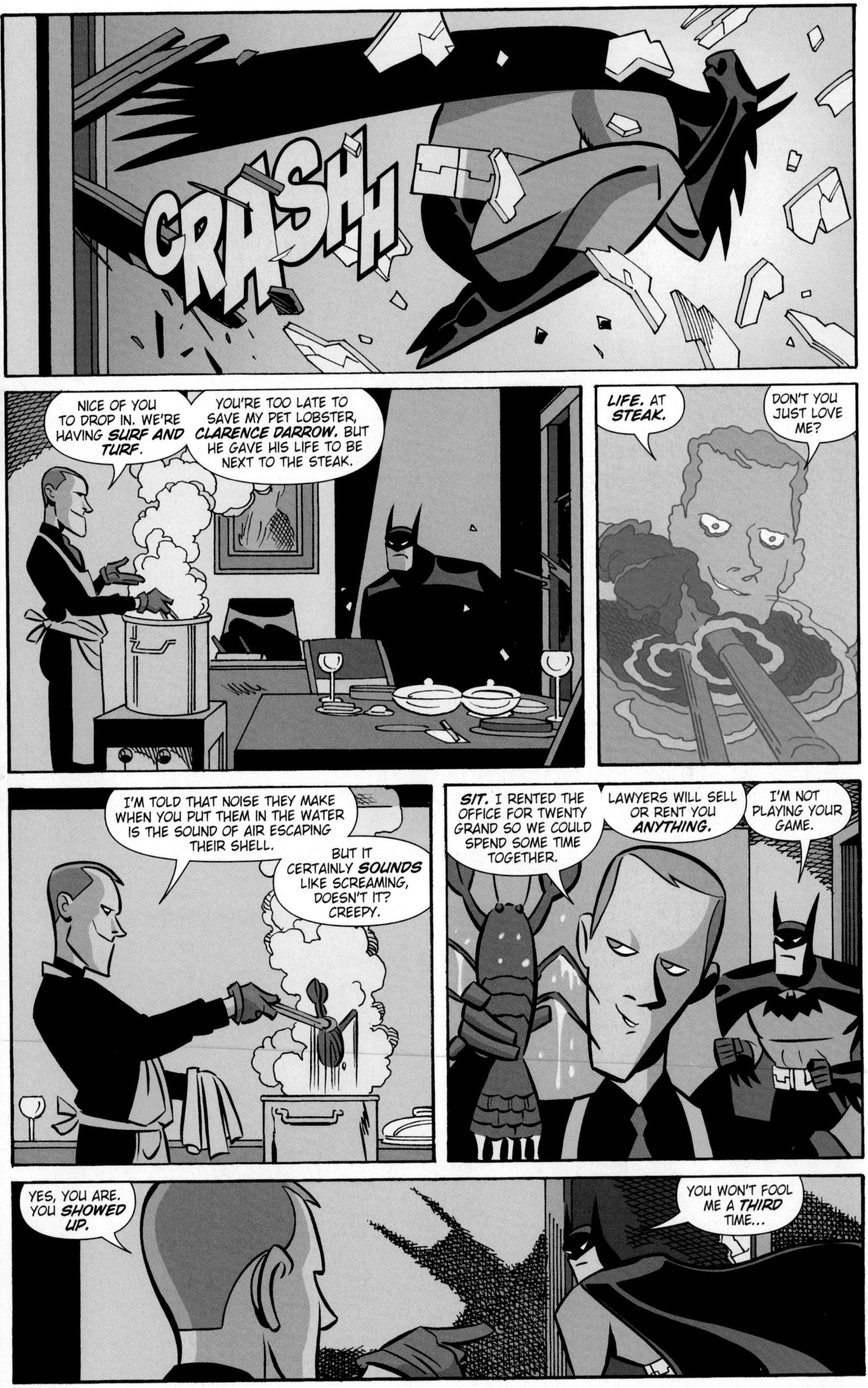
CRASHH
NICE OF YOU TO DROP IN. WE'RE HAVING SURF AND TURF.
YOU'RE TOO LATE TO SAVE MY PET LOBSTER, CLARENCE DARROW. BUT HE GAVE HIS LIFE TO BE NEXT TO THE STEAK.
LIFE. AT STEAK.
DON'T YOU JUST LOVE ME?
I'M TOLD THAT NOISE THEY MAKE WHEN YOU PUT THEM IN THE WATER IS THE SOUND OF AIR ESCAPING THEIR SHELL.
BUT IT CERTAINLY SOUNDS LIKE SCREAMING, DOESN'T IT? CREEPY.
SIT. I RENTED THE OFFICE FOR TWENTY GRAND SO WE COULD SPEND SOME TIME TOGETHER.
LAWYERS WILL SELL OR RENT YOU ANYTHING.
I'M NOT PLAYING YOUR GAME.
YES, YOU ARE. YOU SHOWED UP.
YOU WON'T FOOL ME A THIRD TIME...

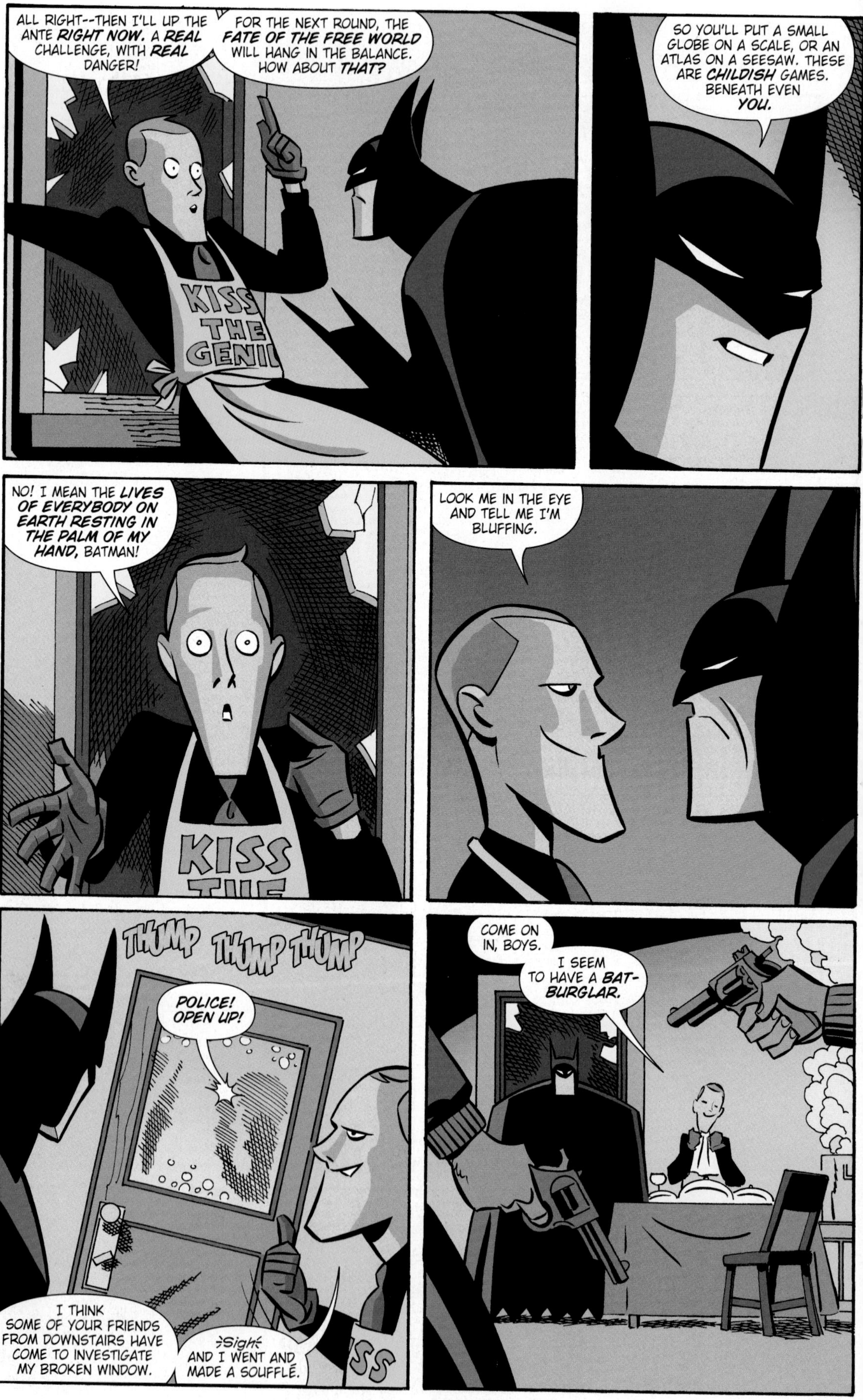
ALL RIGHT--THEN I'LL UP THE ANTE *RIGHT NOW*. A *REAL* CHALLENGE, WITH *REAL* DANGER!
FOR THE NEXT ROUND, THE *FATE OF THE FREE WORLD* WILL HANG IN THE BALANCE. HOW ABOUT *THAT?*
KISS THE GENIU
SO YOU'LL PUT A SMALL GLOBE ON A SCALE, OR AN ATLAS ON A SEESAW. THESE ARE *CHILDISH* GAMES. BENEATH EVEN *YOU.*
NO! I MEAN THE *LIVES OF EVERYBODY ON EARTH RESTING IN THE PALM OF MY HAND,* BATMAN!
KISS
LOOK ME IN THE EYE AND TELL ME I'M BLUFFING.
THUMP THUMP THUMP
POLICE! OPEN UP!
I THINK SOME OF YOUR FRIENDS FROM DOWNSTAIRS HAVE COME TO INVESTIGATE MY BROKEN WINDOW.
Sigh AND I WENT AND MADE A SOUFFLÉ.
COME ON IN, BOYS.
I SEEM TO HAVE A *BAT-BURGLAR.*

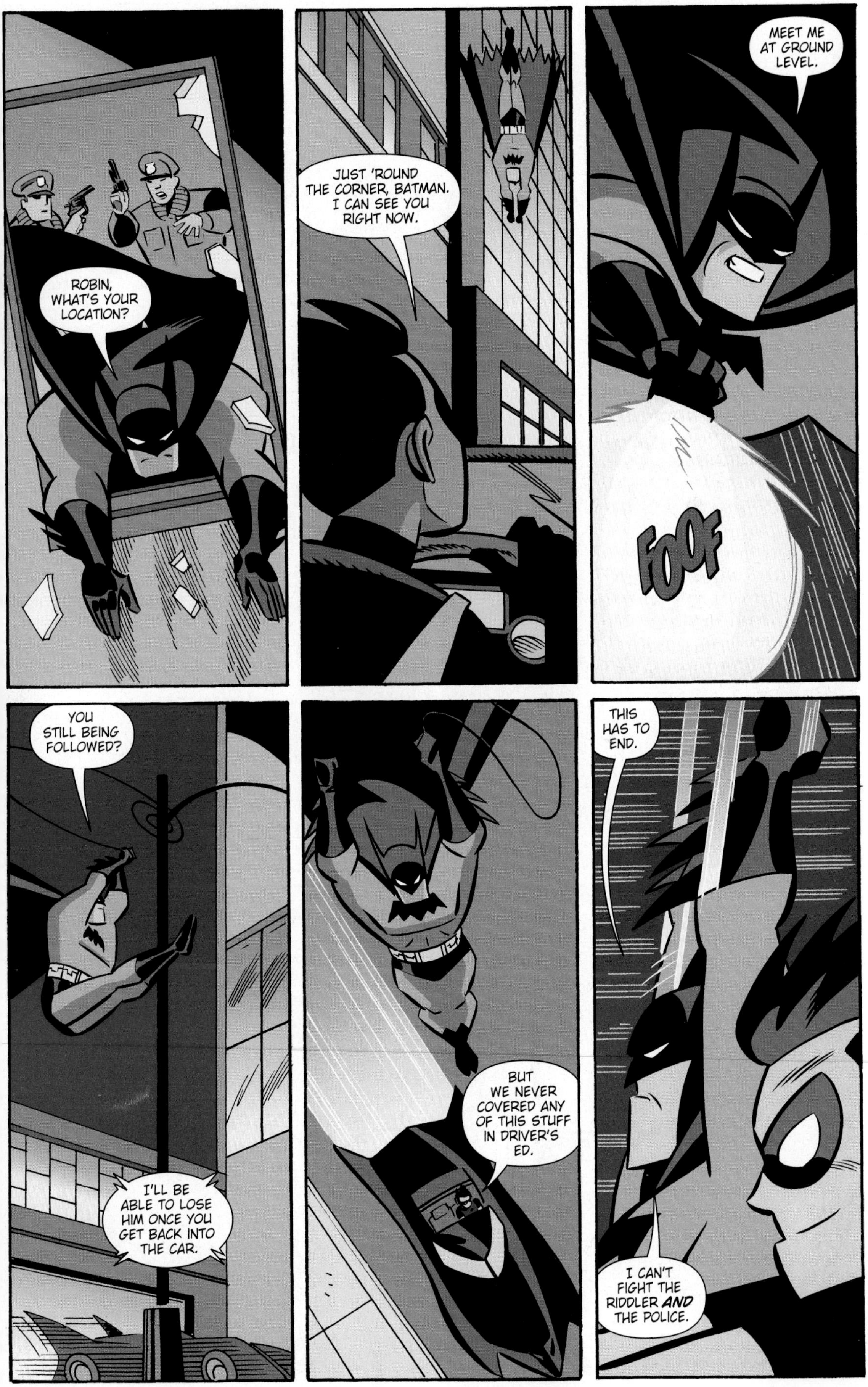
ROBIN, WHAT'S YOUR LOCATION?
JUST 'ROUND THE CORNER, BATMAN. I CAN SEE YOU RIGHT NOW.
MEET ME AT GROUND LEVEL.
FOOF
YOU STILL BEING FOLLOWED?
I'LL BE ABLE TO LOSE HIM ONCE YOU GET BACK INTO THE CAR.
BUT WE NEVER COVERED ANY OF THIS STUFF IN DRIVER'S ED.
THIS HAS TO END.
I CAN'T FIGHT THE RIDDLER AND THE POLICE.

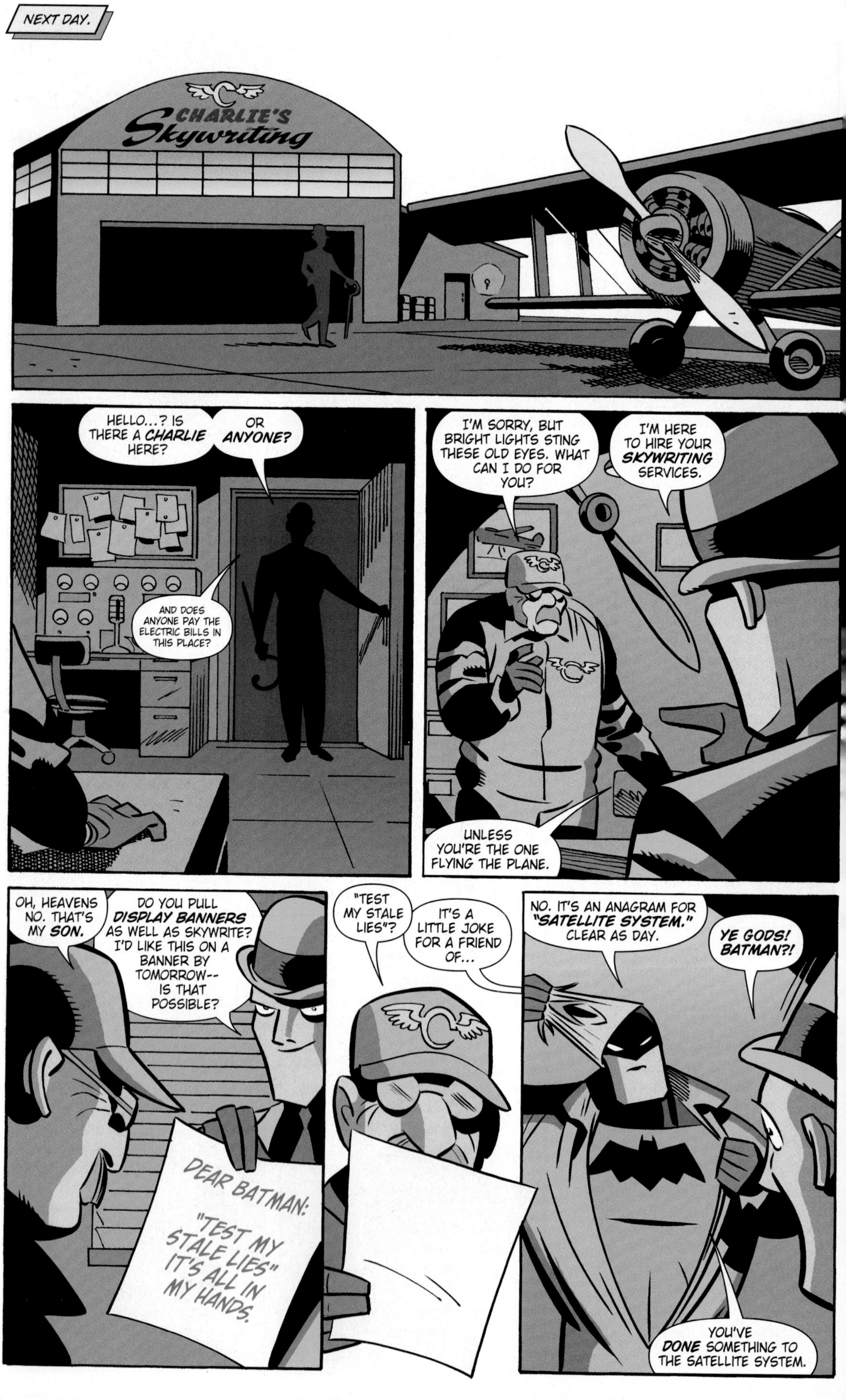
NEXT DAY.
CHARLIE'S Skywriting
HELLO...? IS THERE A CHARLIE HERE?
OR ANYONE?
AND DOES ANYONE PAY THE ELECTRIC BILLS IN THIS PLACE?
I'M SORRY, BUT BRIGHT LIGHTS STING THESE OLD EYES. WHAT CAN I DO FOR YOU?
I'M HERE TO HIRE YOUR SKYWRITING SERVICES.
UNLESS YOU'RE THE ONE FLYING THE PLANE.
OH, HEAVENS NO. THAT'S MY SON.
DO YOU PULL DISPLAY BANNERS AS WELL AS SKYWRITE? I'D LIKE THIS ON A BANNER BY TOMORROW-- IS THAT POSSIBLE?
DEAR BATMAN: "TEST MY STALE LIES" IT'S ALL IN MY HANDS.
"TEST MY STALE LIES"?
IT'S A LITTLE JOKE FOR A FRIEND OF...
NO. IT'S AN ANAGRAM FOR "SATELLITE SYSTEM." CLEAR AS DAY.
YE GODS! BATMAN?!
YOU'VE DONE SOMETHING TO THE SATELLITE SYSTEM.

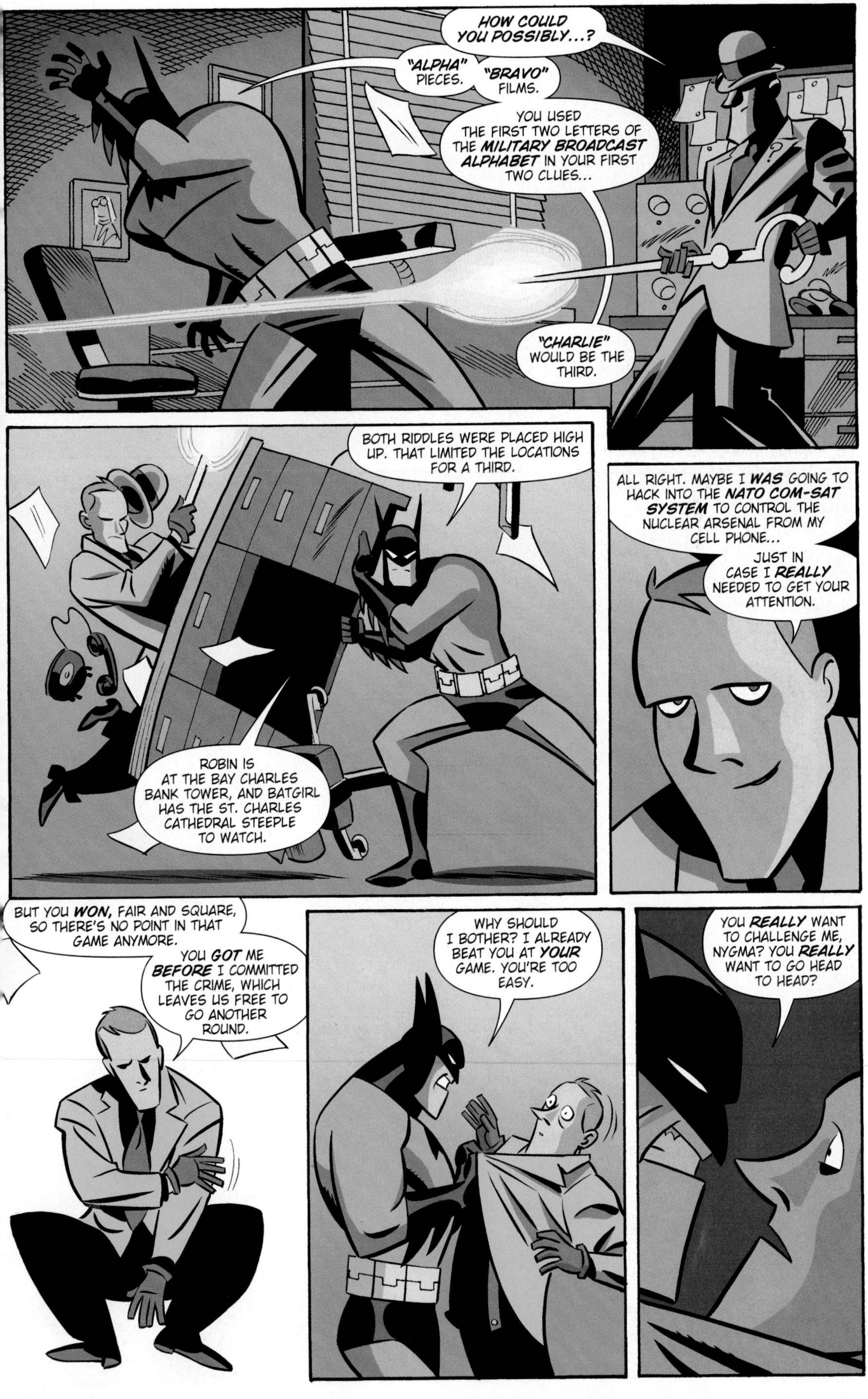
HOW COULD YOU POSSIBLY...?
"ALPHA" PIECES.
"BRAVO" FILMS.
YOU USED THE FIRST TWO LETTERS OF THE MILITARY BROADCAST ALPHABET IN YOUR FIRST TWO CLUES...
"CHARLIE" WOULD BE THE THIRD.
BOTH RIDDLES WERE PLACED HIGH UP. THAT LIMITED THE LOCATIONS FOR A THIRD.
ROBIN IS AT THE BAY CHARLES BANK TOWER, AND BATGIRL HAS THE ST. CHARLES CATHEDRAL STEEPLE TO WATCH.
ALL RIGHT. MAYBE I WAS GOING TO HACK INTO THE NATO COM-SAT SYSTEM TO CONTROL THE NUCLEAR ARSENAL FROM MY CELL PHONE...
JUST IN CASE I REALLY NEEDED TO GET YOUR ATTENTION.
BUT YOU WON, FAIR AND SQUARE, SO THERE'S NO POINT IN THAT GAME ANYMORE.
YOU GOT ME BEFORE I COMMITTED THE CRIME, WHICH LEAVES US FREE TO GO ANOTHER ROUND.
WHY SHOULD I BOTHER? I ALREADY BEAT YOU AT YOUR GAME. YOU'RE TOO EASY.
YOU REALLY WANT TO CHALLENGE ME, NYGMA? YOU REALLY WANT TO GO HEAD TO HEAD?

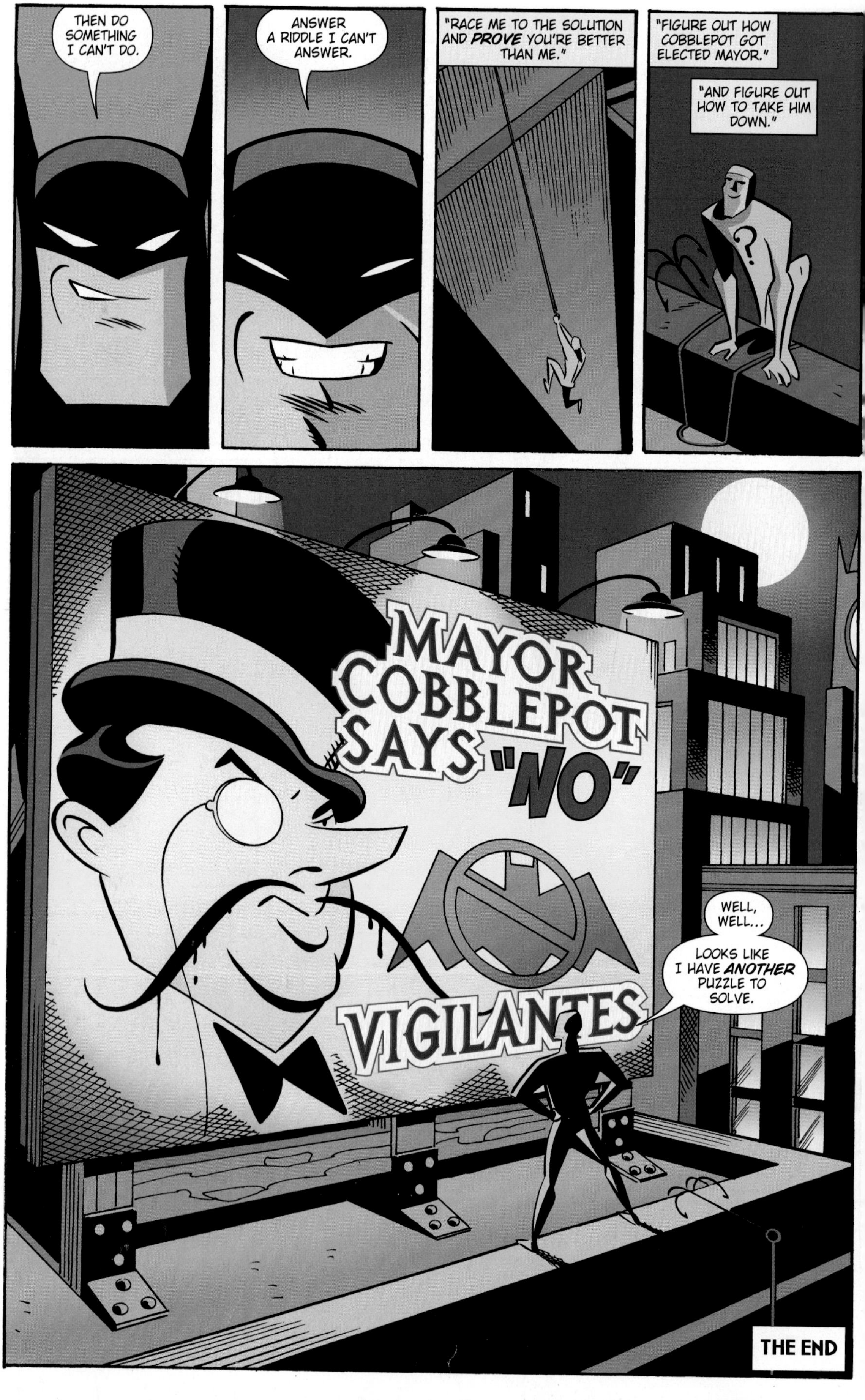
THEN DO SOMETHING I CAN'T DO.
ANSWER A RIDDLE I CAN'T ANSWER.
"RACE ME TO THE SOLUTION AND PROVE YOU'RE BETTER THAN ME."
"FIGURE OUT HOW COBBLEPOT GOT ELECTED MAYOR."
"AND FIGURE OUT HOW TO TAKE HIM DOWN."
MAYOR COBBLEPOT SAYS "NO" VIGILANTES
WELL, WELL...
LOOKS LIKE I HAVE ANOTHER PUZZLE TO SOLVE.
THE END

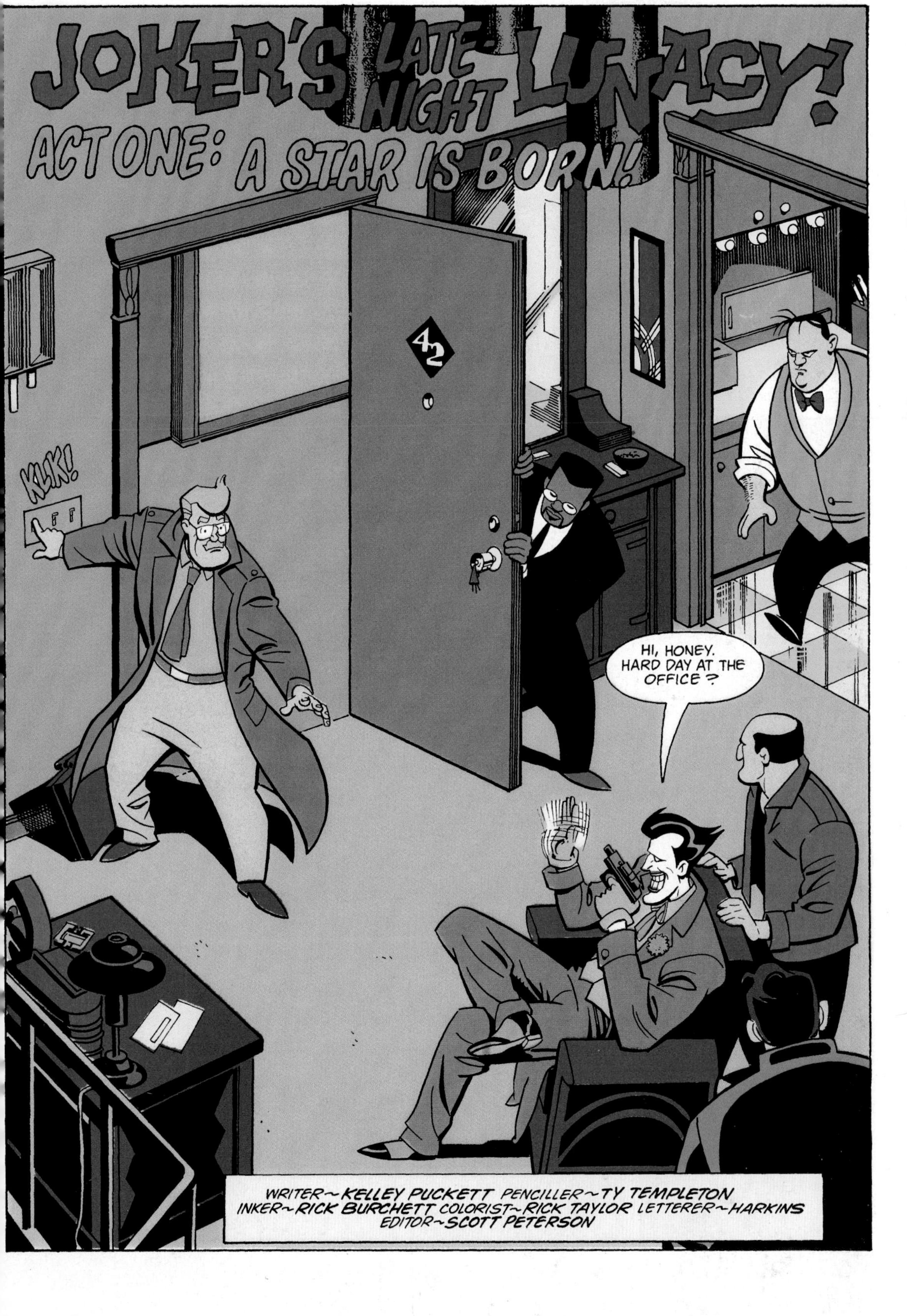
JOKER'S LATE-NIGHT LUNACY!
ACT ONE: A STAR IS BORN!
KLIK!
HI, HONEY. HARD DAY AT THE OFFICE?
WRITER~KELLEY PUCKETT PENCILLER~TY TEMPLETON
INKER~RICK BURCHETT COLORIST~RICK TAYLOR LETTERER~HARKINS
EDITOR~SCOTT PETERSON

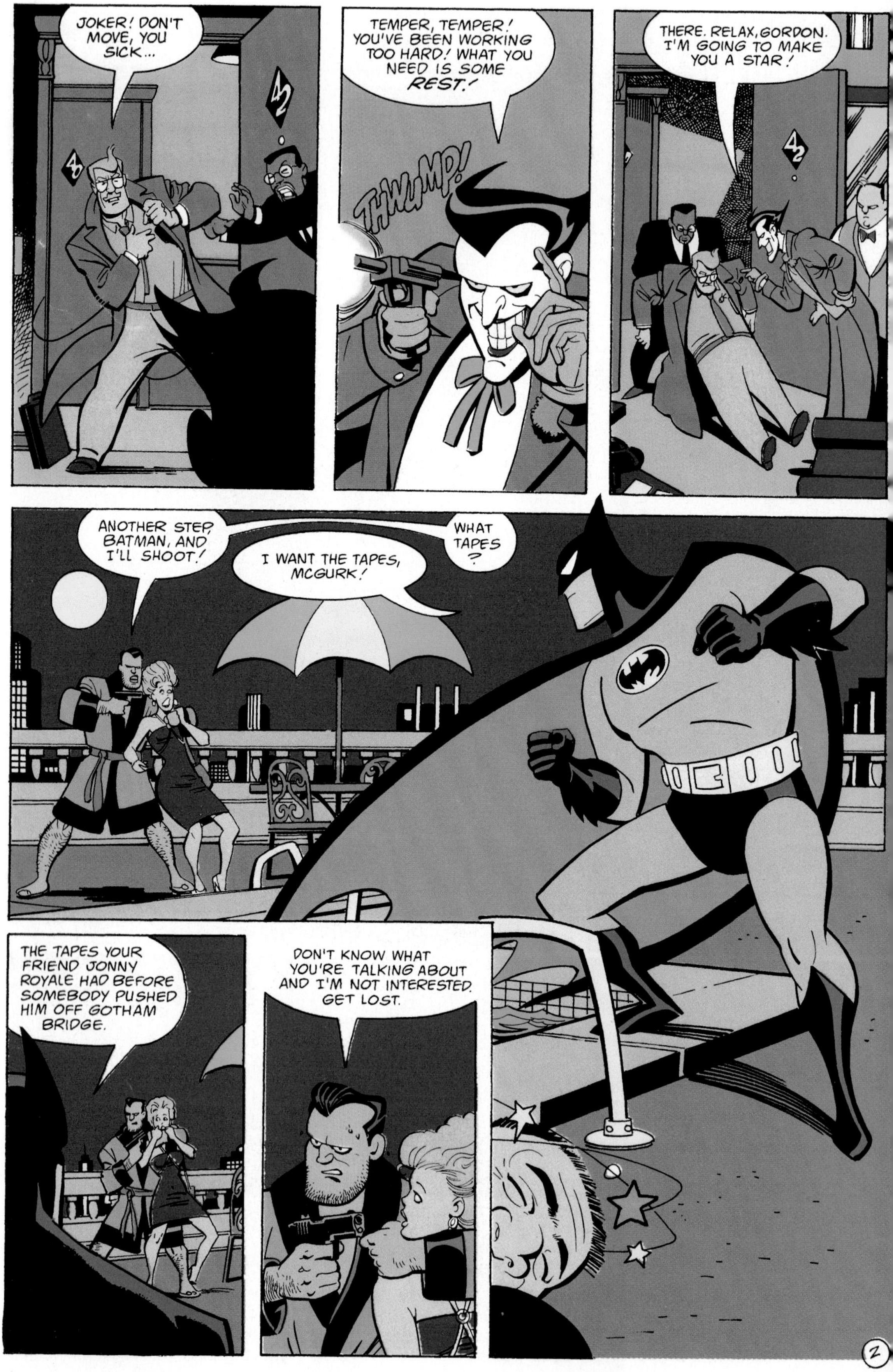

JOKER! DON'T MOVE, YOU SICK...
TEMPER, TEMPER! YOU'VE BEEN WORKING TOO HARD! WHAT YOU NEED IS SOME REST!
THWUMP!
THERE. RELAX, GORDON. I'M GOING TO MAKE YOU A STAR!
ANOTHER STEP, BATMAN, AND I'LL SHOOT!
I WANT THE TAPES, MCGURK!
WHAT TAPES?
THE TAPES YOUR FRIEND JONNY ROYALE HAD BEFORE SOMEBODY PUSHED HIM OFF GOTHAM BRIDGE.
DON'T KNOW WHAT YOU'RE TALKING ABOUT AND I'M NOT INTERESTED. GET LOST.

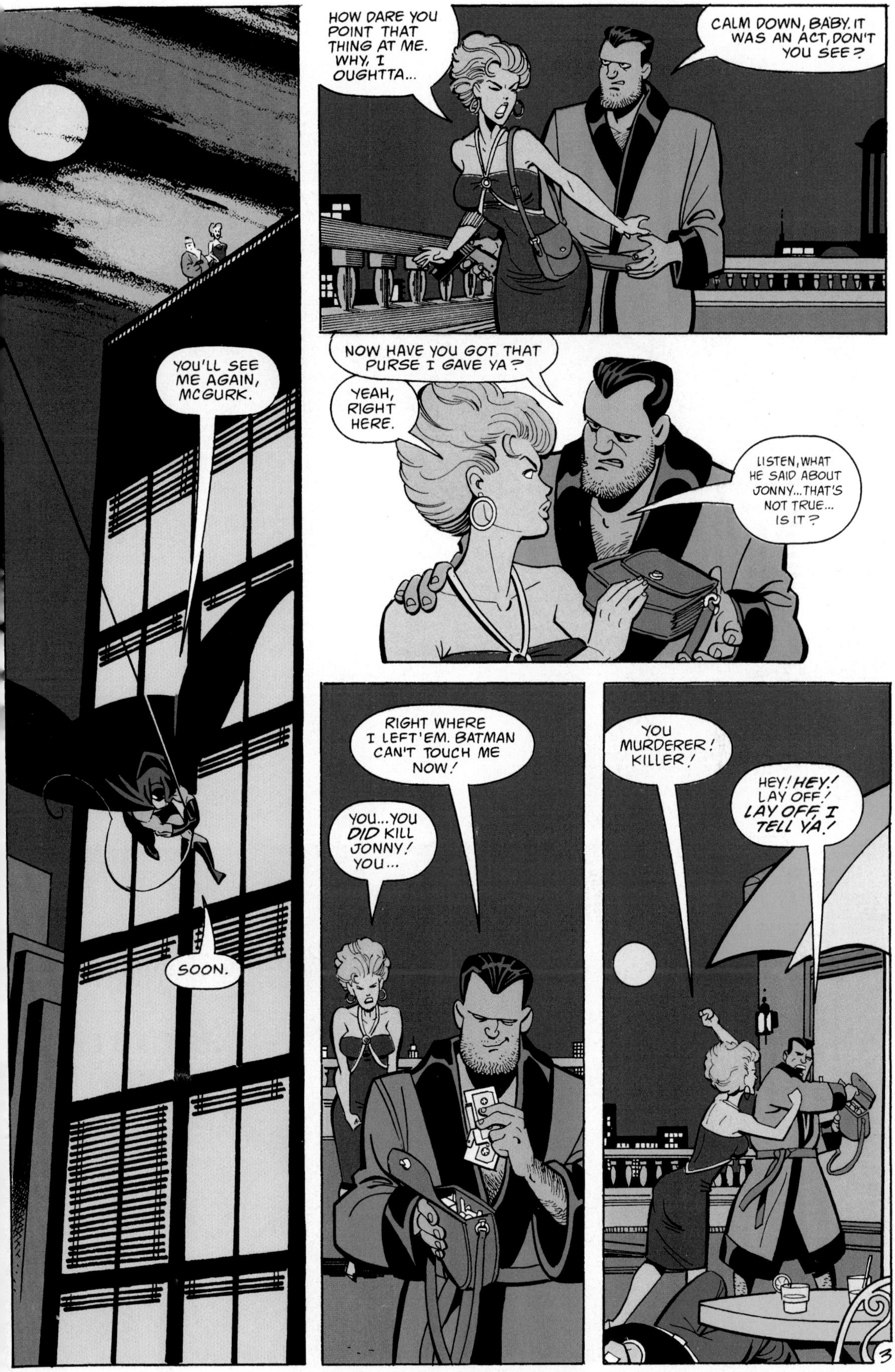
YOU'LL SEE ME AGAIN, MCGURK.
SOON.
HOW DARE YOU POINT THAT THING AT ME. WHY, I OUGHTTA...
CALM DOWN, BABY. IT WAS AN ACT, DON'T YOU SEE?
NOW HAVE YOU GOT THAT PURSE I GAVE YA?
YEAH, RIGHT HERE.
LISTEN, WHAT HE SAID ABOUT JONNY... THAT'S NOT TRUE... IS IT?
RIGHT WHERE I LEFT'EM. BATMAN CAN'T TOUCH ME NOW!
YOU... YOU DID KILL JONNY! YOU...
YOU MURDERER! KILLER!
HEY! HEY! LAY OFF! LAY OFF, I TELL YA!

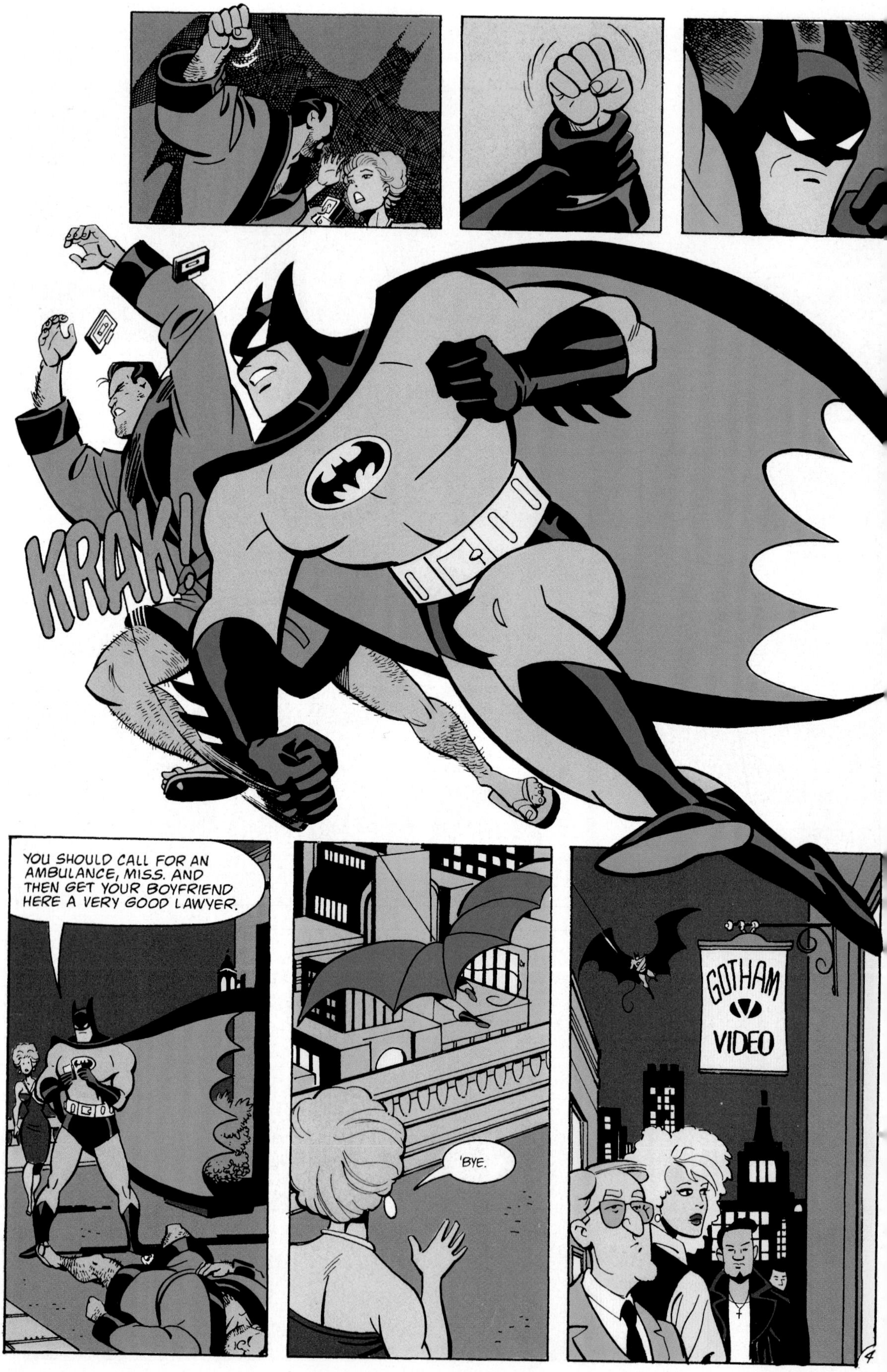
KRAK!
YOU SHOULD CALL FOR AN AMBULANCE, MISS. AND THEN GET YOUR BOYFRIEND HERE A VERY GOOD LAWYER.
'BYE.
GOTHAM
VIDEO

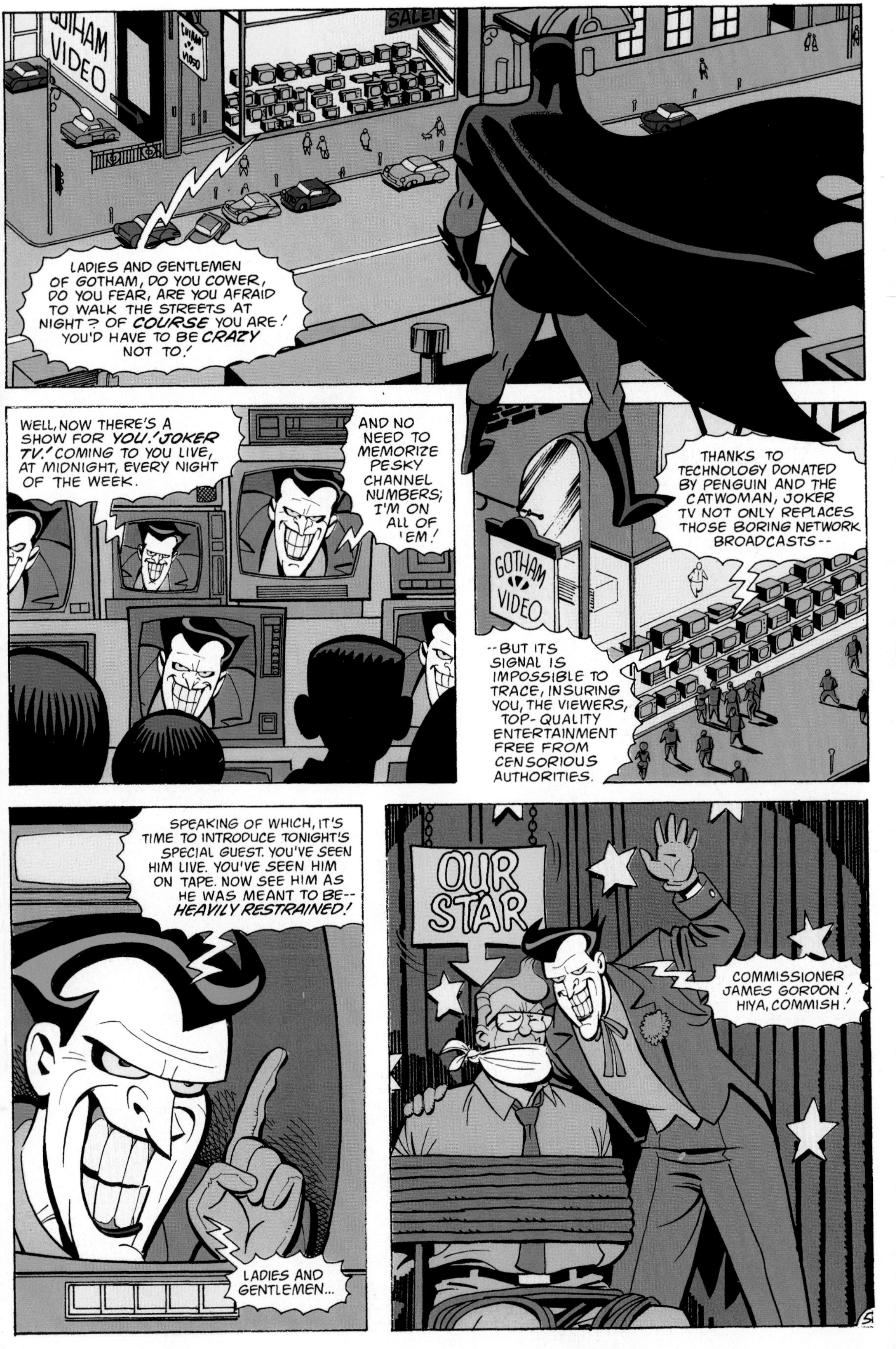
GOTHAM VIDEO
SALE!
LADIES AND GENTLEMEN OF GOTHAM, DO YOU COWER, DO YOU FEAR, ARE YOU AFRAID TO WALK THE STREETS AT NIGHT? OF COURSE YOU ARE! YOU'D HAVE TO BE CRAZY NOT TO!
WELL, NOW THERE'S A SHOW FOR YOU! JOKER TV! COMING TO YOU LIVE, AT MIDNIGHT, EVERY NIGHT OF THE WEEK.
AND NO NEED TO MEMORIZE PESKY CHANNEL NUMBERS; I'M ON ALL OF 'EM!
THANKS TO TECHNOLOGY DONATED BY PENGUIN AND THE CATWOMAN, JOKER TV NOT ONLY REPLACES THOSE BORING NETWORK BROADCASTS--
GOTHAM VIDEO
--BUT ITS SIGNAL IS IMPOSSIBLE TO TRACE, INSURING YOU, THE VIEWERS, TOP-QUALITY ENTERTAINMENT FREE FROM CENSORIOUS AUTHORITIES.
SPEAKING OF WHICH, IT'S TIME TO INTRODUCE TONIGHT'S SPECIAL GUEST. YOU'VE SEEN HIM LIVE. YOU'VE SEEN HIM ON TAPE. NOW SEE HIM AS HE WAS MEANT TO BE-- HEAVILY RESTRAINED!
LADIES AND GENTLEMEN...
OUR STAR
COMMISSIONER JAMES GORDON! HIYA, COMMISH!

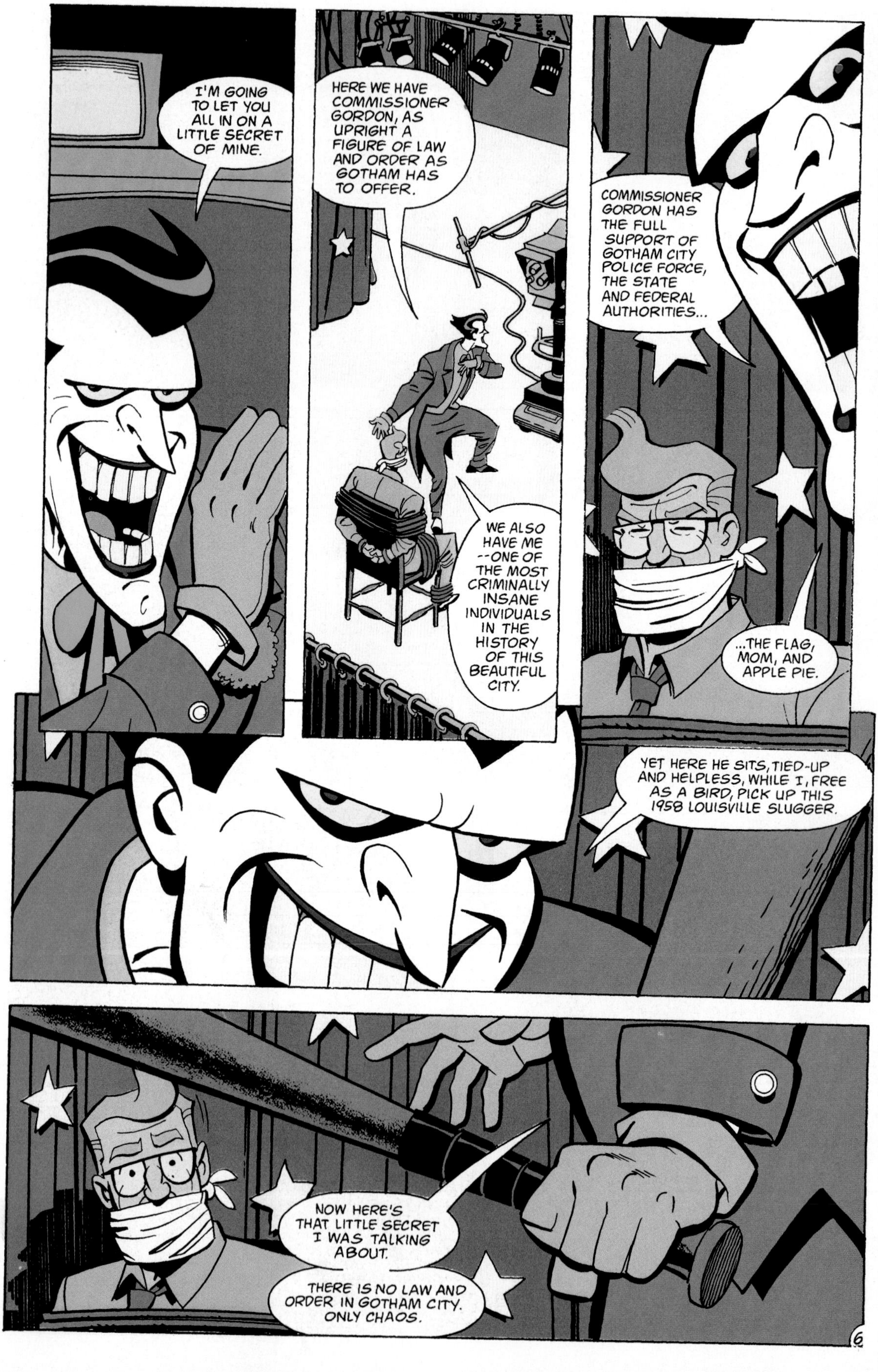
I'M GOING TO LET YOU ALL IN ON A LITTLE SECRET OF MINE.
HERE WE HAVE COMMISSIONER GORDON, AS UPRIGHT A FIGURE OF LAW AND ORDER AS GOTHAM HAS TO OFFER.
WE ALSO HAVE ME --ONE OF THE MOST CRIMINALLY INSANE INDIVIDUALS IN THE HISTORY OF THIS BEAUTIFUL CITY.
COMMISSIONER GORDON HAS THE FULL SUPPORT OF GOTHAM CITY POLICE FORCE, THE STATE AND FEDERAL AUTHORITIES...
...THE FLAG, MOM, AND APPLE PIE.
YET HERE HE SITS, TIED-UP AND HELPLESS, WHILE I, FREE AS A BIRD, PICK UP THIS 1958 LOUISVILLE SLUGGER.
NOW HERE'S THAT LITTLE SECRET I WAS TALKING ABOUT.
THERE IS NO LAW AND ORDER IN GOTHAM CITY. ONLY CHAOS.

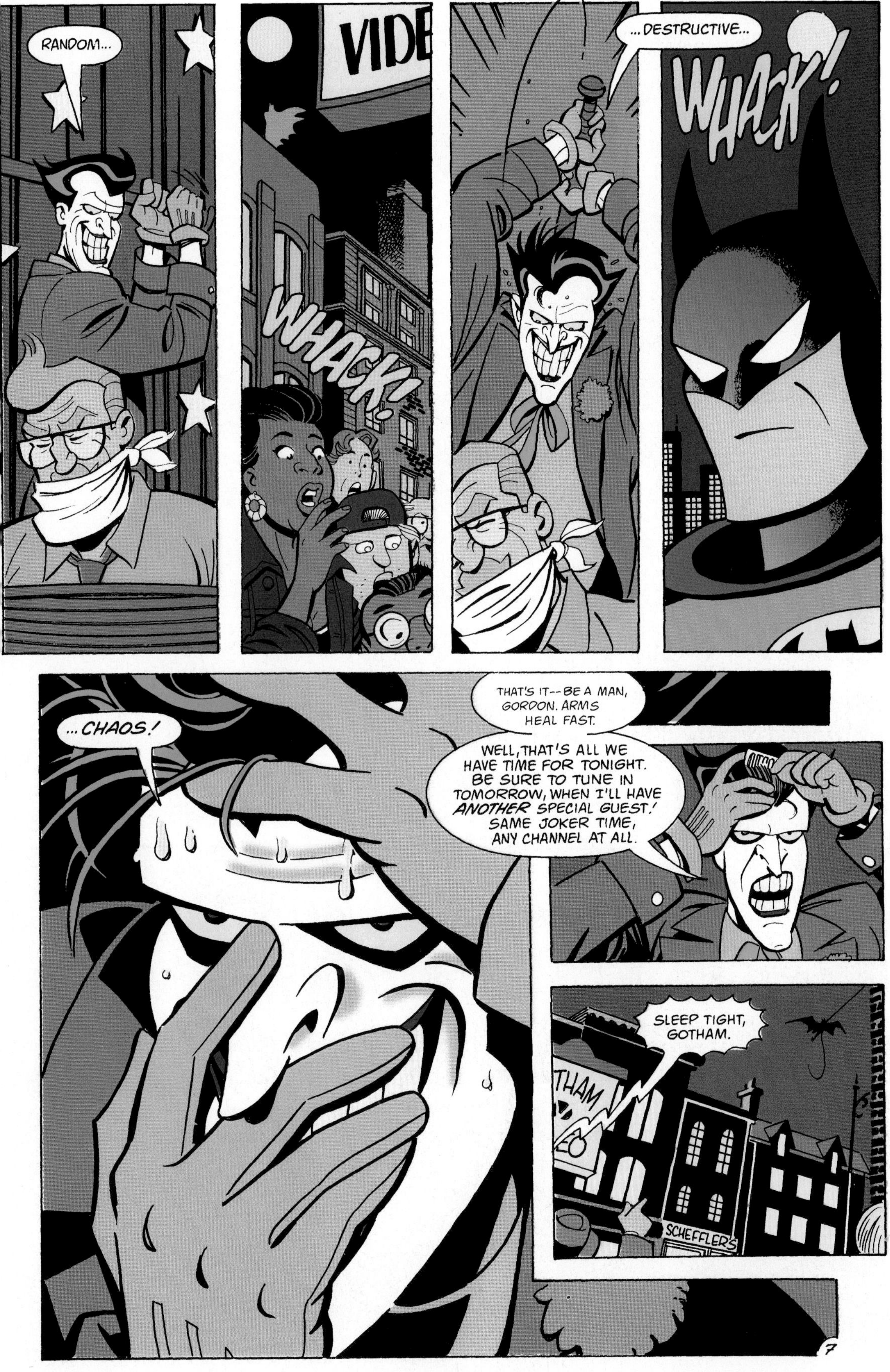

RANDOM...
VIDE
WHACK!
...DESTRUCTIVE...
WHACK!
...CHAOS!
THAT'S IT--BE A MAN, GORDON. ARMS HEAL FAST.
WELL, THAT'S ALL WE HAVE TIME FOR TONIGHT. BE SURE TO TUNE IN TOMORROW, WHEN I'LL HAVE ANOTHER SPECIAL GUEST! SAME JOKER TIME, ANY CHANNEL AT ALL.
SLEEP TIGHT, GOTHAM.
THAM
SCHEFFLERS

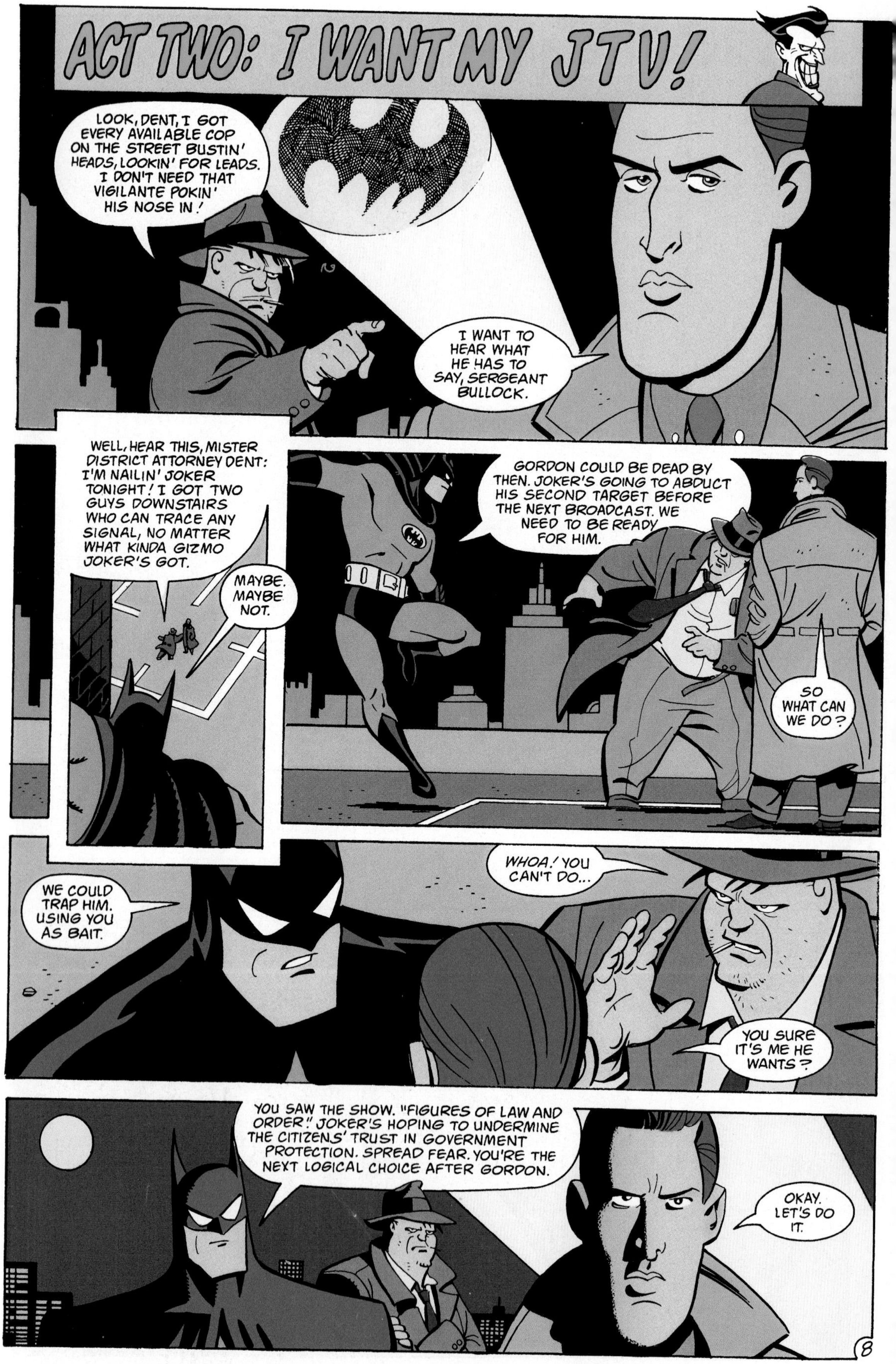
ACT TWO: I WANT MY JTV!
LOOK, DENT, I GOT EVERY AVAILABLE COP ON THE STREET BUSTIN' HEADS, LOOKIN' FOR LEADS. I DON'T NEED THAT VIGILANTE POKIN' HIS NOSE IN!
I WANT TO HEAR WHAT HE HAS TO SAY, SERGEANT BULLOCK.
WELL, HEAR THIS, MISTER DISTRICT ATTORNEY DENT: I'M NAILIN' JOKER TONIGHT! I GOT TWO GUYS DOWNSTAIRS WHO CAN TRACE ANY SIGNAL, NO MATTER WHAT KINDA GIZMO JOKER'S GOT.
MAYBE. MAYBE NOT.
GORDON COULD BE DEAD BY THEN. JOKER'S GOING TO ABDUCT HIS SECOND TARGET BEFORE THE NEXT BROADCAST. WE NEED TO BE READY FOR HIM.
SO WHAT CAN WE DO?
WE COULD TRAP HIM. USING YOU AS BAIT.
WHOA! YOU CAN'T DO...
YOU SURE IT'S ME HE WANTS?
YOU SAW THE SHOW. "FIGURES OF LAW AND ORDER." JOKER'S HOPING TO UNDERMINE THE CITIZENS' TRUST IN GOVERNMENT PROTECTION. SPREAD FEAR. YOU'RE THE NEXT LOGICAL CHOICE AFTER GORDON.
OKAY. LET'S DO IT.

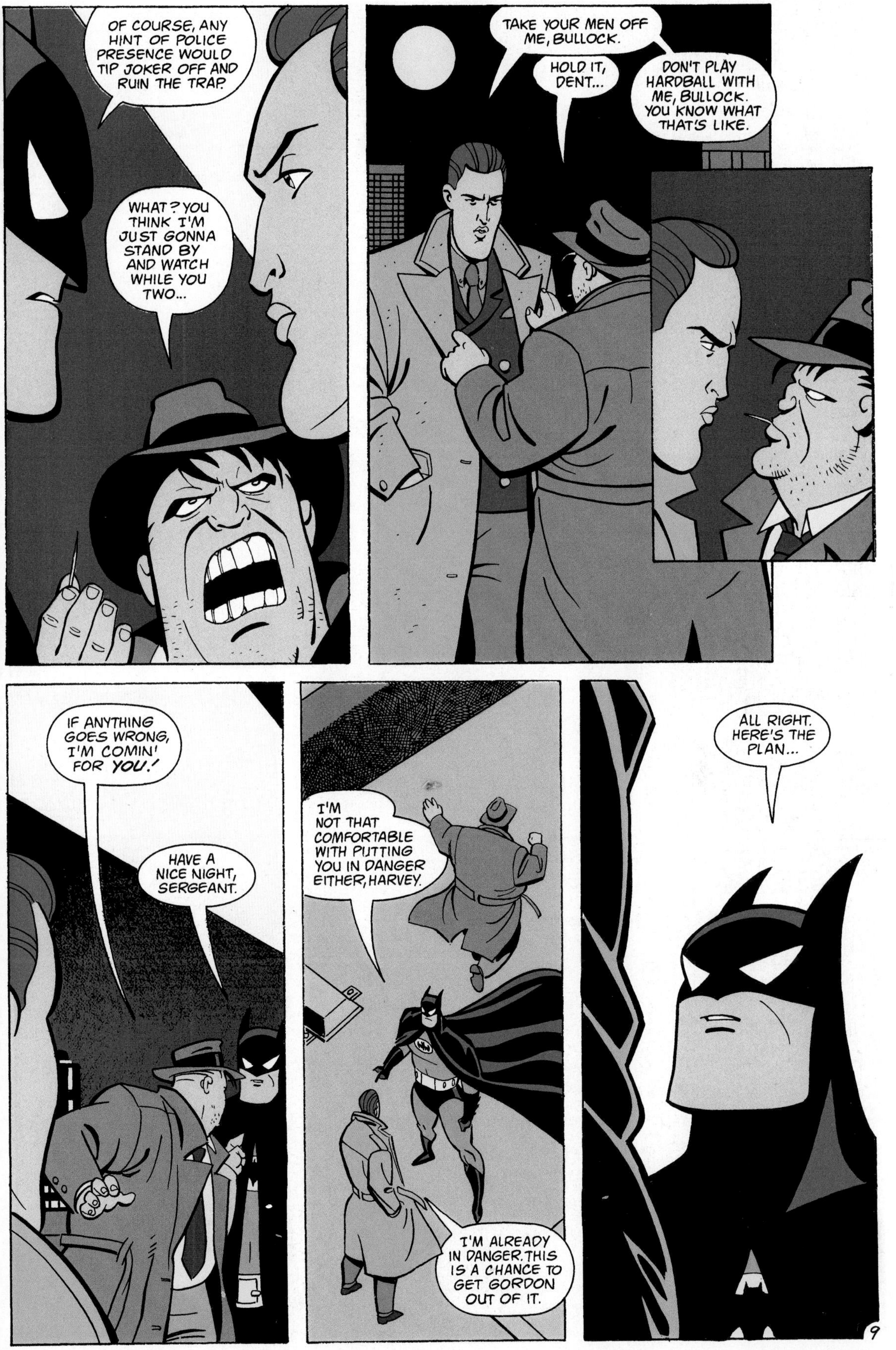

OF COURSE, ANY HINT OF POLICE PRESENCE WOULD TIP JOKER OFF AND RUIN THE TRAP.
WHAT? YOU THINK I'M JUST GONNA STAND BY AND WATCH WHILE YOU TWO...
TAKE YOUR MEN OFF ME, BULLOCK.
HOLD IT, DENT...
DON'T PLAY HARDBALL WITH ME, BULLOCK. YOU KNOW WHAT THAT'S LIKE.
IF ANYTHING GOES WRONG, I'M COMIN' FOR YOU!
HAVE A NICE NIGHT, SERGEANT.
I'M NOT THAT COMFORTABLE WITH PUTTING YOU IN DANGER EITHER, HARVEY.
I'M ALREADY IN DANGER. THIS IS A CHANCE TO GET GORDON OUT OF IT.
ALL RIGHT. HERE'S THE PLAN...

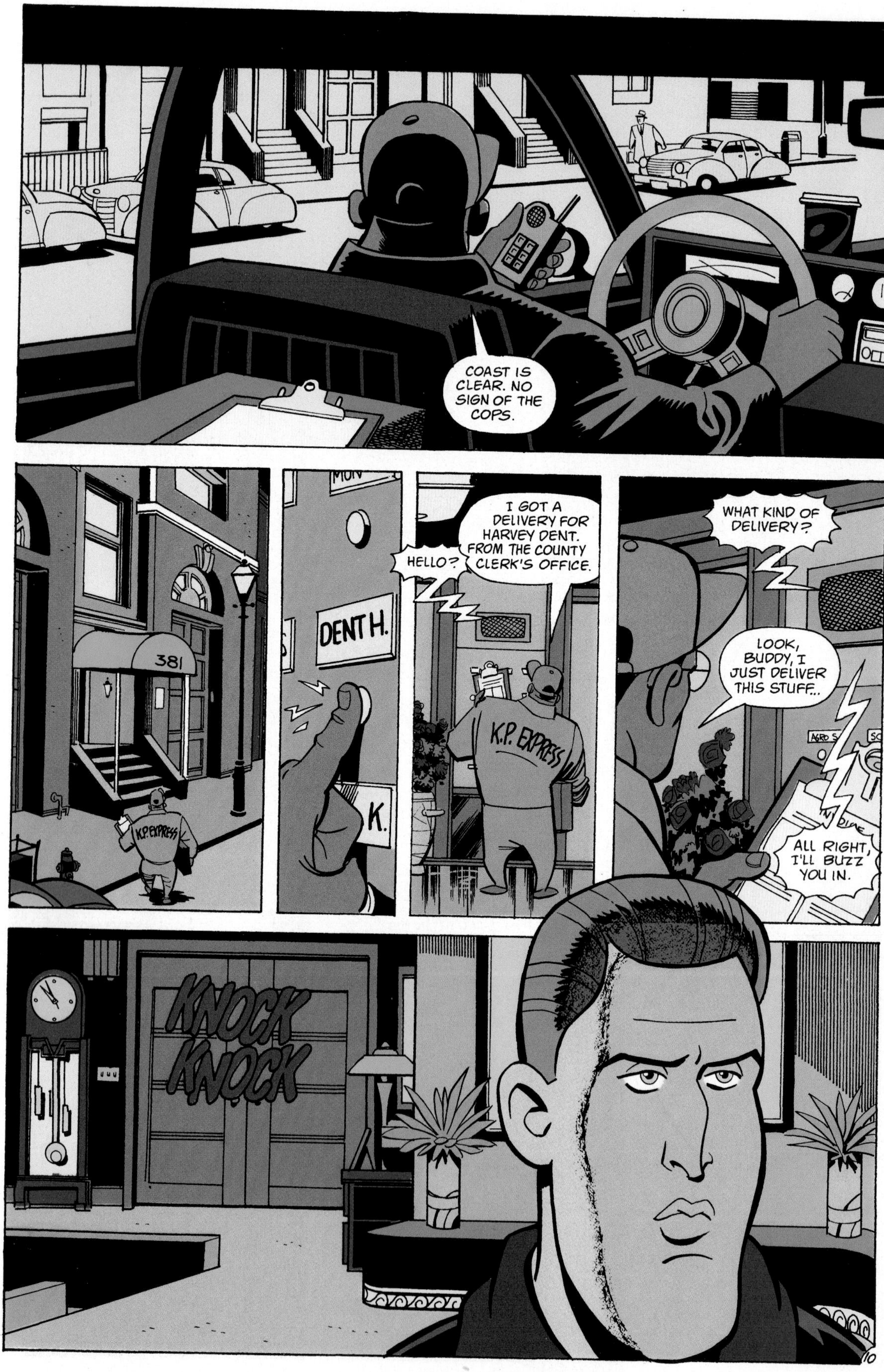

COAST IS CLEAR. NO SIGN OF THE COPS.
381
K.P. EXPRESS
DENT H.
K.
HELLO?
I GOT A DELIVERY FOR HARVEY DENT. FROM THE COUNTY CLERK'S OFFICE.
K.P. EXPRESS
WHAT KIND OF DELIVERY?
LOOK, BUDDY, I JUST DELIVER THIS STUFF...
ALL RIGHT, I'LL BUZZ YOU IN.
KNOCK KNOCK

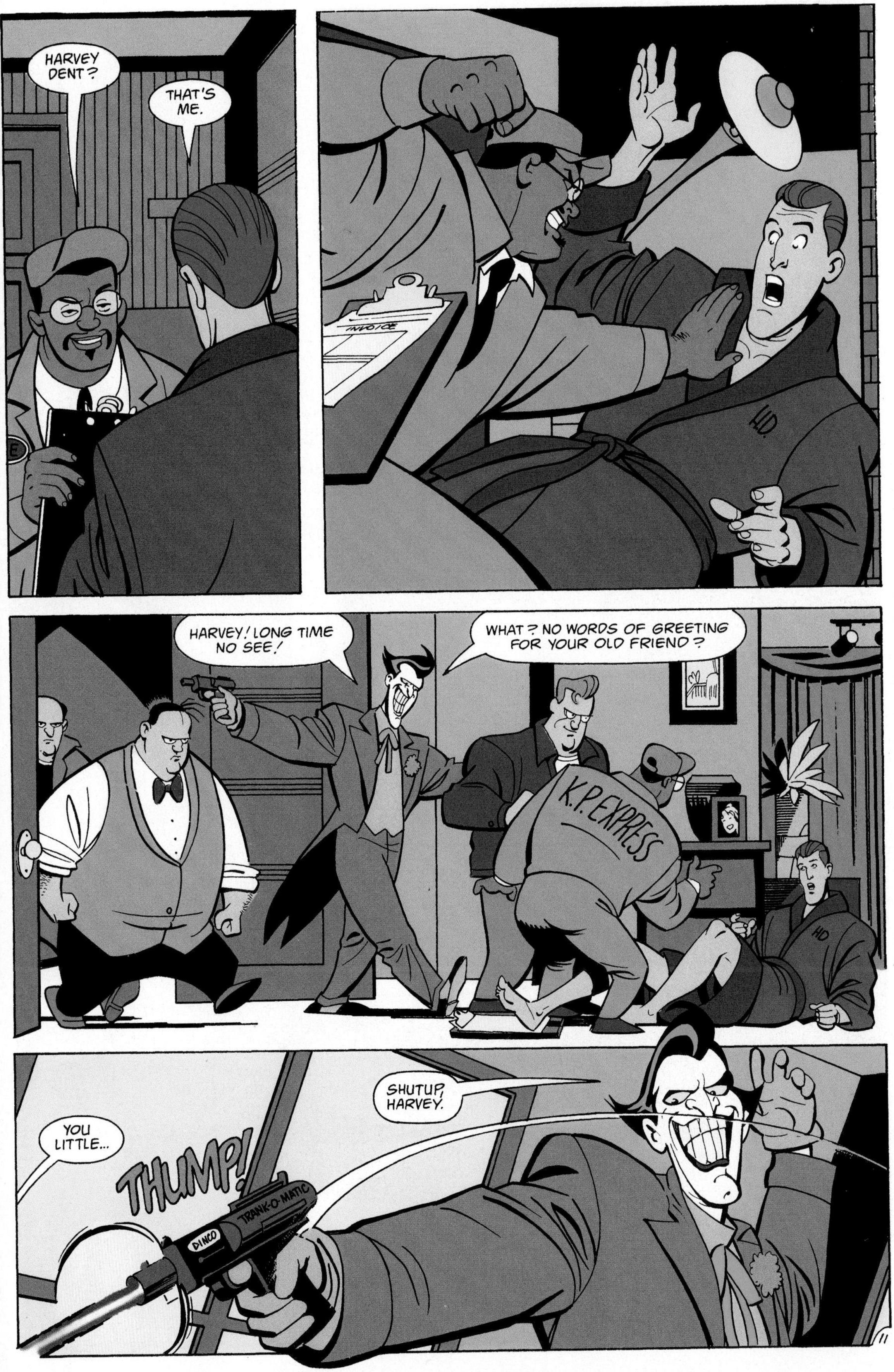
HARVEY DENT?
THAT'S ME.
INVOICE
H.D.
HARVEY! LONG TIME NO SEE!
WHAT? NO WORDS OF GREETING FOR YOUR OLD FRIEND?
K.P. EXPRESS
HD
SHUTUP, HARVEY.
YOU LITTLE...
THUMP!
TRANK-O-MATIC
DINCO

THIS IS WAY, WAY, *WAY* TOO EASY. BATMAN'S CLOSE BY. I CAN SMELL HIM.

MOVE OUT CAREFULLY AND WATCH YOUR BACKS.

LET'S GO.

DON'T DAWDLE!

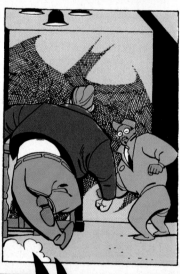

CHOK!

12

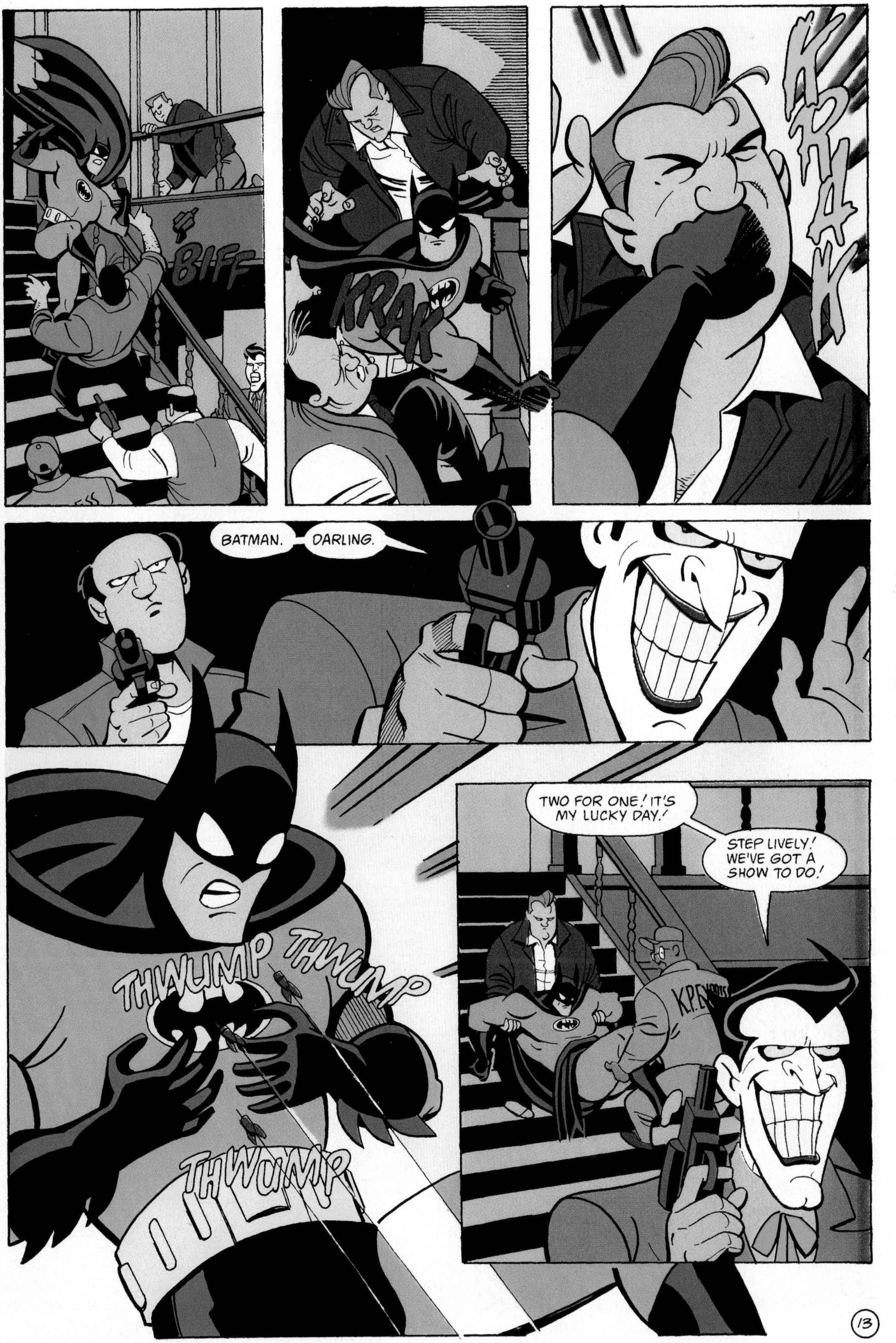
BIFF
KRAK
KRAK
BATMAN.
DARLING.
THWUMP THWUMP
THWUMP
TWO FOR ONE! IT'S MY LUCKY DAY!
STEP LIVELY! WE'VE GOT A SHOW TO DO!

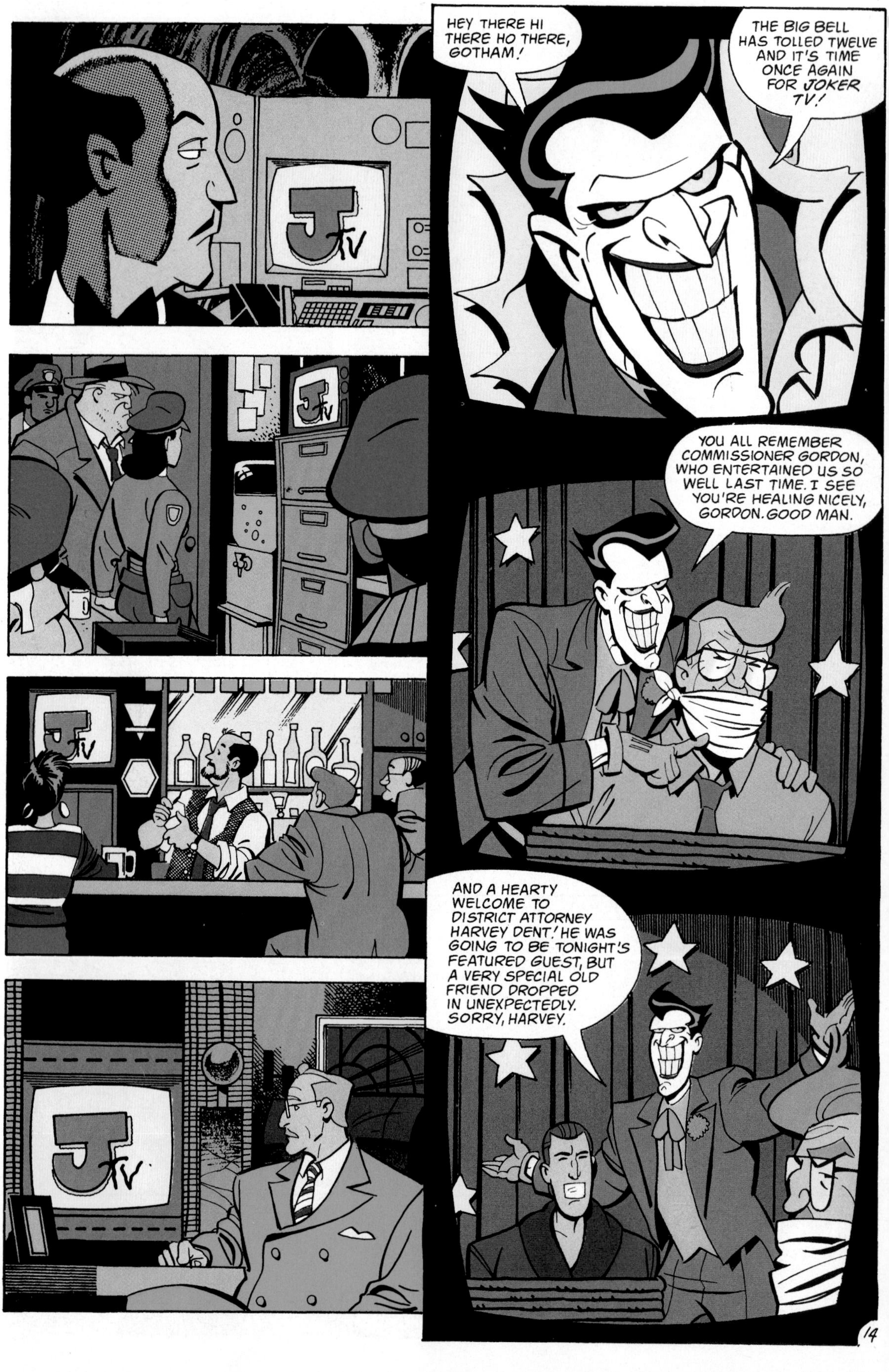

J TV
HEY THERE HI THERE HO THERE, GOTHAM!
THE BIG BELL HAS TOLLED TWELVE AND IT'S TIME ONCE AGAIN FOR JOKER TV!
YOU ALL REMEMBER COMMISSIONER GORDON, WHO ENTERTAINED US SO WELL LAST TIME. I SEE YOU'RE HEALING NICELY, GORDON. GOOD MAN.
AND A HEARTY WELCOME TO DISTRICT ATTORNEY HARVEY DENT! HE WAS GOING TO BE TONIGHT'S FEATURED GUEST, BUT A VERY SPECIAL OLD FRIEND DROPPED IN UNEXPECTEDLY. SORRY, HARVEY.

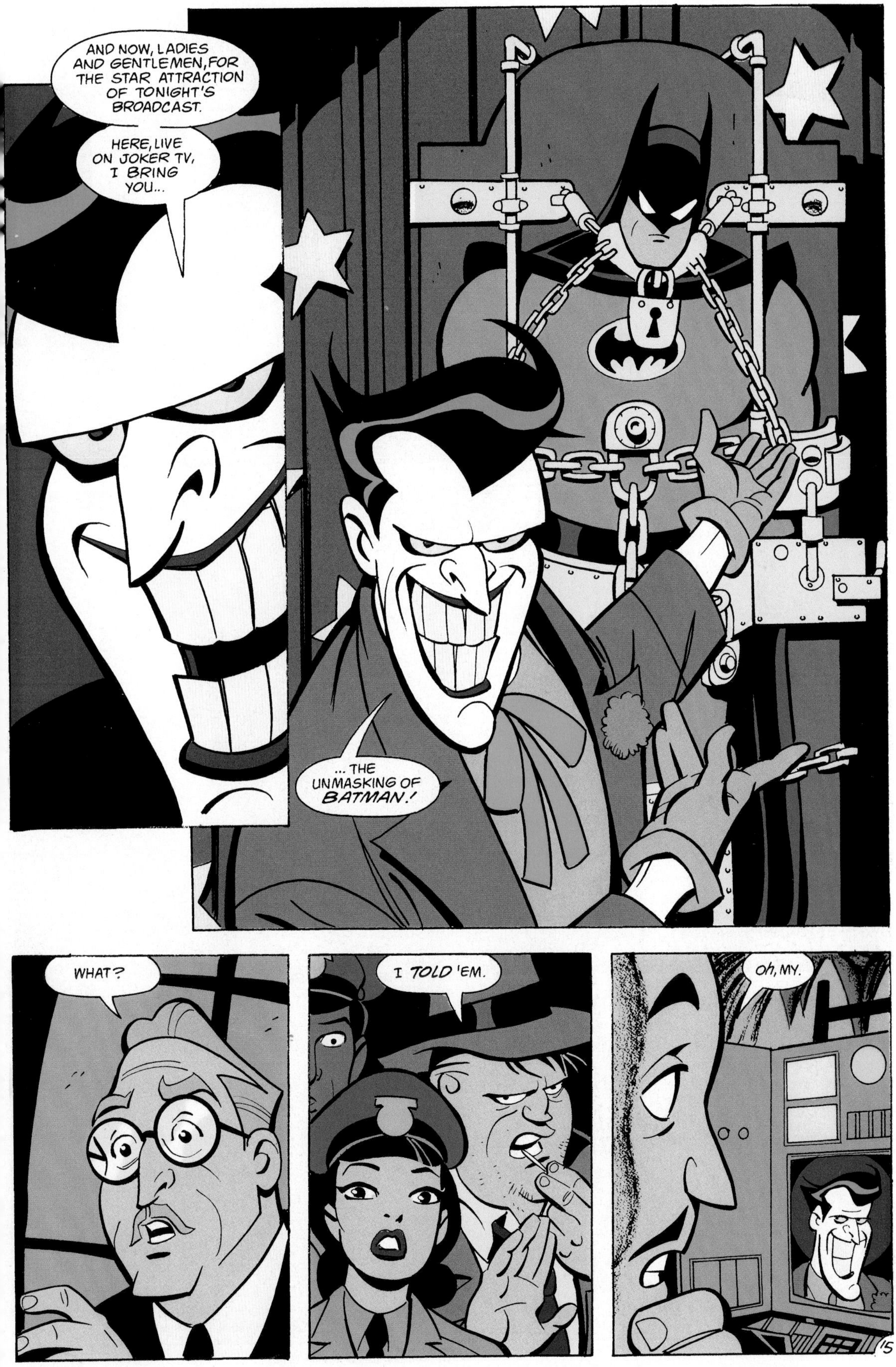

AND NOW, LADIES AND GENTLEMEN, FOR THE STAR ATTRACTION OF TONIGHT'S BROADCAST.
HERE, LIVE ON JOKER TV, I BRING YOU...
... THE UNMASKING OF BATMAN!
WHAT?
I TOLD 'EM.
Oh, MY.

ACT THREE: FLASH IN THE PAN!

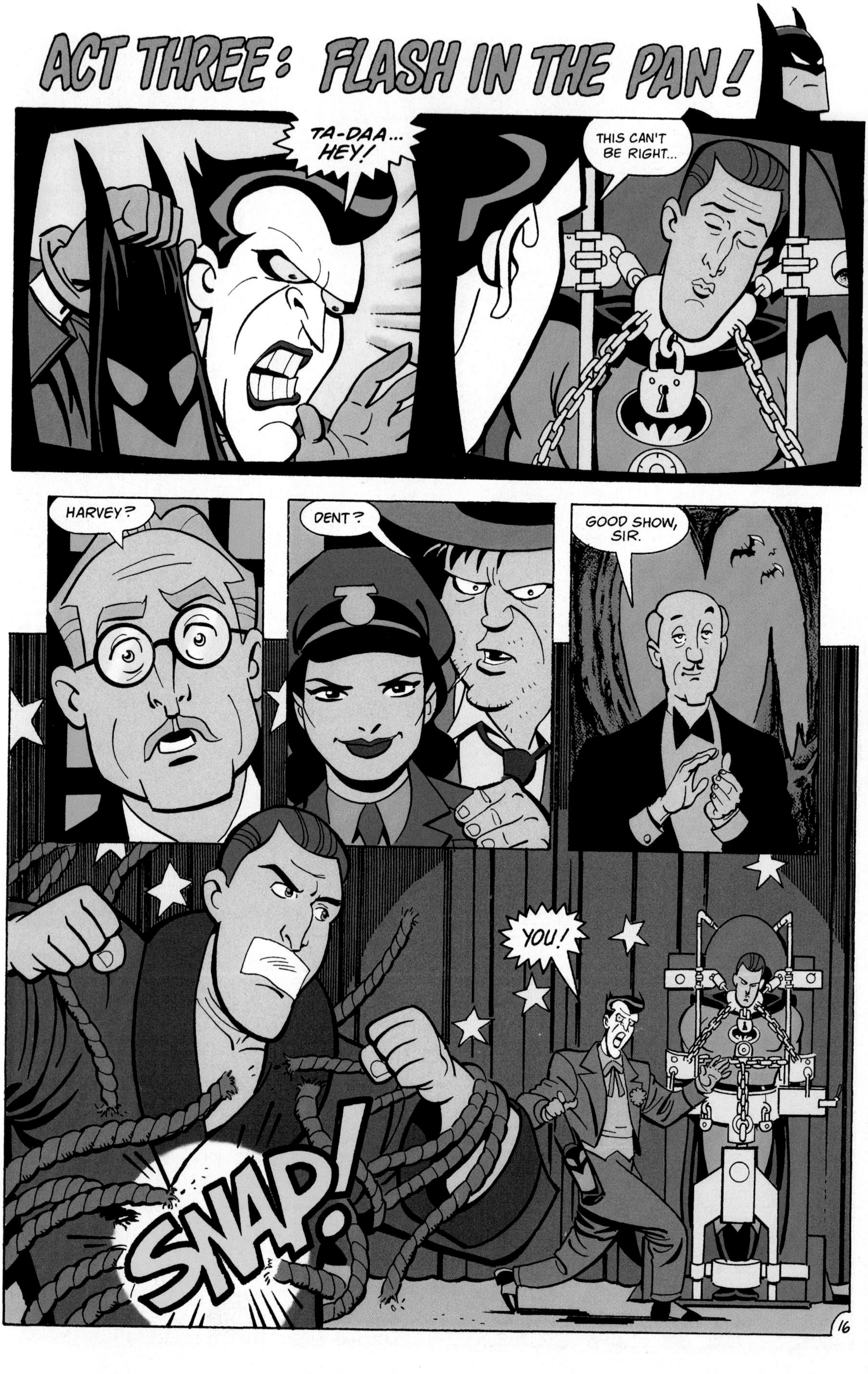

TA-DAA... HEY!
THIS CAN'T BE RIGHT...
HARVEY?
DENT?
GOOD SHOW, SIR.
YOU!
SNAP!

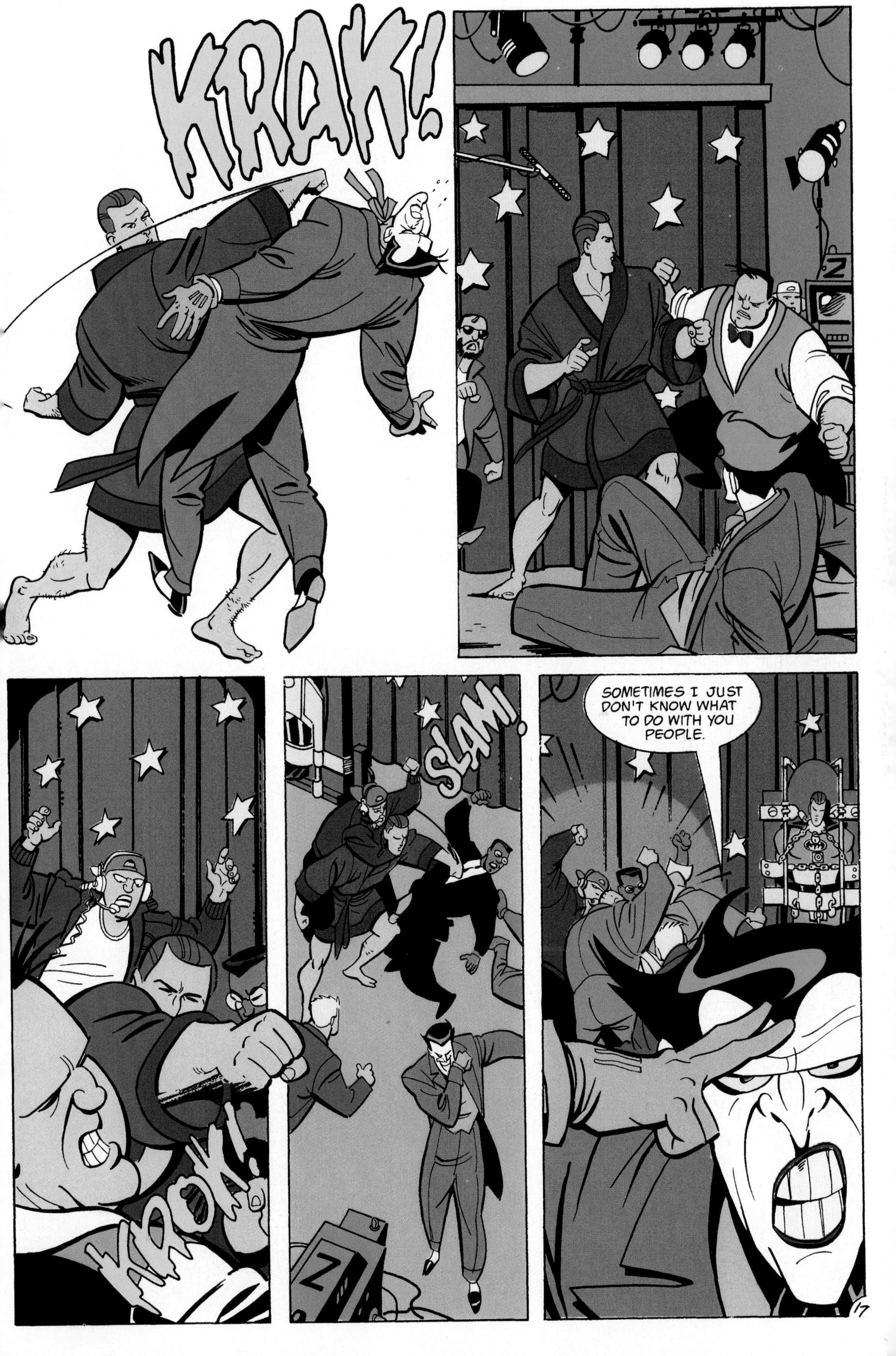
KRAK!
SLAM!
SOMETIMES I JUST DON'T KNOW WHAT TO DO WITH YOU PEOPLE.

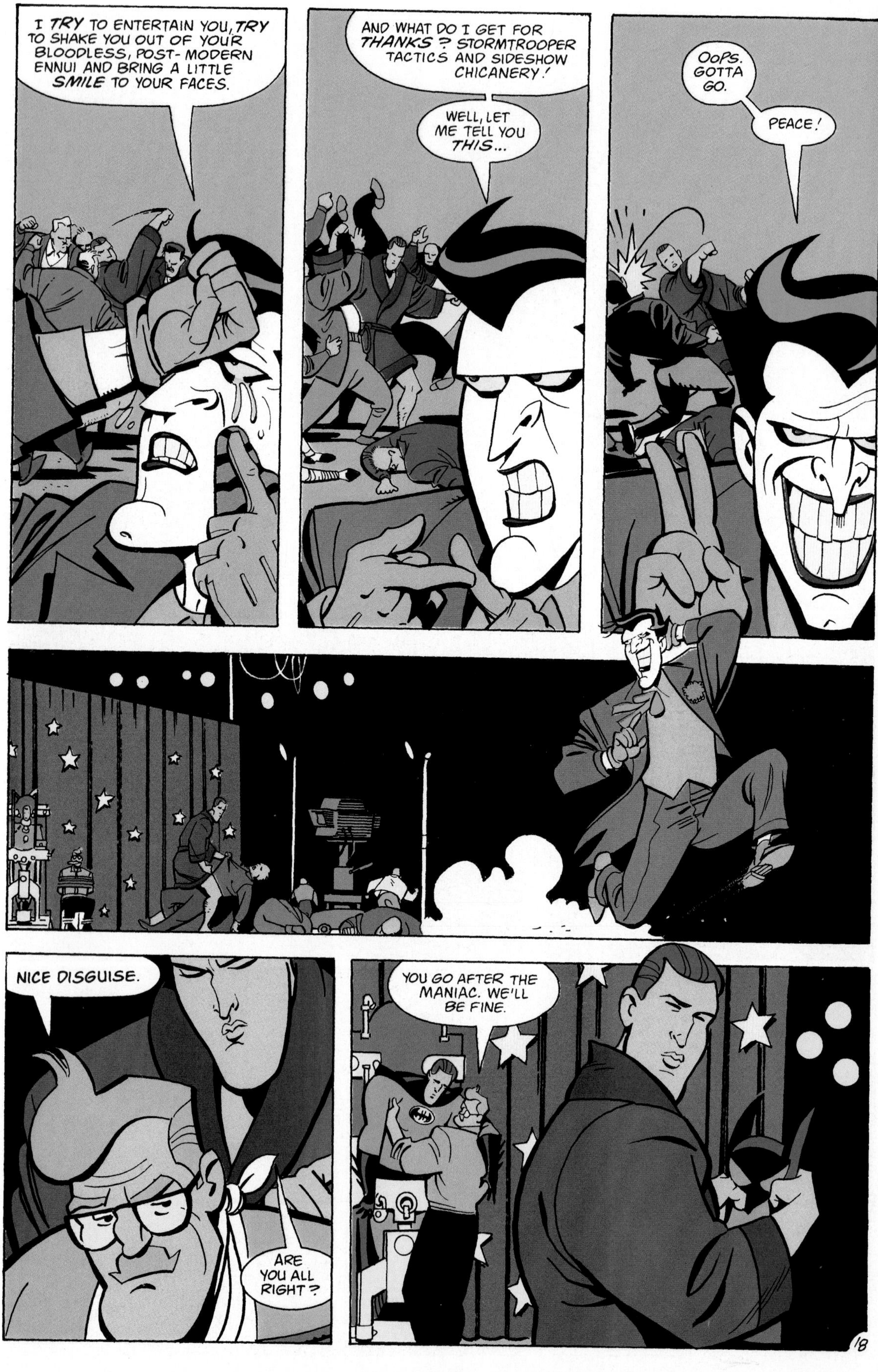
I TRY TO ENTERTAIN YOU, TRY TO SHAKE YOU OUT OF YOUR BLOODLESS, POST-MODERN ENNUI AND BRING A LITTLE SMILE TO YOUR FACES.
AND WHAT DO I GET FOR THANKS? STORMTROOPER TACTICS AND SIDESHOW CHICANERY!
WELL, LET ME TELL YOU THIS...
OOPS. GOTTA GO.
PEACE!
NICE DISGUISE.
ARE YOU ALL RIGHT?
YOU GO AFTER THE MANIAC. WE'LL BE FINE.

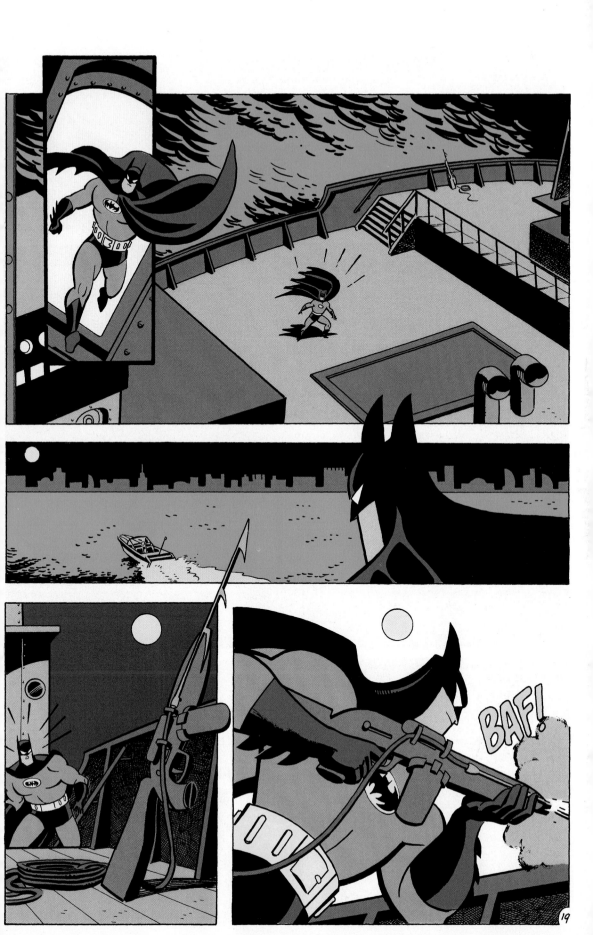

BAF!

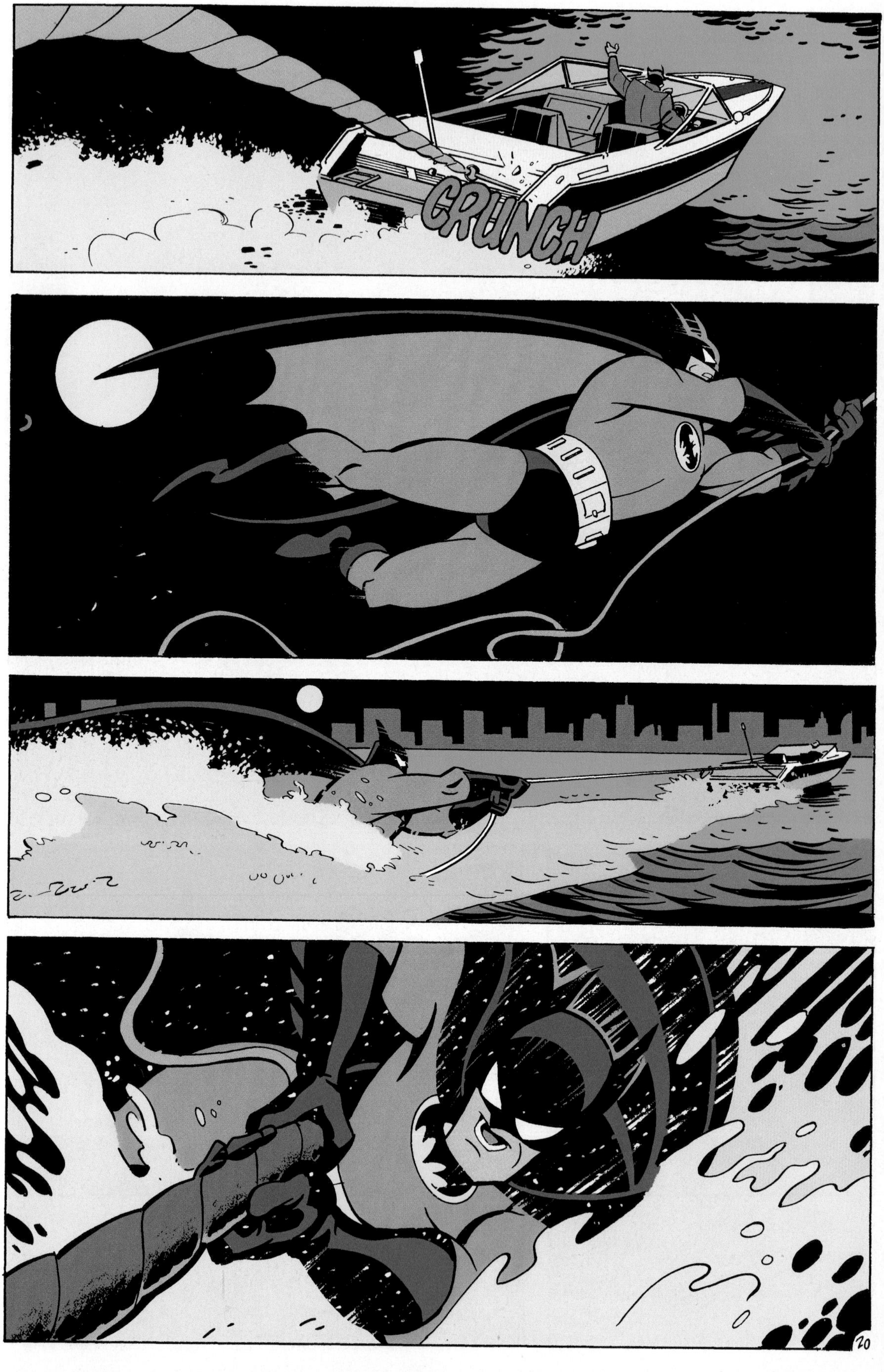
CRUNCH

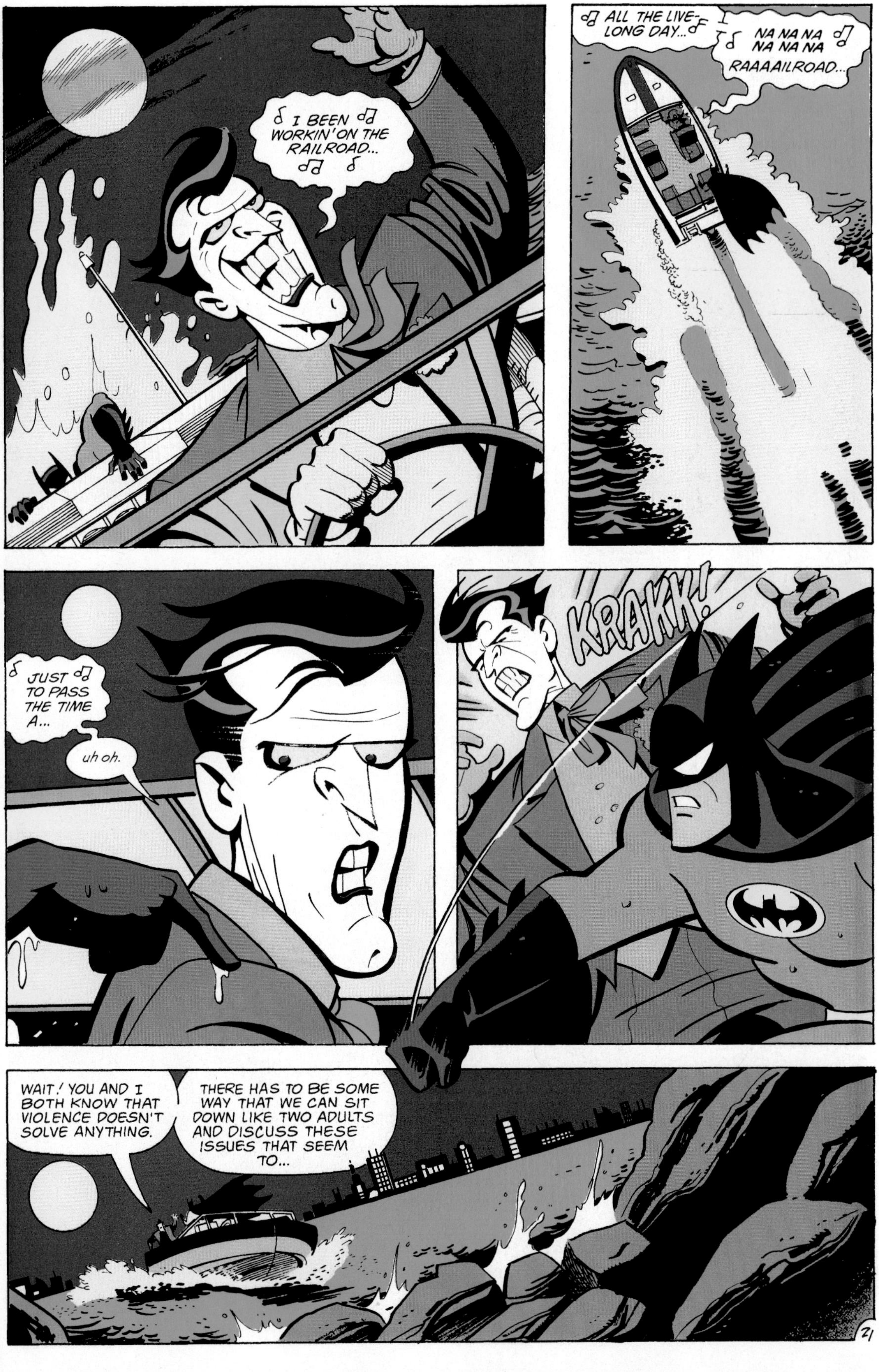
I BEEN WORKIN' ON THE RAILROAD...
ALL THE LIVE-LONG DAY...
NA NA NA NA NA NA RAAAAILROAD...
JUST TO PASS THE TIME A...
uh oh.
KRAKK!
WAIT! YOU AND I BOTH KNOW THAT VIOLENCE DOESN'T SOLVE ANYTHING.
THERE HAS TO BE SOME WAY THAT WE CAN SIT DOWN LIKE TWO ADULTS AND DISCUSS THESE ISSUES THAT SEEM TO...

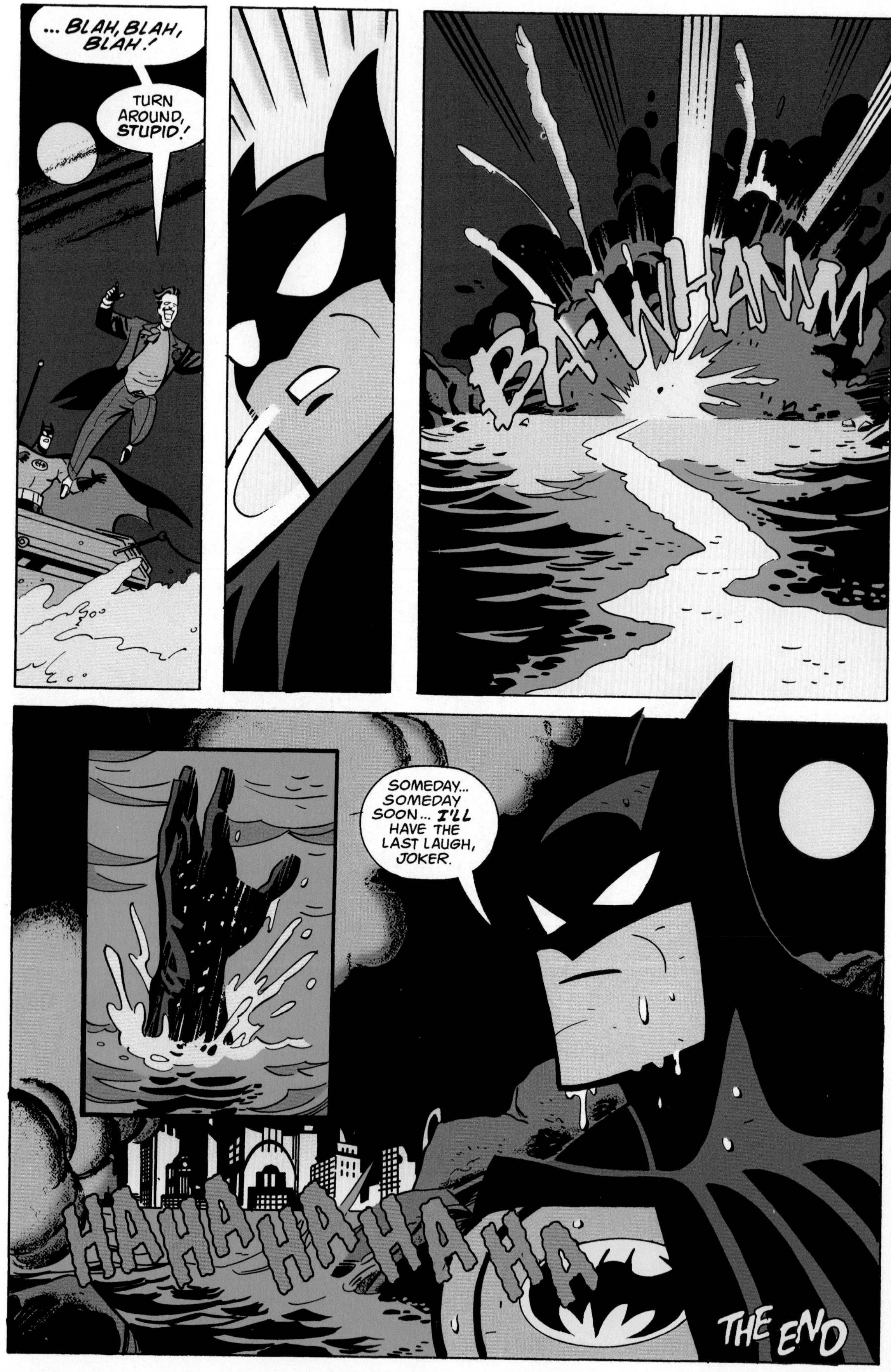

...BLAH, BLAH, BLAH!
TURN AROUND, STUPID!
BA-WHAMM
SOMEDAY... SOMEDAY SOON... I'LL HAVE THE LAST LAUGH, JOKER.
HA HA HA HA HA HA HA HA
THE END

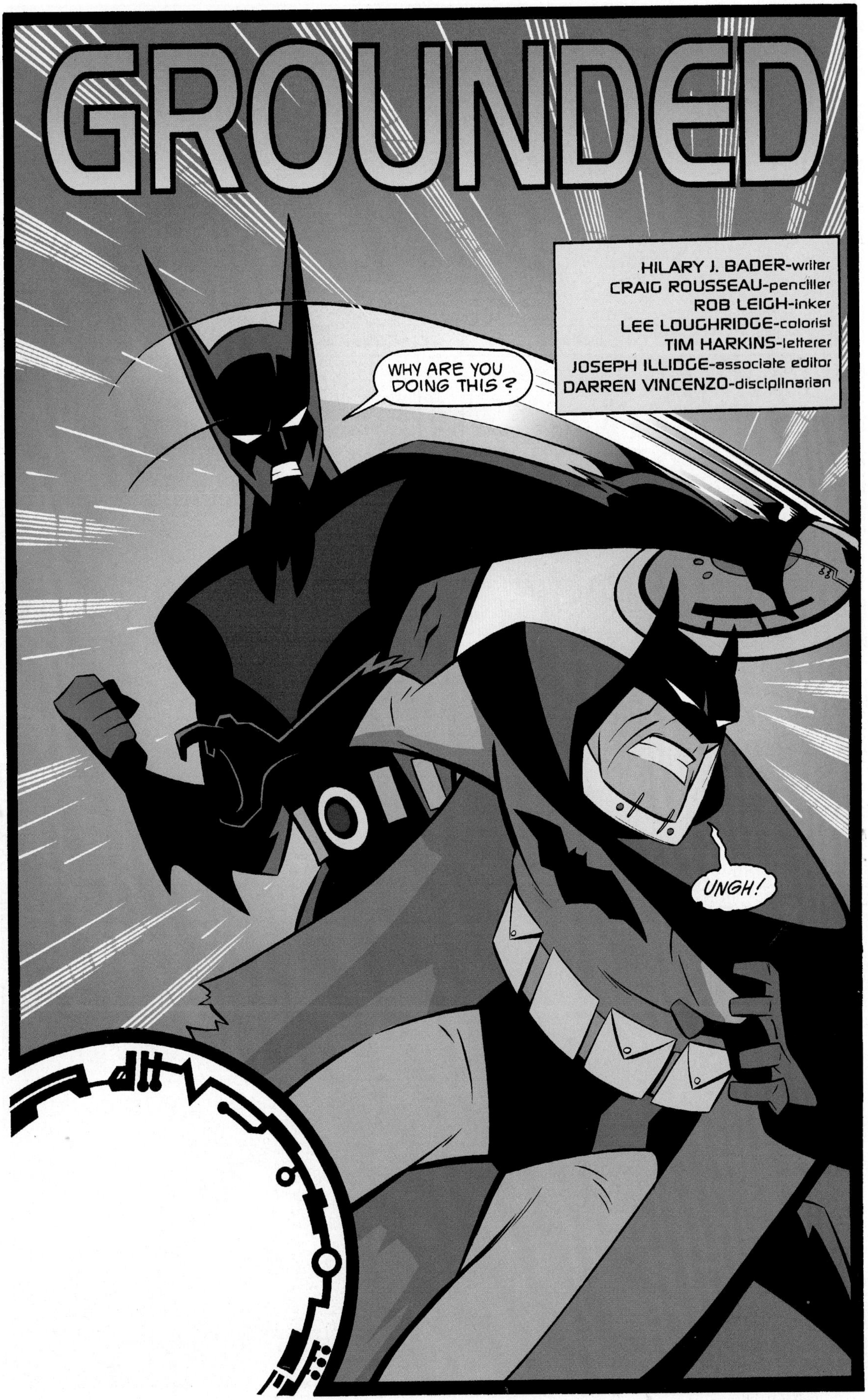
GROUNDED
HILARY J. BADER-writer
CRAIG ROUSSEAU-penciller
ROB LEIGH-inker
LEE LOUGHRIDGE-colorist
TIM HARKINS-letterer
JOSEPH ILLIDGE-associate editor
DARREN VINCENZO-disciplinarian
WHY ARE YOU DOING THIS?
UNGH!

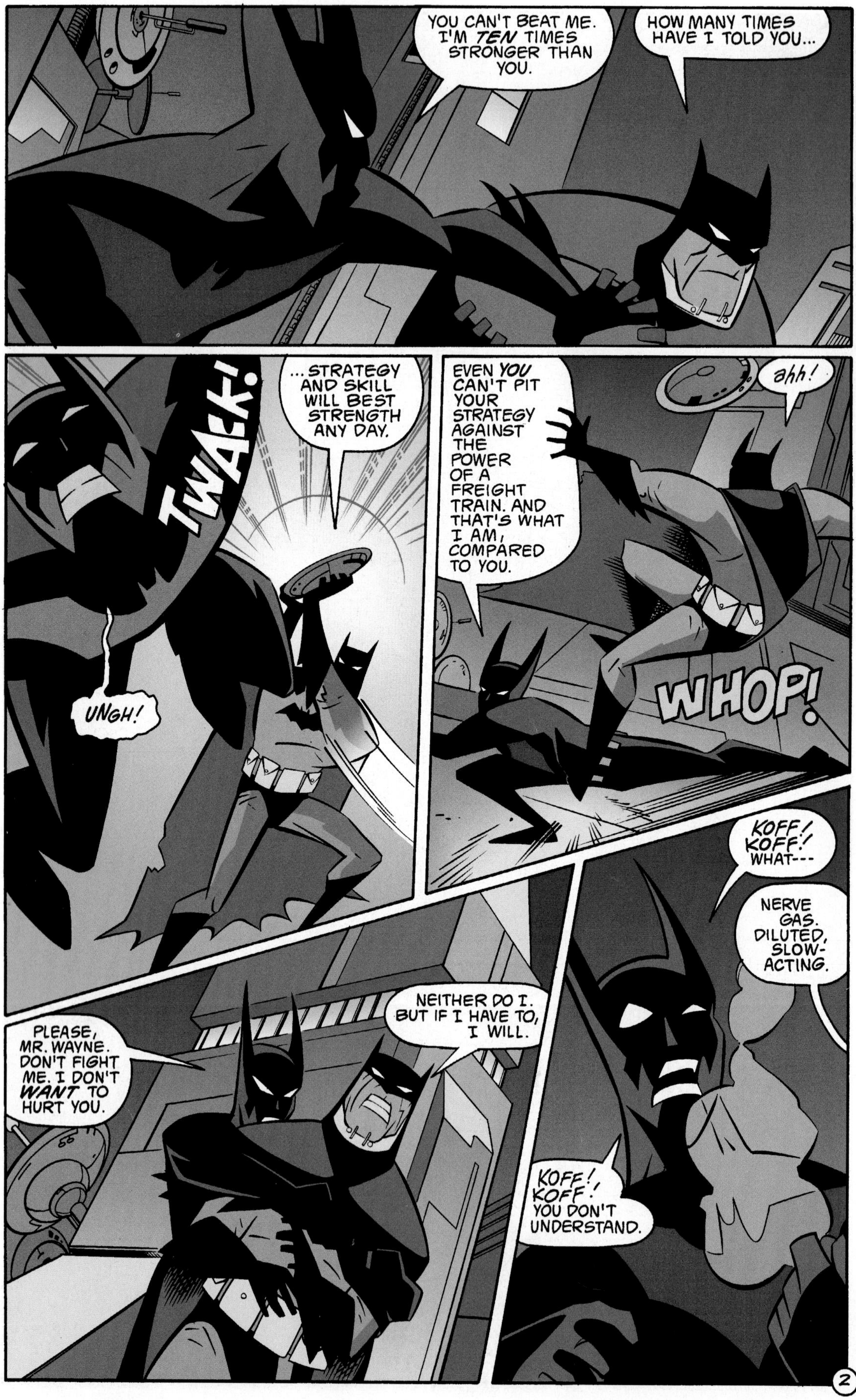

YOU CAN'T BEAT ME. I'M TEN TIMES STRONGER THAN YOU.
HOW MANY TIMES HAVE I TOLD YOU...
...STRATEGY AND SKILL WILL BEST STRENGTH ANY DAY.
TWAK!
UNGH!
EVEN YOU CAN'T PIT YOUR STRATEGY AGAINST THE POWER OF A FREIGHT TRAIN. AND THAT'S WHAT I AM, COMPARED TO YOU.
ahh!
WHOP!
KOFF! KOFF! WHAT---
NERVE GAS. DILUTED, SLOW-ACTING.
PLEASE, MR. WAYNE. DON'T FIGHT ME. I DON'T WANT TO HURT YOU.
NEITHER DO I. BUT IF I HAVE TO, I WILL.
KOFF! KOFF! YOU DON'T UNDERSTAND.

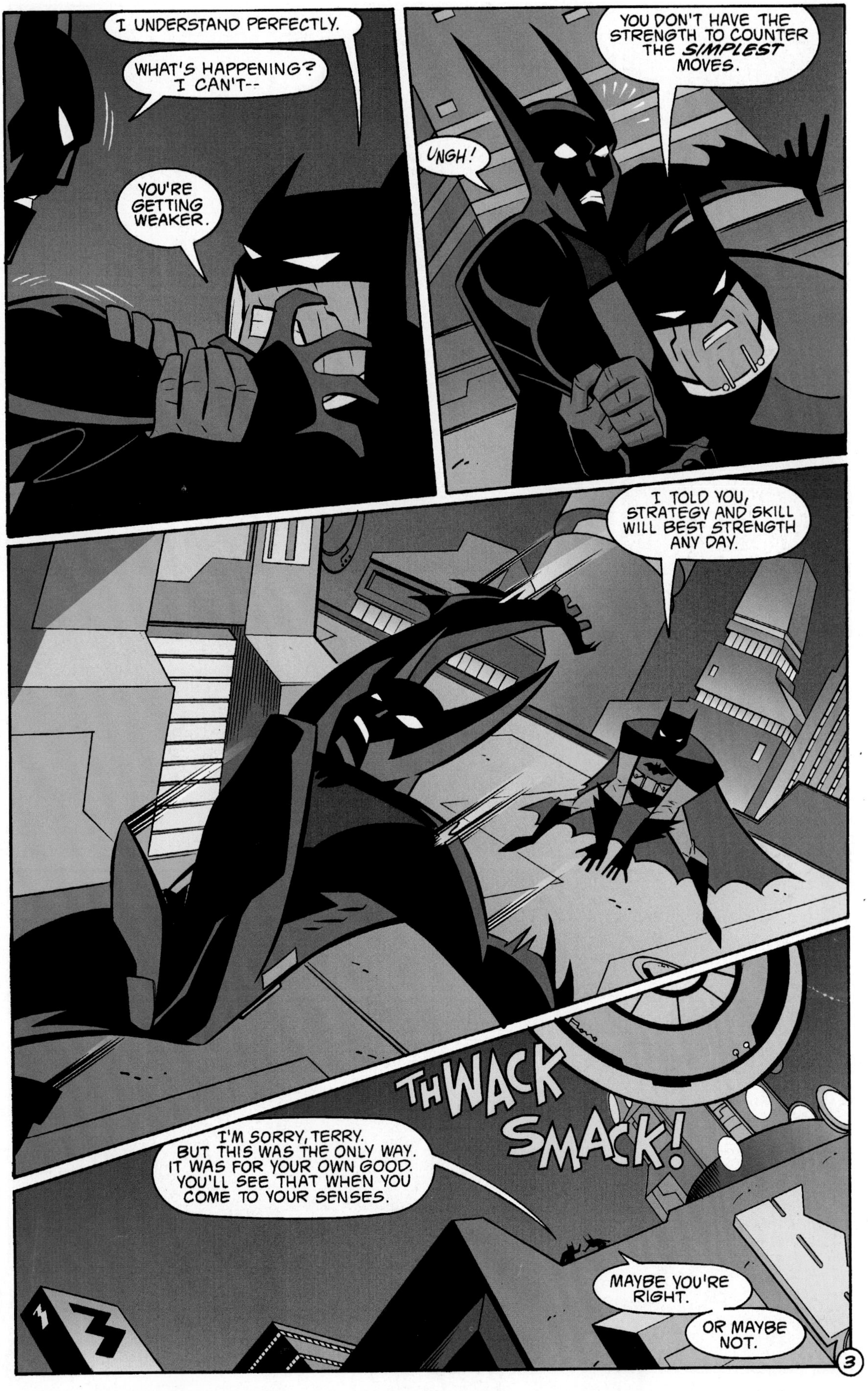
I UNDERSTAND PERFECTLY.
WHAT'S HAPPENING? I CAN'T--
YOU'RE GETTING WEAKER.
YOU DON'T HAVE THE STRENGTH TO COUNTER THE SIMPLEST MOVES.
UNGH!
I TOLD YOU, STRATEGY AND SKILL WILL BEST STRENGTH ANY DAY.
THWACK
SMACK!
I'M SORRY, TERRY. BUT THIS WAS THE ONLY WAY. IT WAS FOR YOUR OWN GOOD. YOU'LL SEE THAT WHEN YOU COME TO YOUR SENSES.
MAYBE YOU'RE RIGHT.
OR MAYBE NOT.

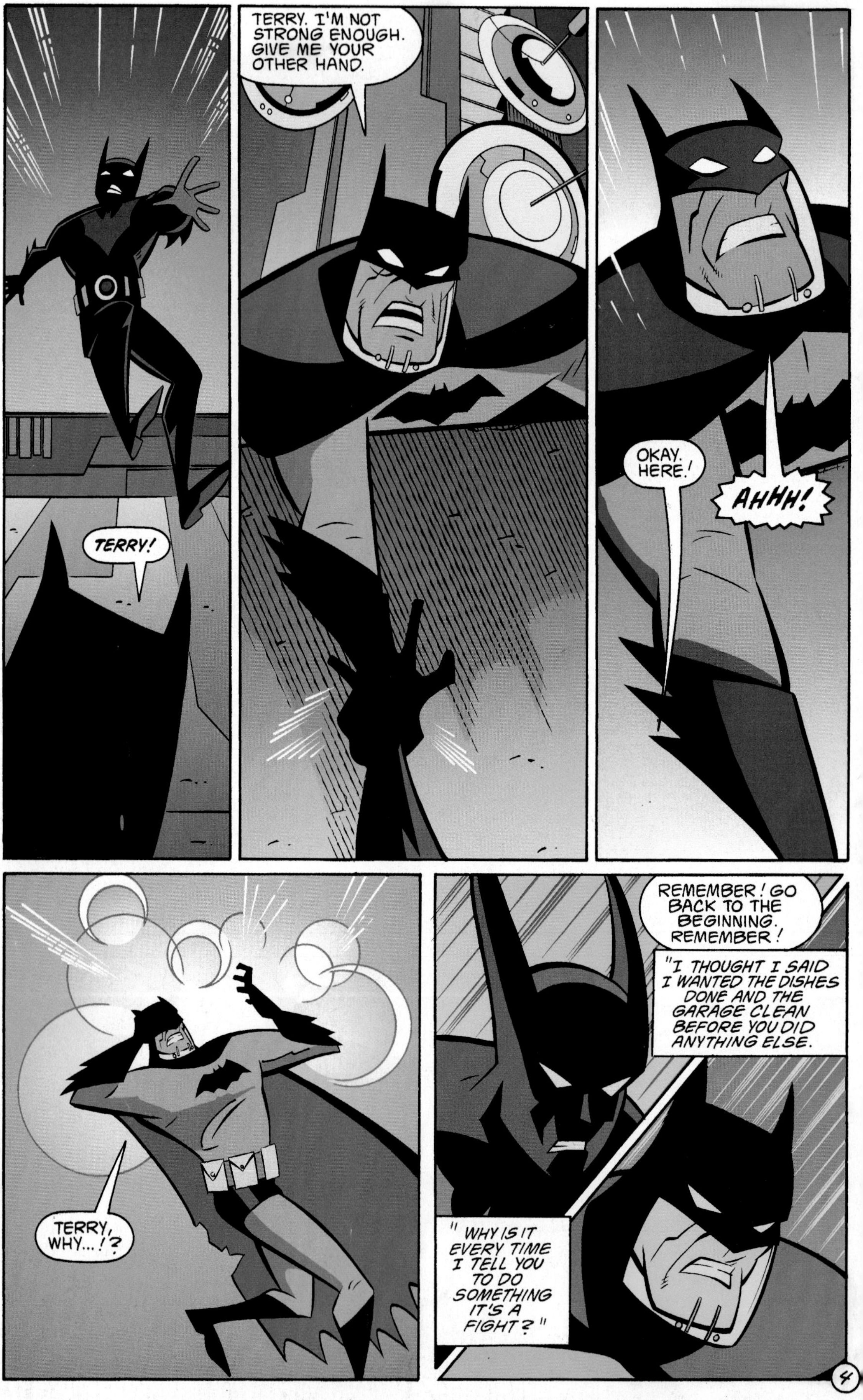
TERRY!
TERRY. I'M NOT STRONG ENOUGH. GIVE ME YOUR OTHER HAND.
OKAY. HERE!
AHHH!
TERRY, WHY...!?
REMEMBER! GO BACK TO THE BEGINNING. REMEMBER!
"I THOUGHT I SAID I WANTED THE DISHES DONE AND THE GARAGE CLEAN BEFORE YOU DID ANYTHING ELSE.
" WHY IS IT EVERY TIME I TELL YOU TO DO SOMETHING IT'S A FIGHT?"

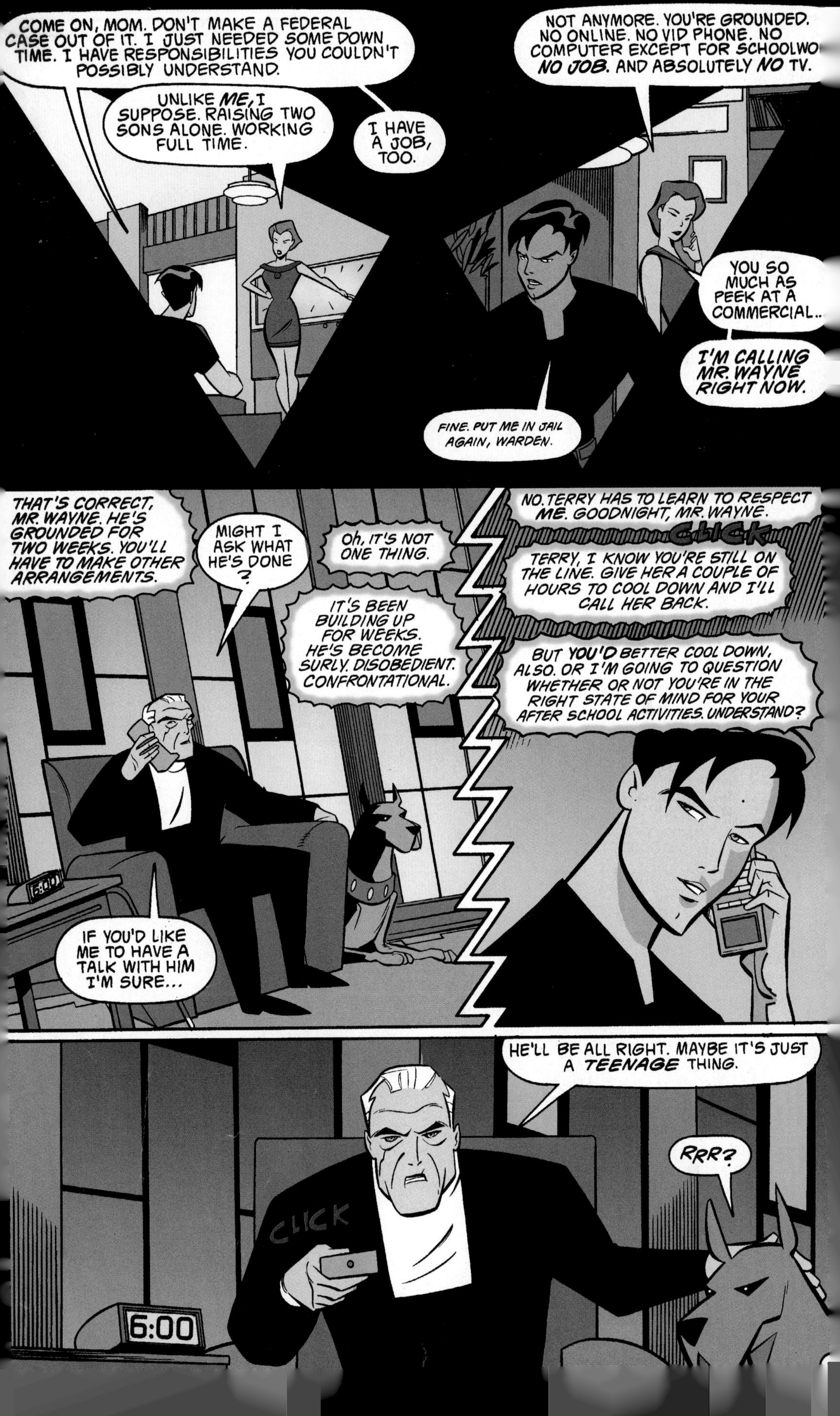
COME ON, MOM. DON'T MAKE A FEDERAL CASE OUT OF IT. I JUST NEEDED SOME DOWN TIME. I HAVE RESPONSIBILITIES YOU COULDN'T POSSIBLY UNDERSTAND.
UNLIKE ME, I SUPPOSE. RAISING TWO SONS ALONE. WORKING FULL TIME.
I HAVE A JOB, TOO.
NOT ANYMORE. YOU'RE GROUNDED. NO ONLINE. NO VID PHONE. NO COMPUTER EXCEPT FOR SCHOOLWO
NO JOB. AND ABSOLUTELY NO TV.
YOU SO MUCH AS PEEK AT A COMMERCIAL...
I'M CALLING MR. WAYNE RIGHT NOW.
FINE. PUT ME IN JAIL AGAIN, WARDEN.
THAT'S CORRECT, MR. WAYNE. HE'S GROUNDED FOR TWO WEEKS. YOU'LL HAVE TO MAKE OTHER ARRANGEMENTS.
MIGHT I ASK WHAT HE'S DONE?
Oh, IT'S NOT ONE THING.
IT'S BEEN BUILDING UP FOR WEEKS. HE'S BECOME SURLY. DISOBEDIENT. CONFRONTATIONAL.
IF YOU'D LIKE ME TO HAVE A TALK WITH HIM I'M SURE...
NO. TERRY HAS TO LEARN TO RESPECT ME. GOODNIGHT, MR. WAYNE.
CLICK
TERRY, I KNOW YOU'RE STILL ON THE LINE. GIVE HER A COUPLE OF HOURS TO COOL DOWN AND I'LL CALL HER BACK.
BUT YOU'D BETTER COOL DOWN, ALSO. OR I'M GOING TO QUESTION WHETHER OR NOT YOU'RE IN THE RIGHT STATE OF MIND FOR YOUR AFTER SCHOOL ACTIVITIES. UNDERSTAND?
6:00
HE'LL BE ALL RIGHT. MAYBE IT'S JUST A TEENAGE THING.
RRR?
CLICK
6:00

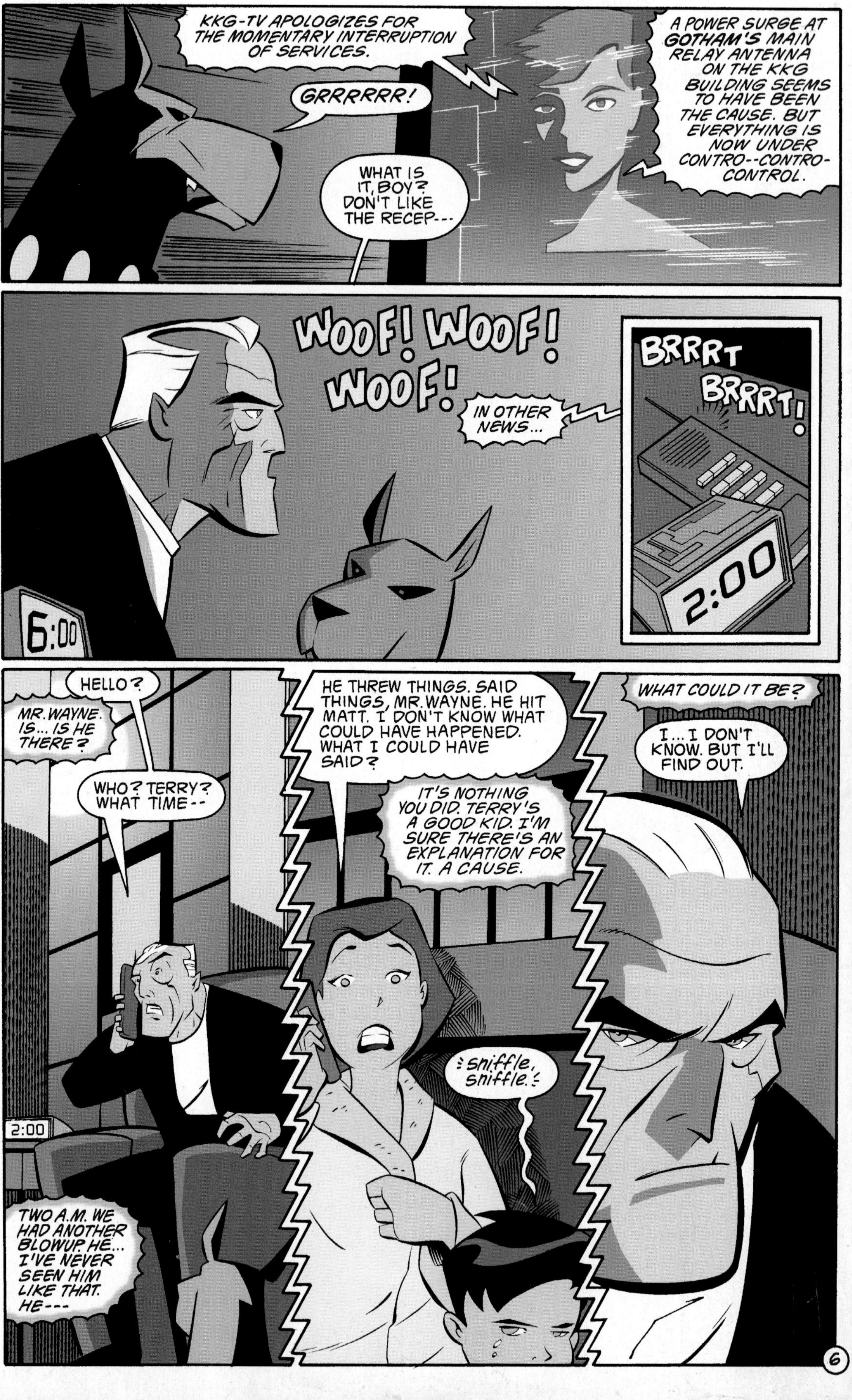
KKG-TV APOLOGIZES FOR THE MOMENTARY INTERRUPTION OF SERVICES.
A POWER SURGE AT GOTHAM'S MAIN RELAY ANTENNA ON THE KKG BUILDING SEEMS TO HAVE BEEN THE CAUSE. BUT EVERYTHING IS NOW UNDER CONTRO--CONTRO-CONTROL.
GRRRRRR!
WHAT IS IT, BOY? DON'T LIKE THE RECEP---
WOOF! WOOF! WOOF!
IN OTHER NEWS...
BRRRT BRRRT!
2:00
6:00
HELLO?
MR. WAYNE. IS... IS HE THERE?
WHO? TERRY? WHAT TIME--
2:00
TWO A.M. WE HAD ANOTHER BLOWUP. HE... I'VE NEVER SEEN HIM LIKE THAT. HE---
HE THREW THINGS. SAID THINGS, MR. WAYNE. HE HIT MATT. I DON'T KNOW WHAT COULD HAVE HAPPENED. WHAT I COULD HAVE SAID?
IT'S NOTHING YOU DID. TERRY'S A GOOD KID. I'M SURE THERE'S AN EXPLANATION FOR IT. A CAUSE.
sniffle, sniffle.
WHAT COULD IT BE?
I... I DON'T KNOW. BUT I'LL FIND OUT.

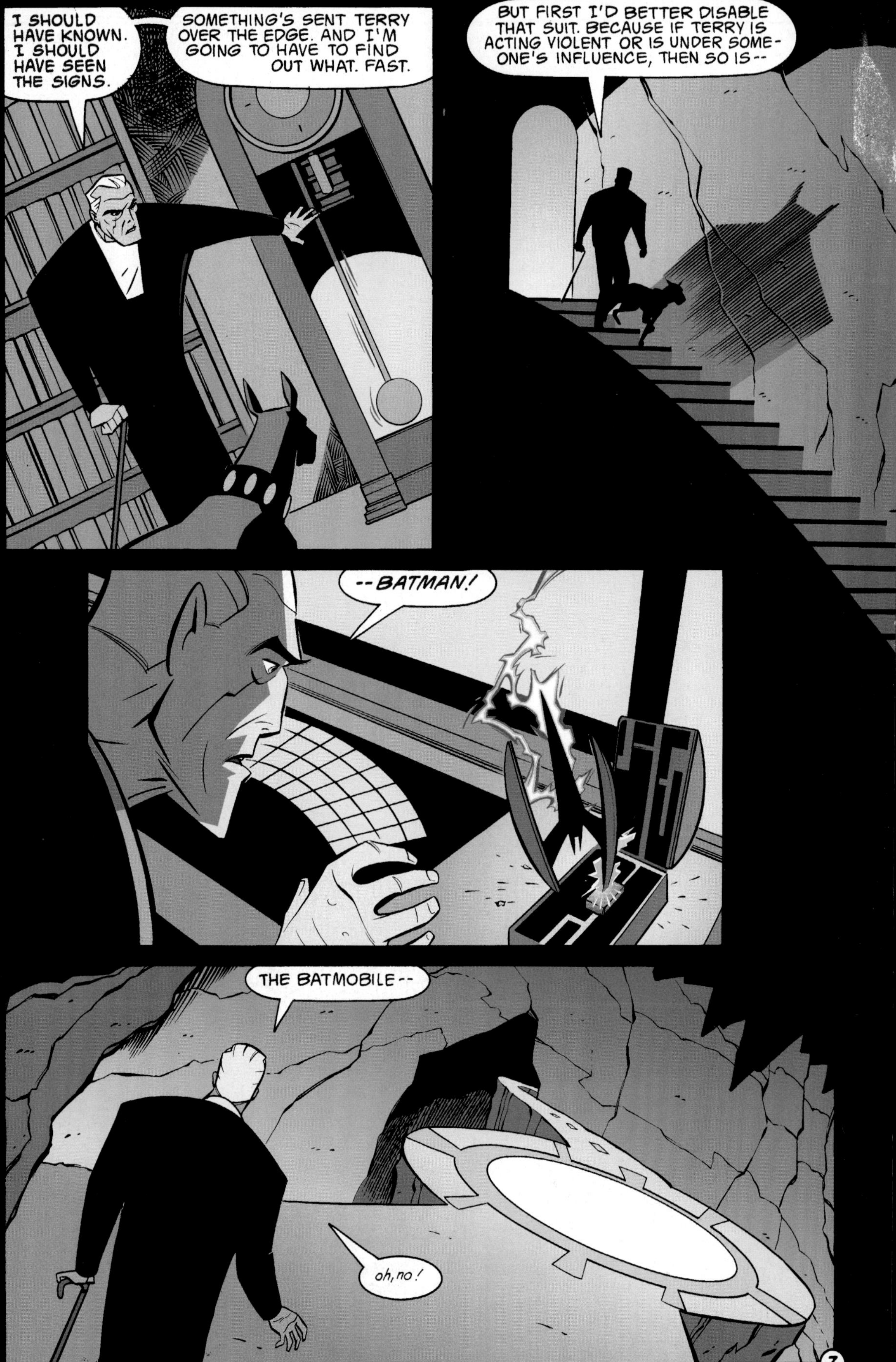

I SHOULD HAVE KNOWN. I SHOULD HAVE SEEN THE SIGNS.
SOMETHING'S SENT TERRY OVER THE EDGE. AND I'M GOING TO HAVE TO FIND OUT WHAT. FAST.
BUT FIRST I'D BETTER DISABLE THAT SUIT. BECAUSE IF TERRY IS ACTING VIOLENT OR IS UNDER SOME-ONE'S INFLUENCE, THEN SO IS--
--BATMAN!
THE BATMOBILE--
oh, no!

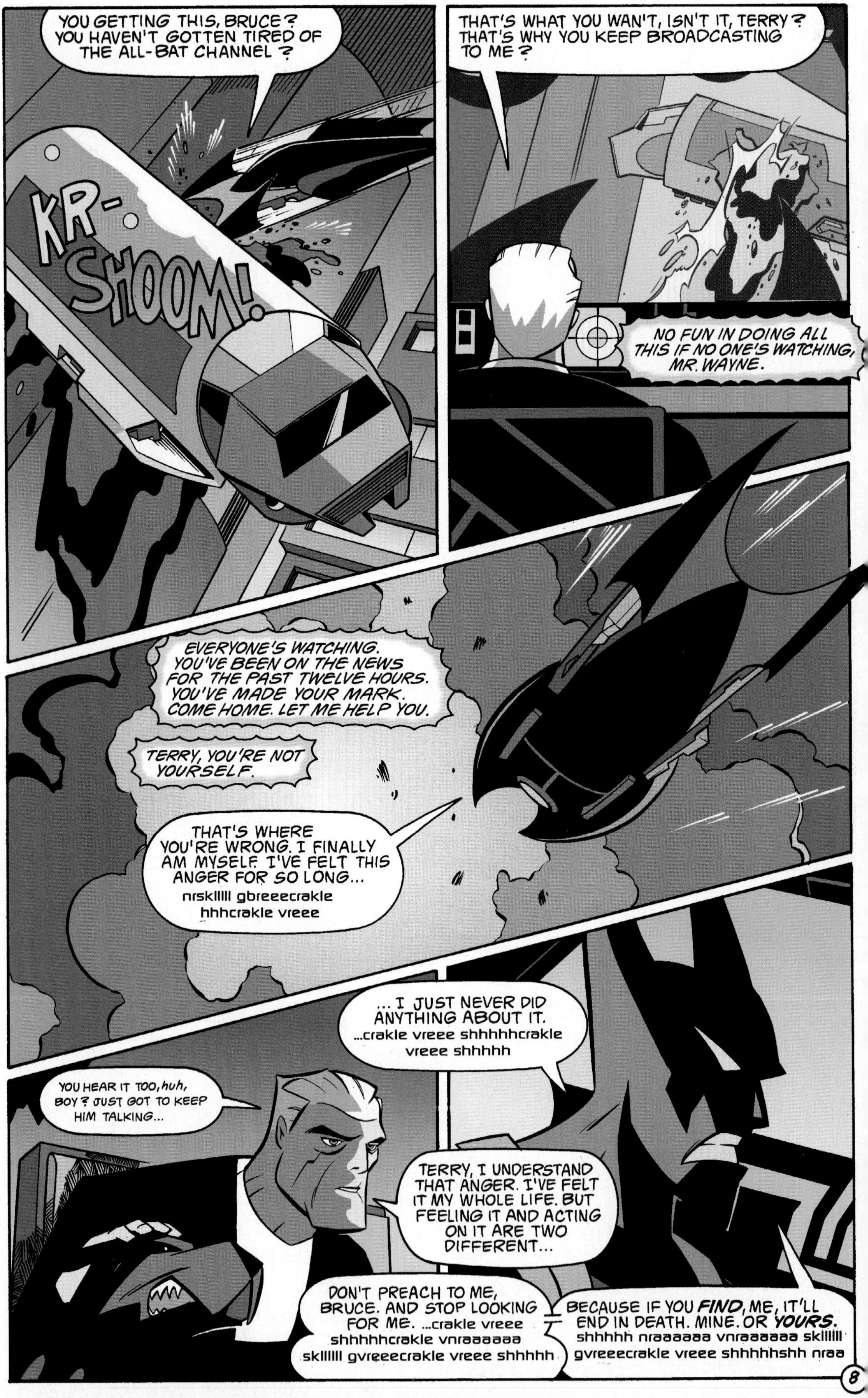
YOU GETTING THIS, BRUCE? YOU HAVEN'T GOTTEN TIRED OF THE ALL-BAT CHANNEL?
KR-SHOOM!
THAT'S WHAT YOU WAN'T, ISN'T IT, TERRY? THAT'S WHY YOU KEEP BROADCASTING TO ME?
NO FUN IN DOING ALL THIS IF NO ONE'S WATCHING, MR. WAYNE.
EVERYONE'S WATCHING. YOU'VE BEEN ON THE NEWS FOR THE PAST TWELVE HOURS. YOU'VE MADE YOUR MARK. COME HOME. LET ME HELP YOU.
TERRY, YOU'RE NOT YOURSELF.
THAT'S WHERE YOU'RE WRONG. I FINALLY AM MYSELF. I'VE FELT THIS ANGER FOR SO LONG... nrsklllll gbreeecrakle hhhcrakle vreee
... I JUST NEVER DID ANYTHING ABOUT IT. ...crakle vreee shhhhhcrakle vreee shhhhh
YOU HEAR IT TOO, huh, BOY? JUST GOT TO KEEP HIM TALKING...
TERRY, I UNDERSTAND THAT ANGER. I'VE FELT IT MY WHOLE LIFE. BUT FEELING IT AND ACTING ON IT ARE TWO DIFFERENT...
DON'T PREACH TO ME, BRUCE. AND STOP LOOKING FOR ME. ...crakle vreee shhhhhcrakle vnraaaaaaa sklllllll gvreeecrakle vreee shhhhh
BECAUSE IF YOU FIND, ME, IT'LL END IN DEATH. MINE. OR YOURS. shhhhh nraaaaaa vnraaaaaaa sklllllll gvreeecrakle vreee shhhhhshh nraa

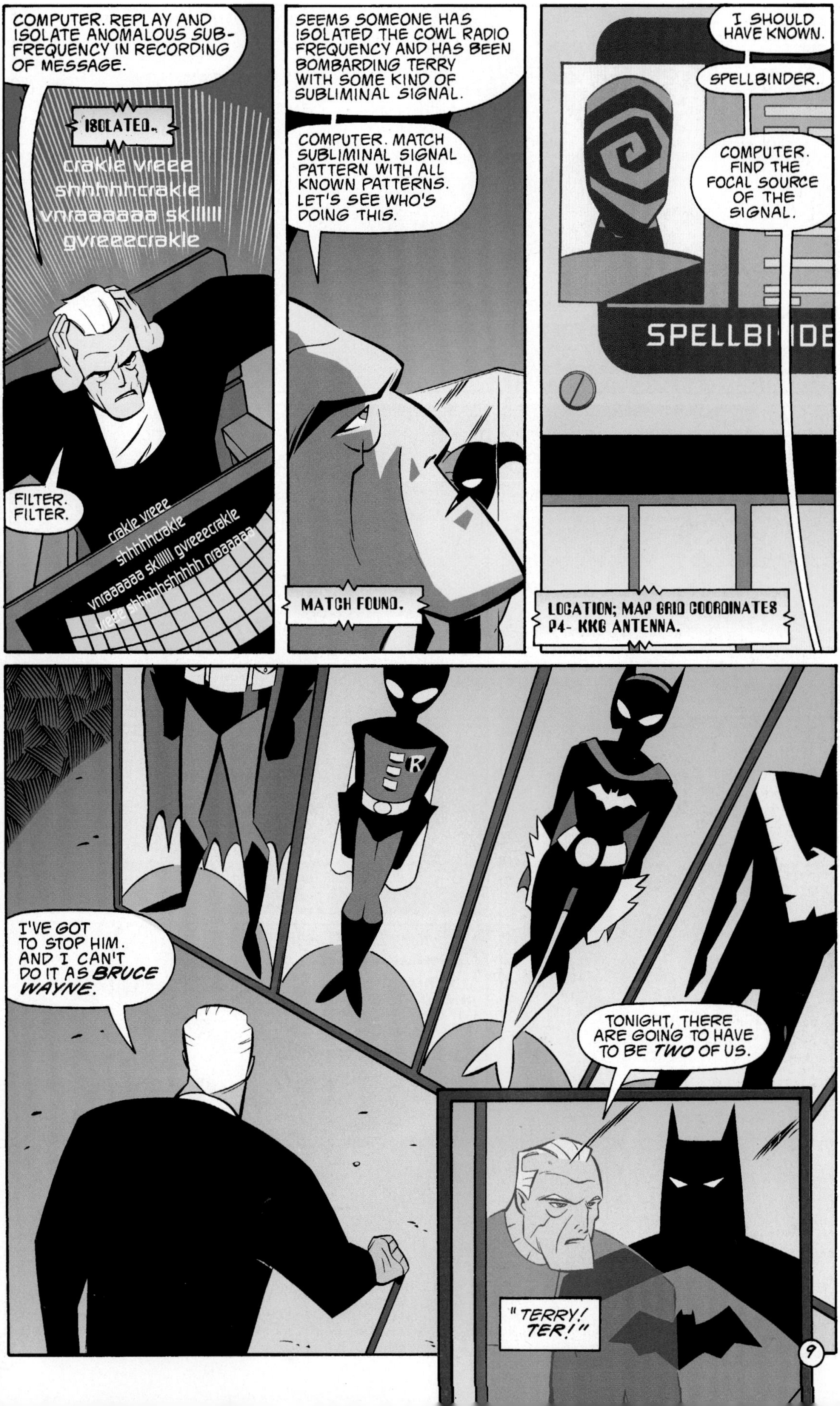
COMPUTER. REPLAY AND ISOLATE ANOMALOUS SUB-FREQUENCY IN RECORDING OF MESSAGE.
ISOLATED.
crakle vieee
shhhhhcrakle
vnraaaaaa skilllll
gvreeecrakle
FILTER. FILTER.
crakle vieee
shhhhhcrakle
vnraaaaaa skilllll gvreeecrakle
SEEMS SOMEONE HAS ISOLATED THE COWL RADIO FREQUENCY AND HAS BEEN BOMBARDING TERRY WITH SOME KIND OF SUBLIMINAL SIGNAL.
COMPUTER. MATCH SUBLIMINAL SIGNAL PATTERN WITH ALL KNOWN PATTERNS. LET'S SEE WHO'S DOING THIS.
MATCH FOUND.
I SHOULD HAVE KNOWN.
SPELLBINDER.
COMPUTER. FIND THE FOCAL SOURCE OF THE SIGNAL.
SPELLBI DE
LOCATION; MAP GRID COORDINATES P4- KKG ANTENNA.
I'VE GOT TO STOP HIM. AND I CAN'T DO IT AS *BRUCE WAYNE*.
TONIGHT, THERE ARE GOING TO HAVE TO BE *TWO* OF US.
"*TERRY! TER!*"

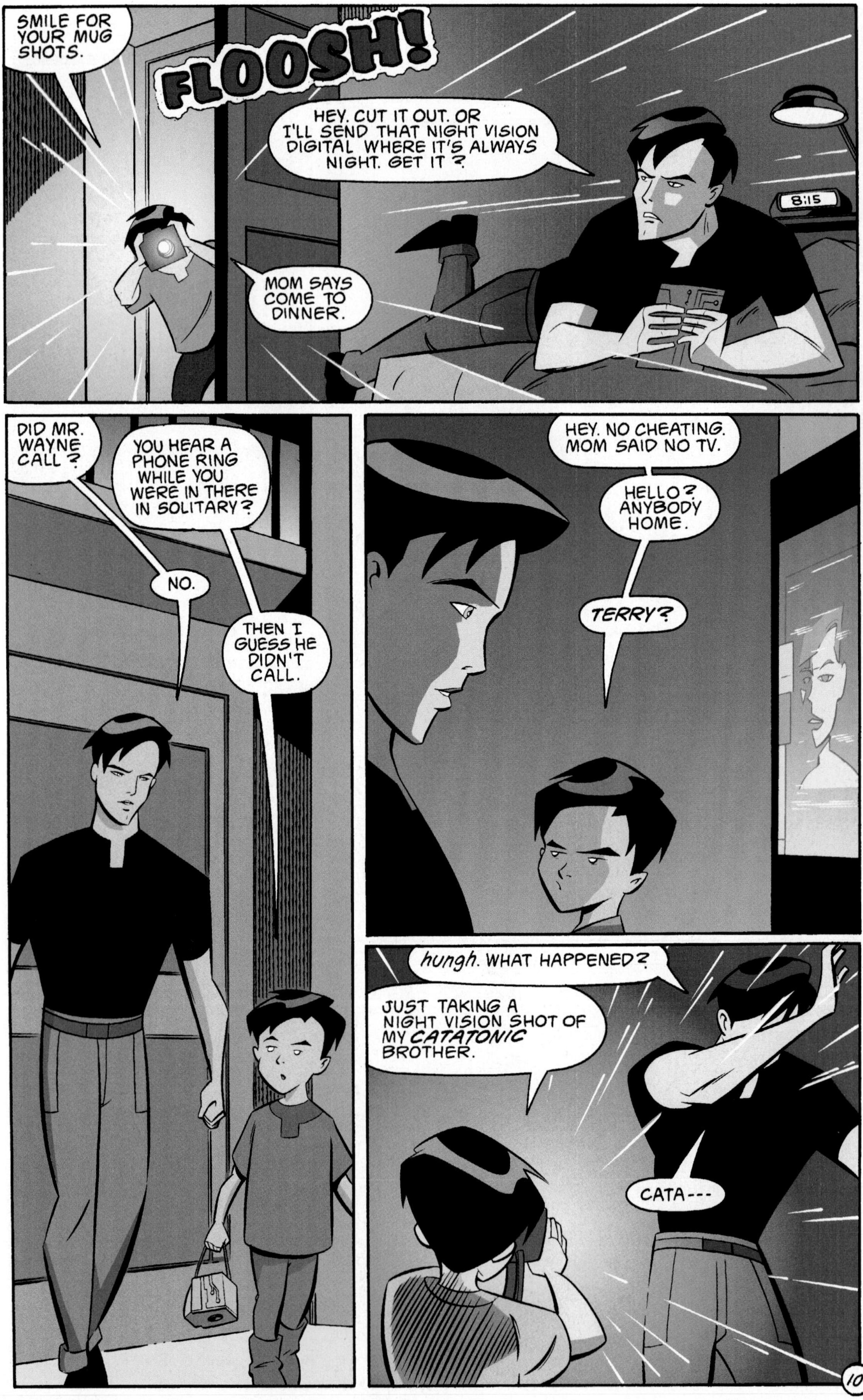

SMILE FOR YOUR MUG SHOTS.
FLOOSH!
HEY. CUT IT OUT. OR I'LL SEND THAT NIGHT VISION DIGITAL WHERE IT'S ALWAYS NIGHT. GET IT ?
8:15
MOM SAYS COME TO DINNER.
DID MR. WAYNE CALL ?
YOU HEAR A PHONE RING WHILE YOU WERE IN THERE IN SOLITARY ?
NO.
THEN I GUESS HE DIDN'T CALL.
HEY. NO CHEATING. MOM SAID NO TV.
HELLO ? ANYBODY HOME.
TERRY ?
hungh. WHAT HAPPENED ?
JUST TAKING A NIGHT VISION SHOT OF MY CATATONIC BROTHER.
CATA---

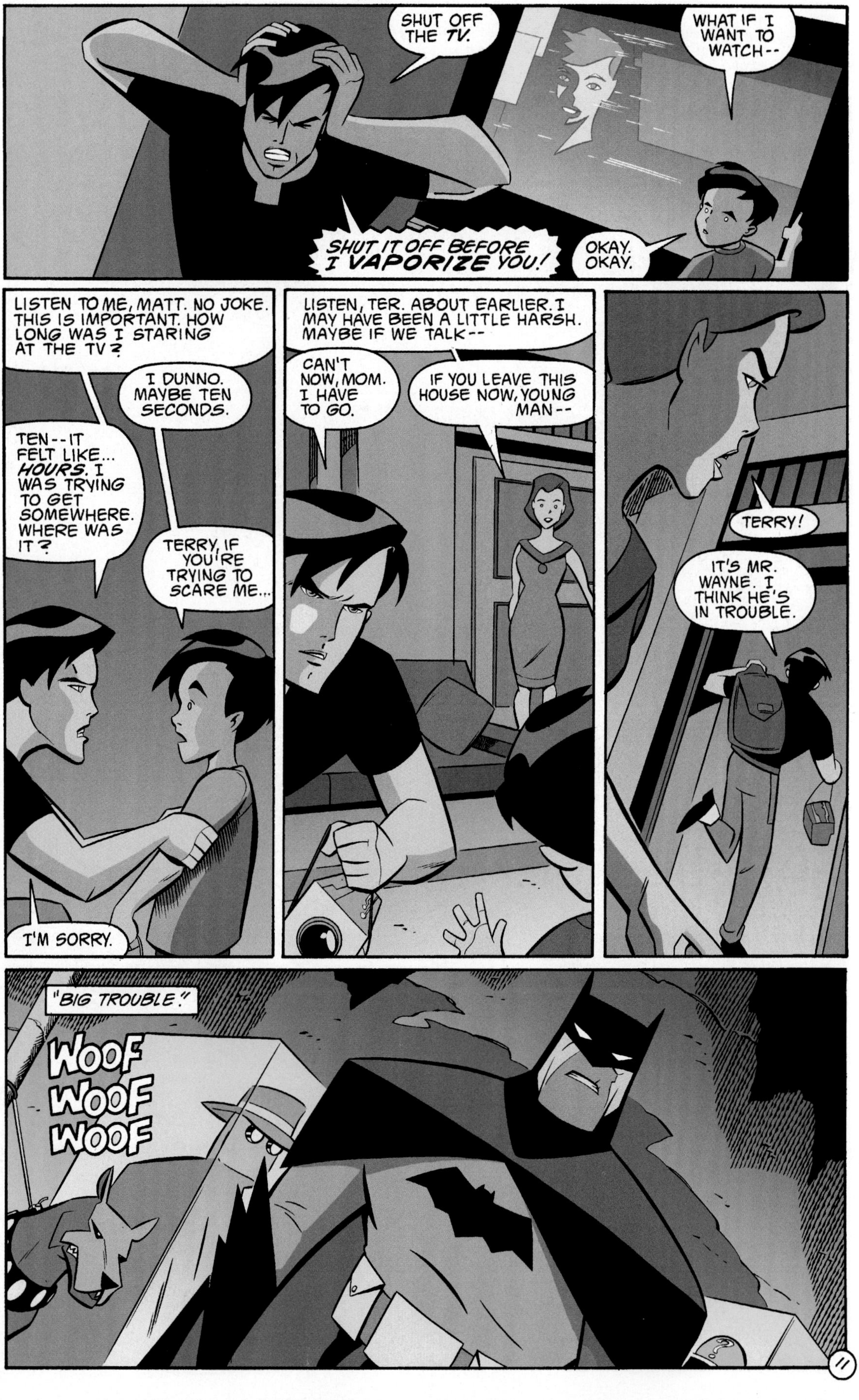
SHUT OFF THE TV.
WHAT IF I WANT TO WATCH--
SHUT IT OFF BEFORE I VAPORIZE YOU!
OKAY. OKAY.
LISTEN TO ME, MATT. NO JOKE. THIS IS IMPORTANT. HOW LONG WAS I STARING AT THE TV?
I DUNNO. MAYBE TEN SECONDS.
TEN--IT FELT LIKE... HOURS. I WAS TRYING TO GET SOMEWHERE. WHERE WAS IT?
TERRY, IF YOU'RE TRYING TO SCARE ME...
I'M SORRY.
LISTEN, TER. ABOUT EARLIER. I MAY HAVE BEEN A LITTLE HARSH. MAYBE IF WE TALK--
CAN'T NOW, MOM. I HAVE TO GO.
IF YOU LEAVE THIS HOUSE NOW, YOUNG MAN--
TERRY!
IT'S MR. WAYNE. I THINK HE'S IN TROUBLE.
"BIG TROUBLE."
WOOF
WOOF
WOOF

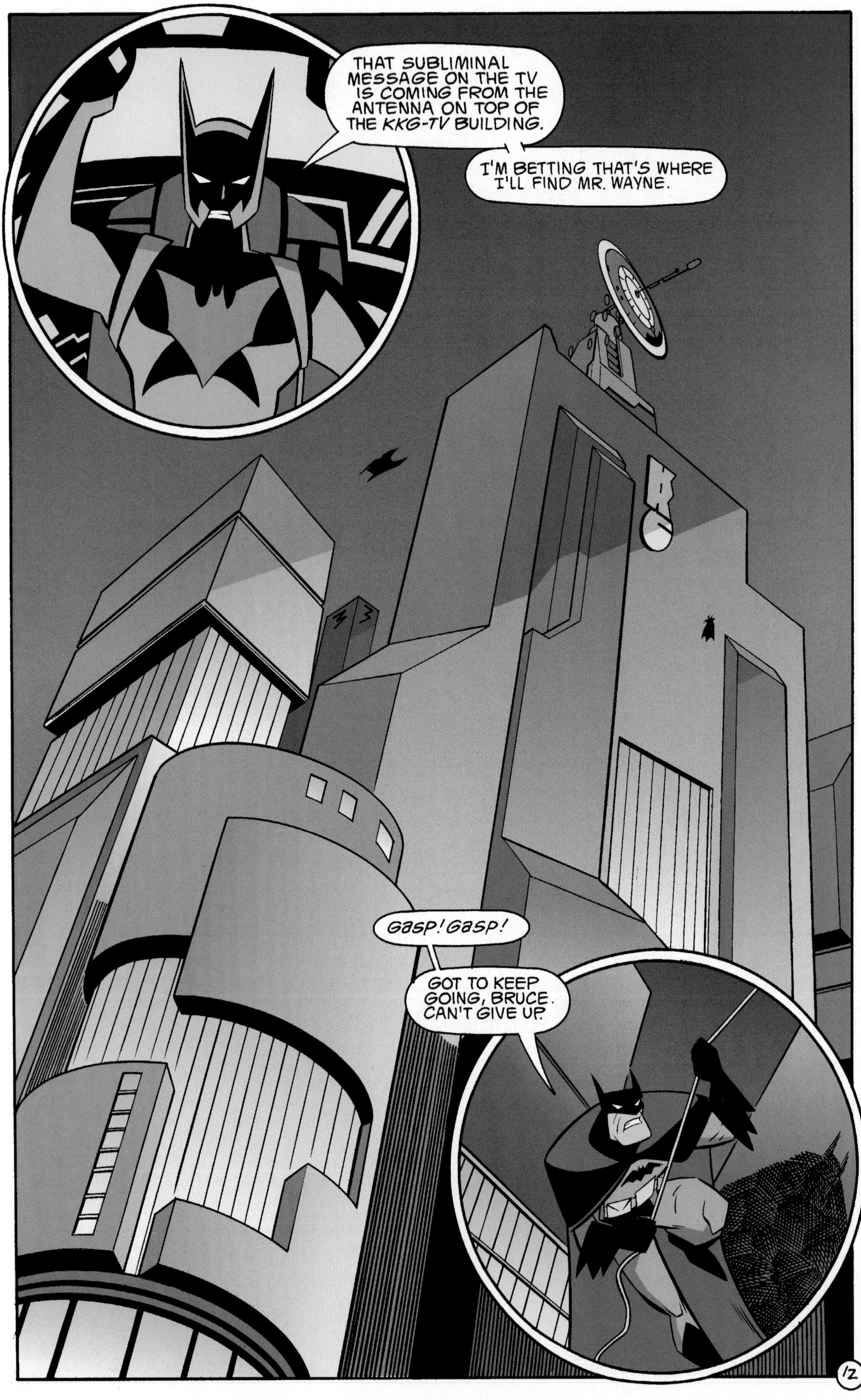
THAT SUBLIMINAL MESSAGE ON THE TV IS COMING FROM THE ANTENNA ON TOP OF THE KKG-TV BUILDING.
I'M BETTING THAT'S WHERE I'LL FIND MR. WAYNE.
Gasp! Gasp!
GOT TO KEEP GOING, BRUCE. CAN'T GIVE UP.

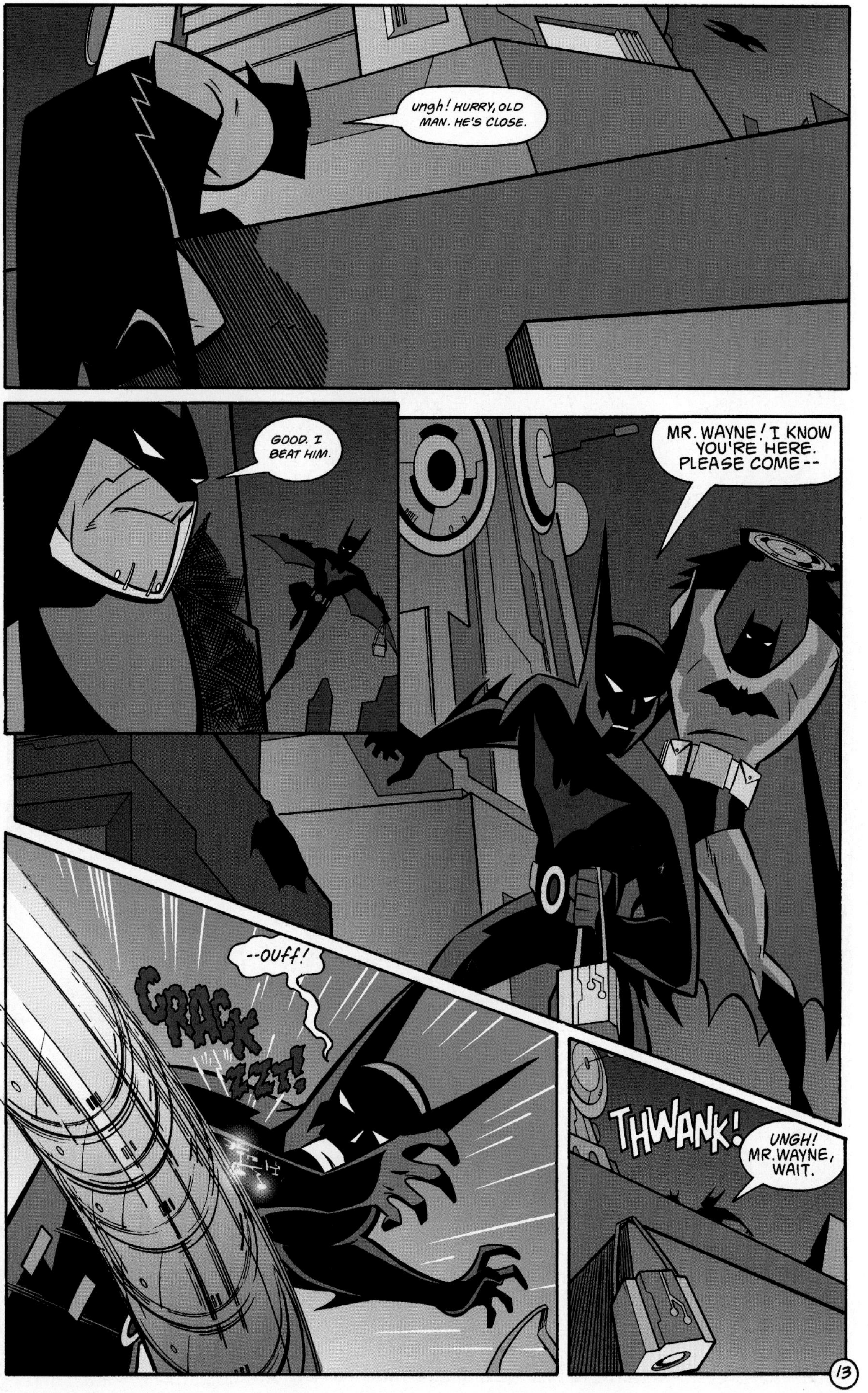
unGh! HURRY, OLD MAN. HE'S CLOSE.
GOOD. I BEAT HIM.
MR. WAYNE! I KNOW YOU'RE HERE. PLEASE COME--
--OUFF!
CRACK
ZZT!
THWANK!
UNGH! MR. WAYNE, WAIT.

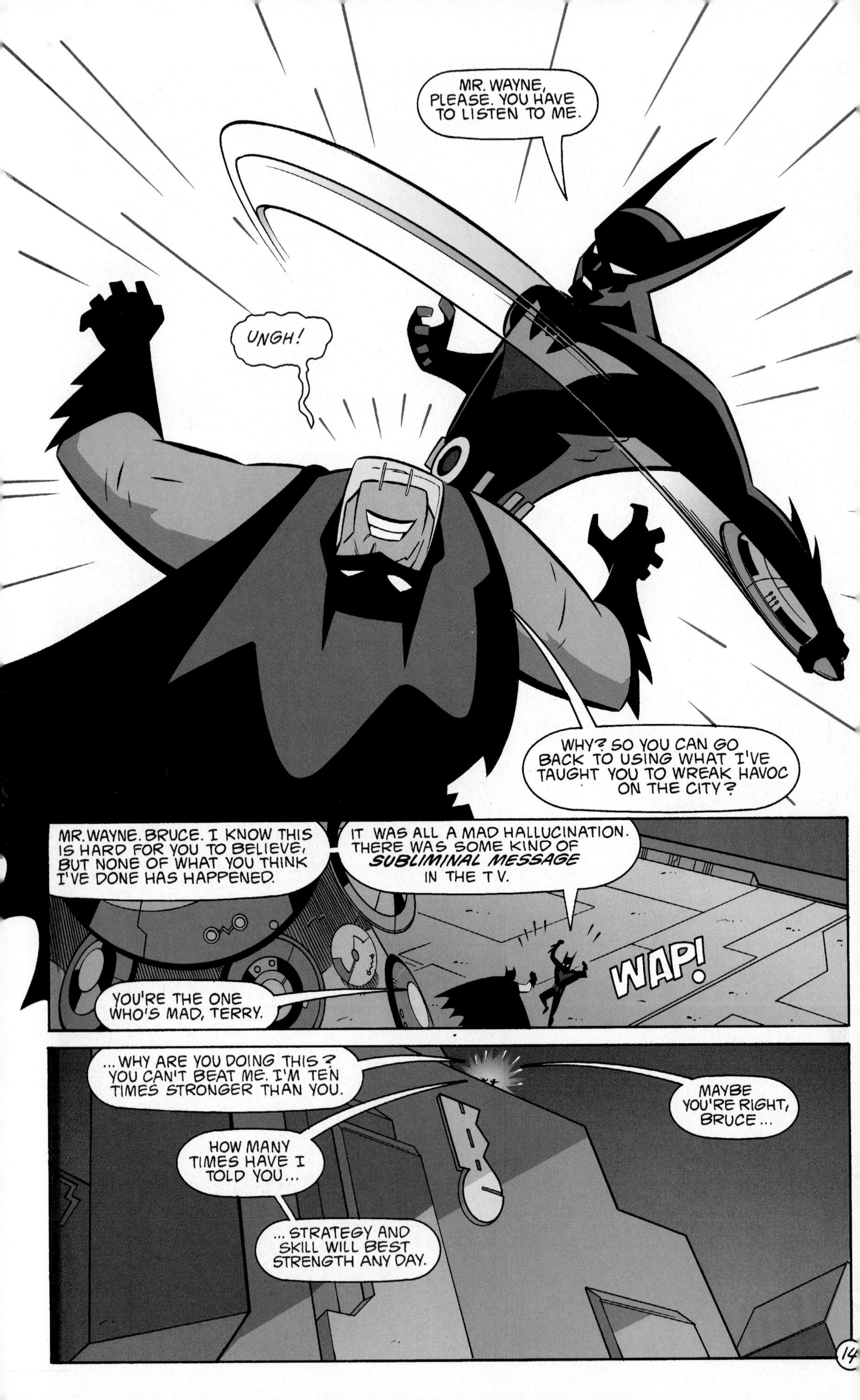
MR. WAYNE, PLEASE. YOU HAVE TO LISTEN TO ME.
UNGH!
WHY? SO YOU CAN GO BACK TO USING WHAT I'VE TAUGHT YOU TO WREAK HAVOC ON THE CITY?
MR. WAYNE. BRUCE. I KNOW THIS IS HARD FOR YOU TO BELIEVE, BUT NONE OF WHAT YOU THINK I'VE DONE HAS HAPPENED.
IT WAS ALL A MAD HALLUCINATION. THERE WAS SOME KIND OF *SUBLIMINAL MESSAGE* IN THE T V.
WAP!
YOU'RE THE ONE WHO'S MAD, TERRY.
...WHY ARE YOU DOING THIS? YOU CAN'T BEAT ME. I'M TEN TIMES STRONGER THAN YOU.
MAYBE YOU'RE RIGHT, BRUCE...
HOW MANY TIMES HAVE I TOLD YOU...
...STRATEGY AND SKILL WILL BEST STRENGTH ANY DAY.

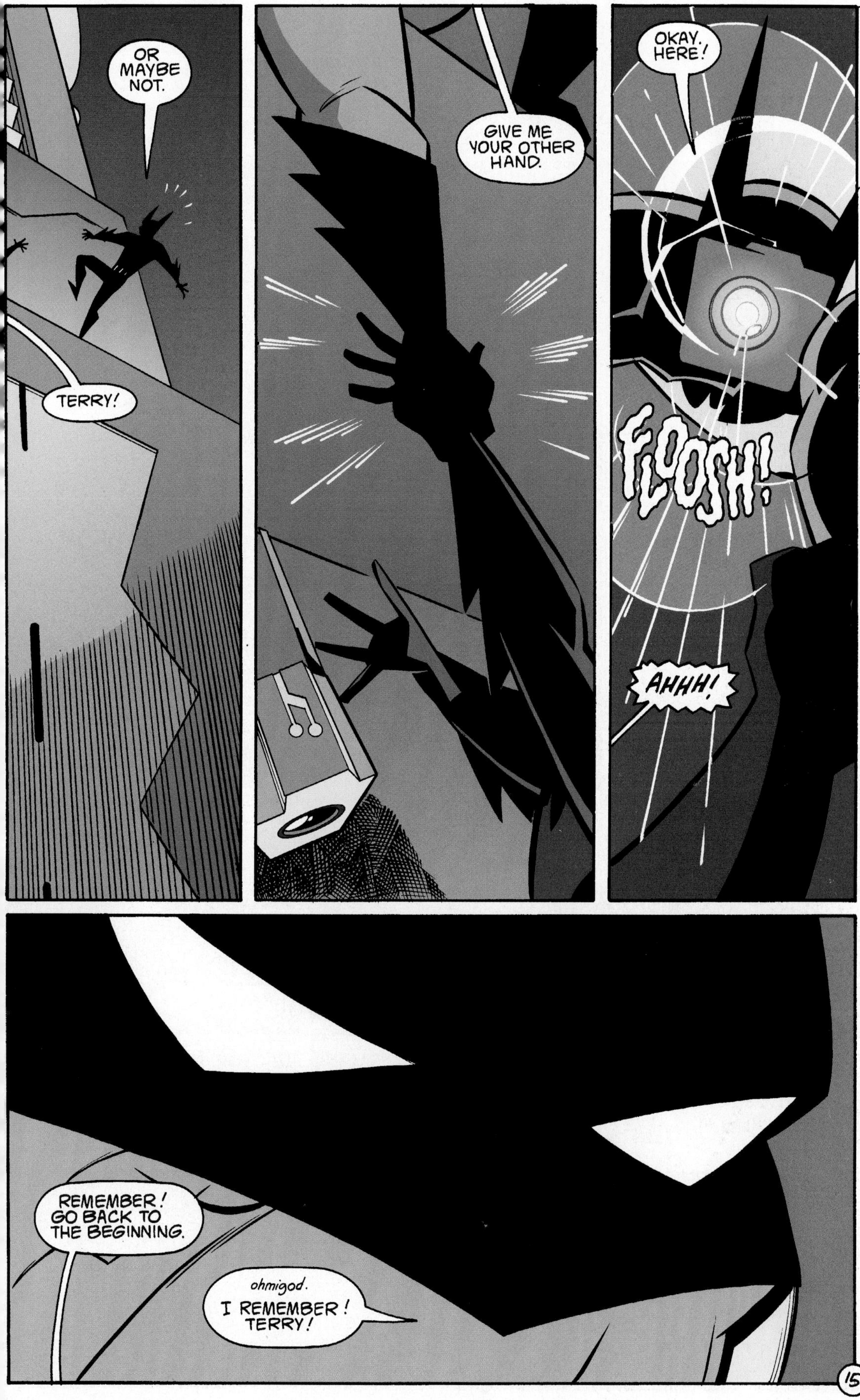
OR MAYBE NOT.
TERRY!
GIVE ME YOUR OTHER HAND.
OKAY. HERE!
FLOOSH!
AHHH!
REMEMBER! GO BACK TO THE BEGINNING.
ohmigod.
I REMEMBER! TERRY!

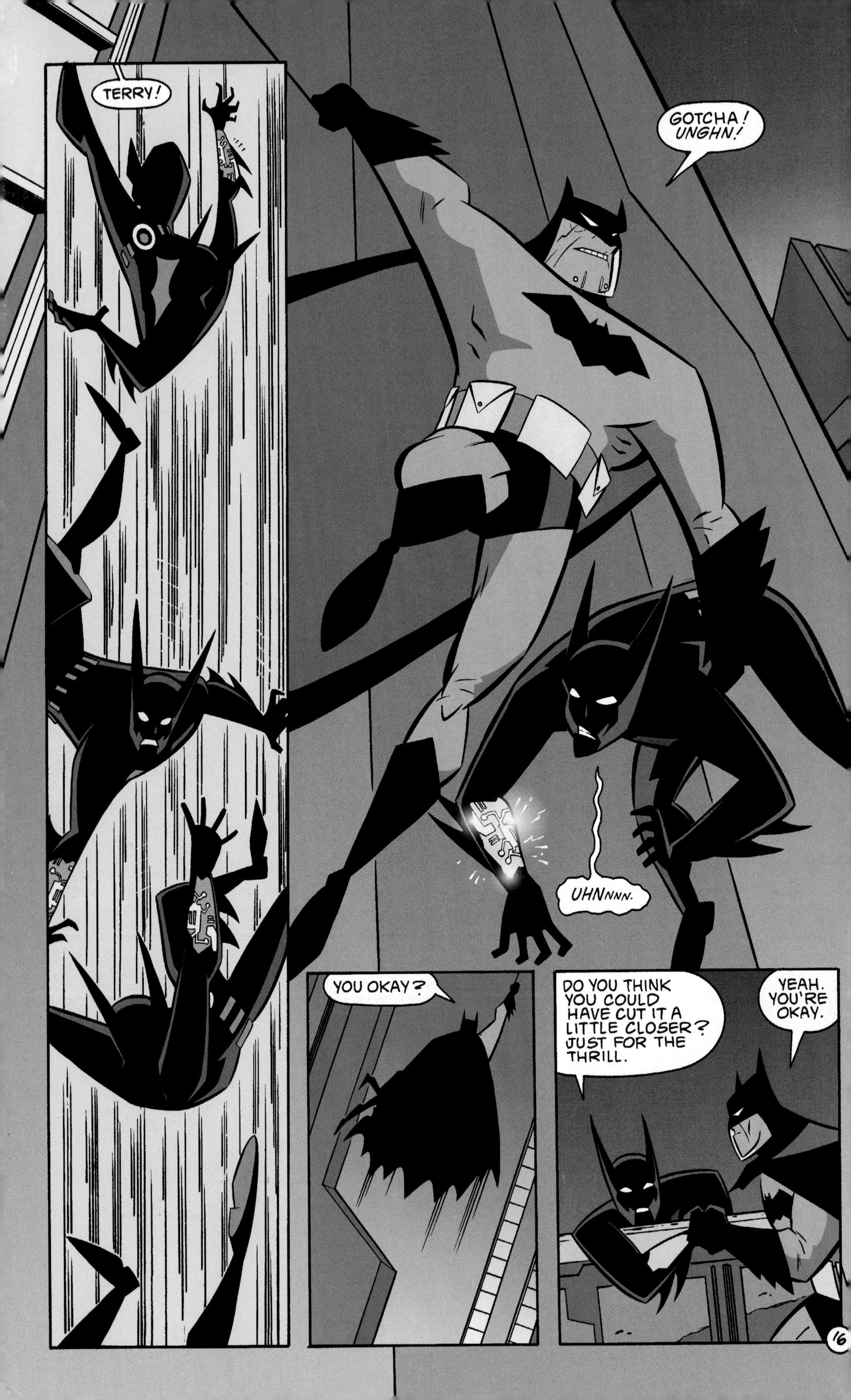
TERRY!
GOTCHA! UNGHN!
UHNNNN.
YOU OKAY?
DO YOU THINK YOU COULD HAVE CUT IT A LITTLE CLOSER? JUST FOR THE THRILL.
YEAH. YOU'RE OKAY.

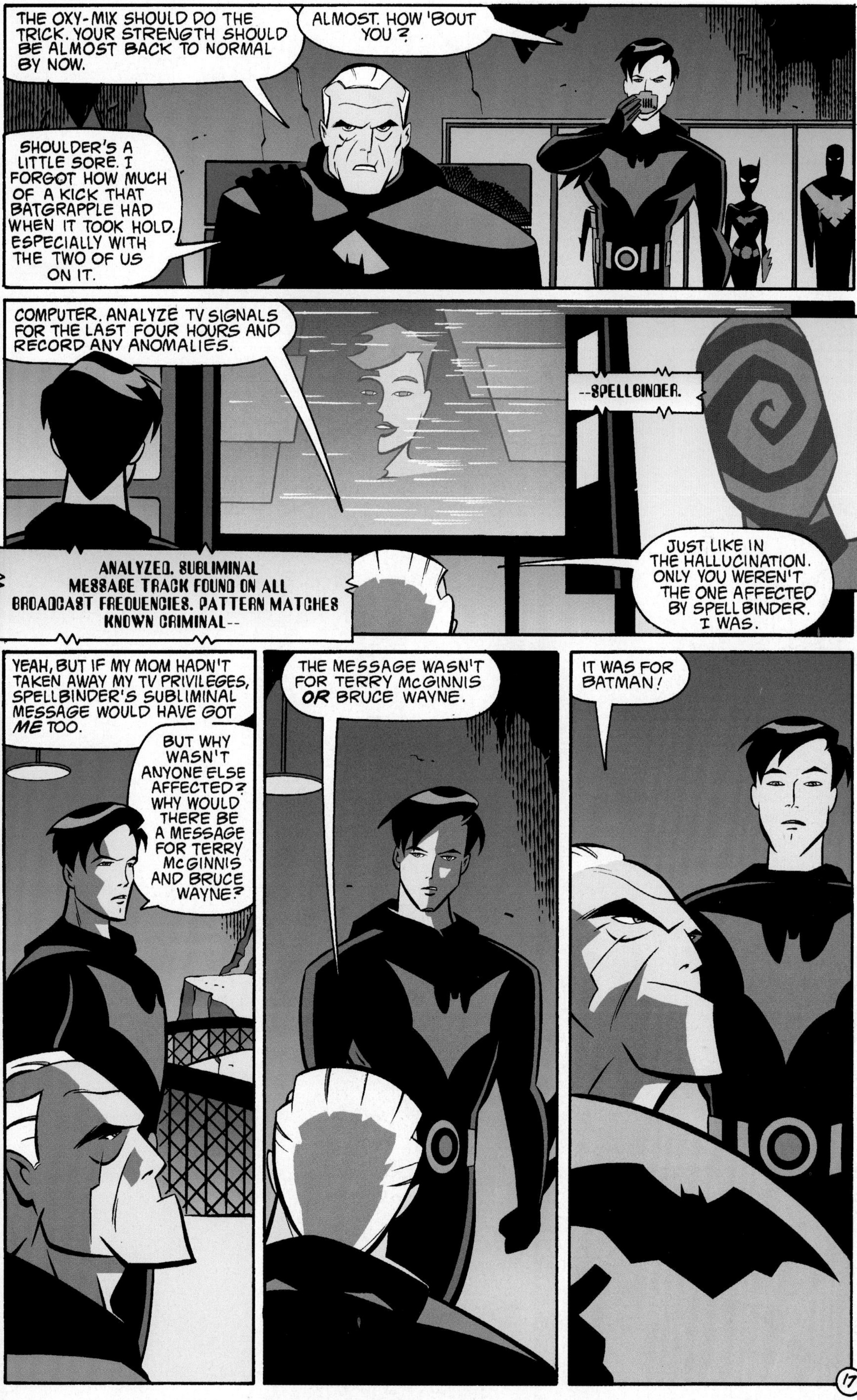
THE OXY-MIX SHOULD DO THE TRICK. YOUR STRENGTH SHOULD BE ALMOST BACK TO NORMAL BY NOW.
ALMOST. HOW 'BOUT YOU?
SHOULDER'S A LITTLE SORE. I FORGOT HOW MUCH OF A KICK THAT BATGRAPPLE HAD WHEN IT TOOK HOLD. ESPECIALLY WITH THE TWO OF US ON IT.
COMPUTER. ANALYZE TV SIGNALS FOR THE LAST FOUR HOURS AND RECORD ANY ANOMALIES.
ANALYZED. SUBLIMINAL MESSAGE TRACK FOUND ON ALL BROADCAST FREQUENCIES. PATTERN MATCHES KNOWN CRIMINAL--
--SPELLBINDER.
JUST LIKE IN THE HALLUCINATION. ONLY YOU WEREN'T THE ONE AFFECTED BY SPELLBINDER. I WAS.
YEAH, BUT IF MY MOM HADN'T TAKEN AWAY MY TV PRIVILEGES, SPELLBINDER'S SUBLIMINAL MESSAGE WOULD HAVE GOT *ME* TOO.
BUT WHY WASN'T ANYONE ELSE AFFECTED? WHY WOULD THERE BE A MESSAGE FOR TERRY McGINNIS AND BRUCE WAYNE?
THE MESSAGE WASN'T FOR TERRY McGINNIS *OR* BRUCE WAYNE.
IT WAS FOR BATMAN!

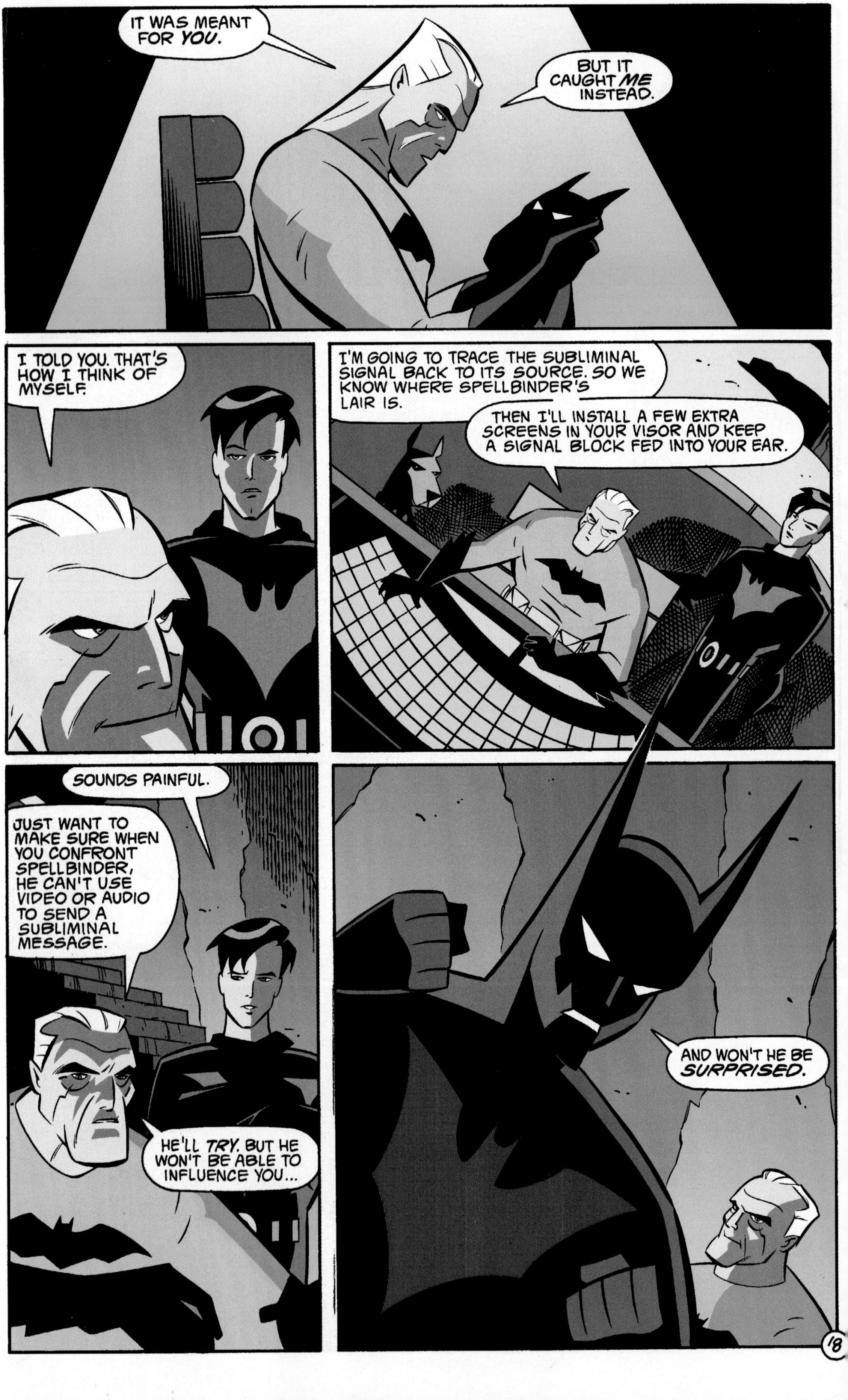
IT WAS MEANT FOR YOU.
BUT IT CAUGHT ME INSTEAD.
I TOLD YOU. THAT'S HOW I THINK OF MYSELF.
I'M GOING TO TRACE THE SUBLIMINAL SIGNAL BACK TO ITS SOURCE. SO WE KNOW WHERE SPELLBINDER'S LAIR IS.
THEN I'LL INSTALL A FEW EXTRA SCREENS IN YOUR VISOR AND KEEP A SIGNAL BLOCK FED INTO YOUR EAR.
SOUNDS PAINFUL.
JUST WANT TO MAKE SURE WHEN YOU CONFRONT SPELLBINDER, HE CAN'T USE VIDEO OR AUDIO TO SEND A SUBLIMINAL MESSAGE.
HE'LL TRY. BUT HE WON'T BE ABLE TO INFLUENCE YOU...
AND WON'T HE BE SURPRISED.
18

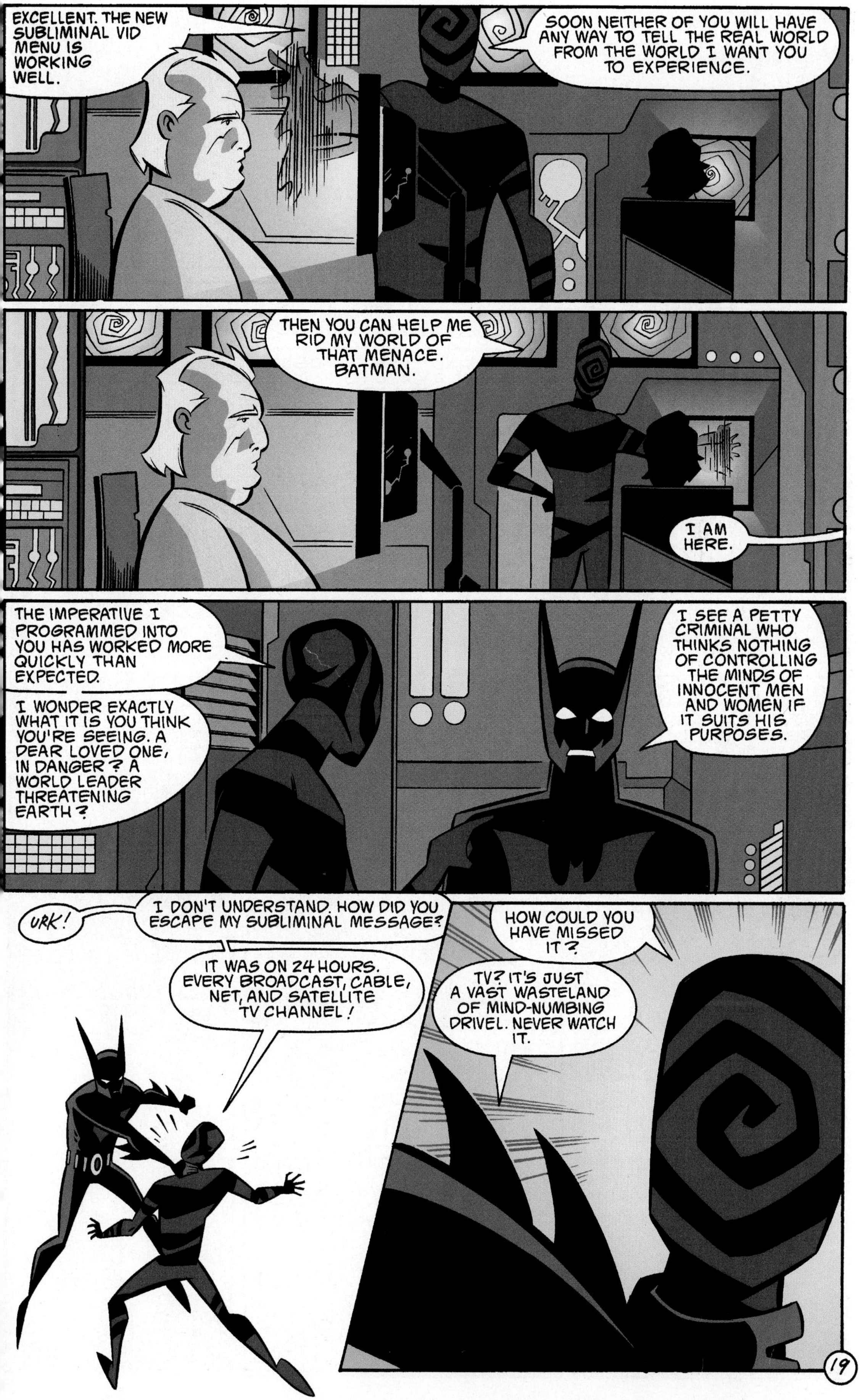
EXCELLENT. THE NEW SUBLIMINAL VID MENU IS WORKING WELL.
SOON NEITHER OF YOU WILL HAVE ANY WAY TO TELL THE REAL WORLD FROM THE WORLD I WANT YOU TO EXPERIENCE.
THEN YOU CAN HELP ME RID MY WORLD OF THAT MENACE. BATMAN.
I AM HERE.
THE IMPERATIVE I PROGRAMMED INTO YOU HAS WORKED MORE QUICKLY THAN EXPECTED.
I WONDER EXACTLY WHAT IT IS YOU THINK YOU'RE SEEING. A DEAR LOVED ONE, IN DANGER? A WORLD LEADER THREATENING EARTH?
I SEE A PETTY CRIMINAL WHO THINKS NOTHING OF CONTROLLING THE MINDS OF INNOCENT MEN AND WOMEN IF IT SUITS HIS PURPOSES.
URK!
I DON'T UNDERSTAND. HOW DID YOU ESCAPE MY SUBLIMINAL MESSAGE?
IT WAS ON 24 HOURS. EVERY BROADCAST, CABLE, NET, AND SATELLITE TV CHANNEL!
HOW COULD YOU HAVE MISSED IT?
TV? IT'S JUST A VAST WASTELAND OF MIND-NUMBING DRIVEL. NEVER WATCH IT.

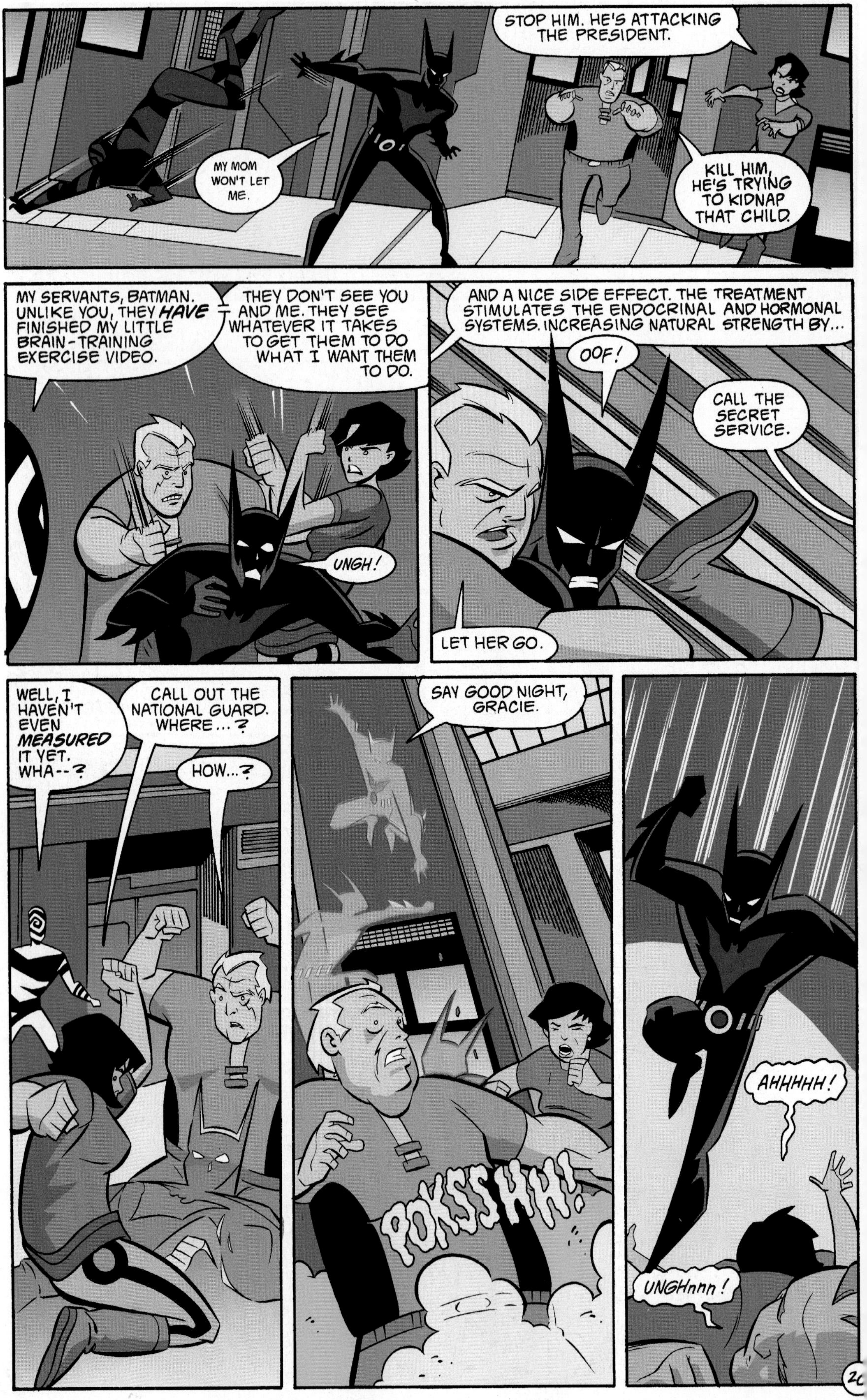
STOP HIM. HE'S ATTACKING THE PRESIDENT.
MY MOM WON'T LET ME.
KILL HIM, HE'S TRYING TO KIDNAP THAT CHILD.
MY SERVANTS, BATMAN. UNLIKE YOU, THEY HAVE FINISHED MY LITTLE BRAIN-TRAINING EXERCISE VIDEO.
THEY DON'T SEE YOU AND ME. THEY SEE WHATEVER IT TAKES TO GET THEM TO DO WHAT I WANT THEM TO DO.
UNGH!
AND A NICE SIDE EFFECT. THE TREATMENT STIMULATES THE ENDOCRINAL AND HORMONAL SYSTEMS. INCREASING NATURAL STRENGTH BY...
OOF!
CALL THE SECRET SERVICE.
LET HER GO.
WELL, I HAVEN'T EVEN MEASURED IT YET. WHA--?
CALL OUT THE NATIONAL GUARD. WHERE...?
HOW...?
SAY GOOD NIGHT, GRACIE.
POKSSHH!
AHHHHH!
UNGHnnn!

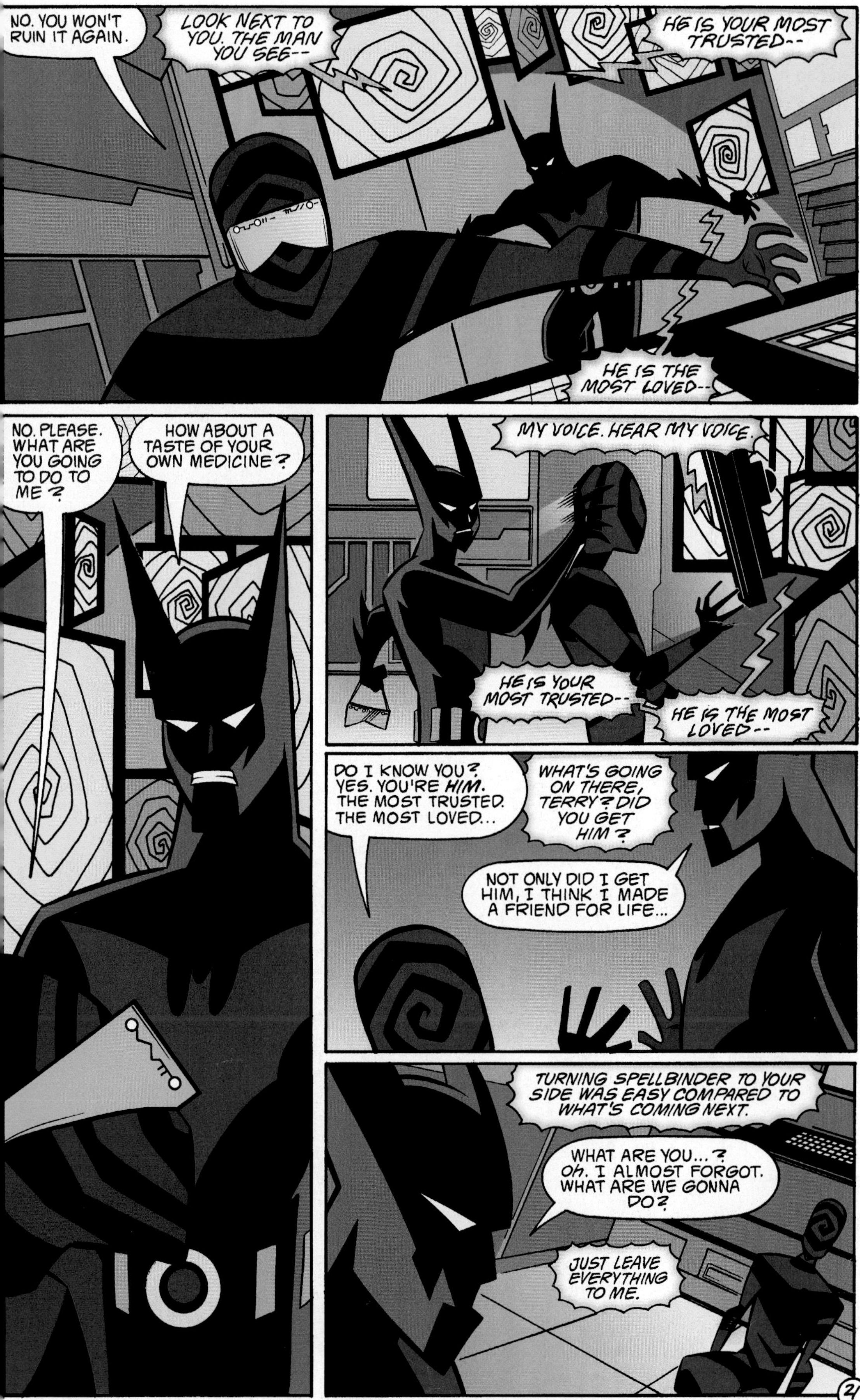
NO. YOU WON'T RUIN IT AGAIN.
LOOK NEXT TO YOU. THE MAN YOU SEE--
HE IS YOUR MOST TRUSTED--
HE IS THE MOST LOVED--
NO. PLEASE. WHAT ARE YOU GOING TO DO TO ME?
HOW ABOUT A TASTE OF YOUR OWN MEDICINE?
MY VOICE. HEAR MY VOICE.
HE IS YOUR MOST TRUSTED--
HE IS THE MOST LOVED--
DO I KNOW YOU? YES. YOU'RE HIM. THE MOST TRUSTED. THE MOST LOVED...
WHAT'S GOING ON THERE, TERRY? DID YOU GET HIM?
NOT ONLY DID I GET HIM, I THINK I MADE A FRIEND FOR LIFE...
TURNING SPELLBINDER TO YOUR SIDE WAS EASY COMPARED TO WHAT'S COMING NEXT.
WHAT ARE YOU...? OH. I ALMOST FORGOT. WHAT ARE WE GONNA DO?
JUST LEAVE EVERYTHING TO ME.

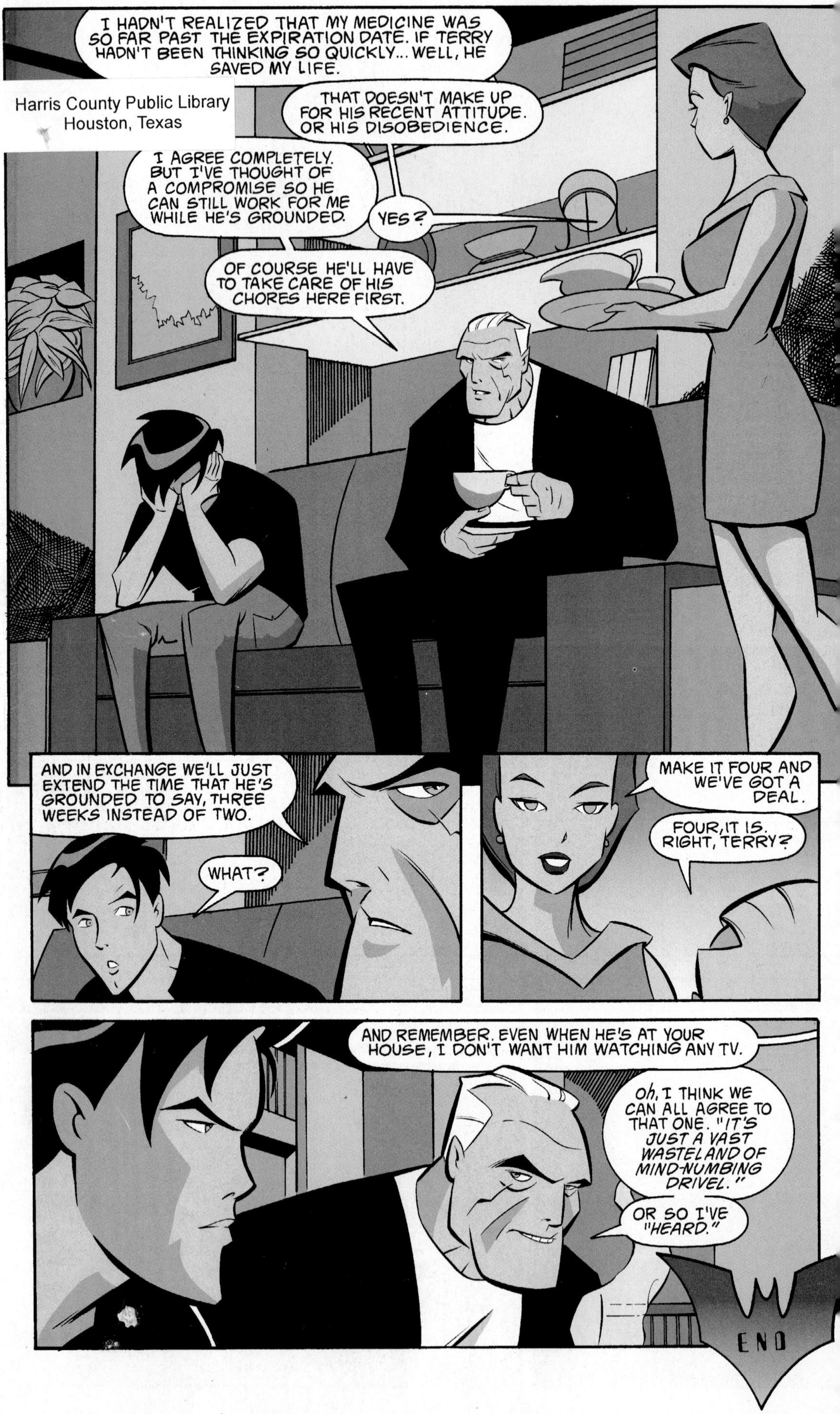
I HADN'T REALIZED THAT MY MEDICINE WAS SO FAR PAST THE EXPIRATION DATE. IF TERRY HADN'T BEEN THINKING SO QUICKLY... WELL, HE SAVED MY LIFE.
THAT DOESN'T MAKE UP FOR HIS RECENT ATTITUDE. OR HIS DISOBEDIENCE.
I AGREE COMPLETELY. BUT I'VE THOUGHT OF A COMPROMISE SO HE CAN STILL WORK FOR ME WHILE HE'S GROUNDED.
YES?
OF COURSE HE'LL HAVE TO TAKE CARE OF HIS CHORES HERE FIRST.
AND IN EXCHANGE WE'LL JUST EXTEND THE TIME THAT HE'S GROUNDED TO SAY, THREE WEEKS INSTEAD OF TWO.
WHAT?
MAKE IT FOUR AND WE'VE GOT A DEAL.
FOUR, IT IS. RIGHT, TERRY?
AND REMEMBER. EVEN WHEN HE'S AT YOUR HOUSE, I DON'T WANT HIM WATCHING ANY TV.
Oh, I THINK WE CAN ALL AGREE TO THAT ONE. "IT'S JUST A VAST WASTELAND OF MIND-NUMBING DRIVEL."
OR SO I'VE "HEARD."
END